CLIMBING UP THE ROUGH SIDE OF THE MOUNTAIN

Sam King

MINERVA PRESS

LONDON
ATLANTA MONTREUX SYDNEY

ISBN 0 75410 478 8

First Published 1998 by
MINERVA PRESS
195 Knightsbridge
London SW7 1RE

Printed in Great Britain for Minerva Press

CLIMBING UP THE ROUGH SIDE OF THE MOUNTAIN

For my wife, Myrtle

Chapter One

Jamaica, the third largest of the West Indian Islands, is small: one hundred and fifty miles long and fifty miles wide, but is blessed with some of the most beautiful countrysides. At the north-eastern end of the island lies Portland, named after the Duke of Portland, the then governor of Jamaica, in 1723. This parish enjoys the highest rainfall in the island and consequently the land is always green and lush.

In early times, Portland was sparsely populated, hence the existence of large properties: Fairy Hill, Content, Castle Comfort (owned by Errol Flynn's family), and Egg Hill, which sweeps down from the Blue Mountain to the sea. All these remain fertile land for livestock and for the production of sugar cane, pimento, coffee and bananas for export. Other crops are also grown for local consumption although some, namely sweet potatoes, yams, coconuts and breadfruit, have found themselves in the export market. The capital, Port Antonio, was once a thriving seaport town thanks to the large banana trade, with weekly sailings of up to seventeen lines of steamers rivalling the Port of Liverpool.

Tourists used to arrive on the banana boats, but with the decline of the banana trade came also the diminution of Port Antonio as a tourist and commercial area. Recently, however, there has been some rejuvenation, due mainly to the beauty of adjacent areas. One such attraction is the mighty Rio Grande river gushing from the Blue Mountain.

It is renowned for its rafting. Anyone who has been on these bamboo rafts will tell you that it is not for the faint-hearted. It is a daunting experience, but the raftsmen are intrepid and skilful on the meandering and scenic five-mile trip from Berrydale to Rafters Rest near Port Antonio where the river meets the sea.

During the Morant Bay Rebellion in 1865, legend has it that a priest was hanged on a wild grape tree at the mouth of the Hope River. He was an Irish priest mistaken for an Englishman (the rebellion was against the English). In memory of this horrible misfortune, the people decided to rename the area Priestman's River. It was in this locality which lies between the two rivers – the River Hope and the River Castle – that I was born to George and Caroline King on the 20th February, 1926, a Sunday morning when worshippers were on their way to church. Mother Thatchel, the self-taught midwife, was in attendance for the birth. She was the only ex-slave then alive, later to die at the age of one hundred and five.

The first child was a girl, but my mother had the premonition that this time she was going to have a boy who would help his people. It was no wonder, then, that she wanted to call him Joseph, but when the family of kings gathered for celebration on the ninth day, the head of the tribe Uncle Adam, the water policeman, prevailed. He insisted that I be named Samuel Beaver King: Samuel because they had all prayed for a son as Hannah in the Bible did, and Beaver because the beaver is a smart and hard-working animal. My mother was so much embraced by the family that she was hereafter referred to as Mother, and this made her extremely happy.

The inhabitants of Priestman's River numbered about six hundred and were largely related. The village regulated itself by means of the head of each family assuming responsibility to run things under the old Victorian values, which no one questioned. The police from the adjacent village of Castle paid occasional visits. There was practically no stealing; people asked for a coconut or a stem of bananas as need dictated – one's property was respected.

The Webbers, my mother's side of the family, were considered people of means. One member was a retired police corporal who owned the village shop, selling everything from foodstuffs to building materials and fabrics. Uncle Unis also owned a truck which hauled bananas on Monday mornings to Port Antonio and on the other days made numerous trips, taking people with their goods, including animals, to the market, the sight of which operation would make one tremble. Animals were loaded first, then people who would clamber over the first layer to end up several feet above the side railings.

My father, on the other hand, loved the land, as did his ancestors. His grandfather had twelve sons and, together with two other families, had grasped the opportunity to purchase Egg Hill, a property of roughly twelve hundred acres from a slave owner who was returning to England. These families subsequently formed the Egg Hill Cooperative. My grandfather also extended his ownership of property by purchasing Harmony, which passed to my father, his only child, and now to us, his children.

Two years after I was born and my mother was expecting her third child, my father unexpectedly left for Cuba to work on the sugar plantation, and then moved on to the United States, returning when I was about four years old. I remember him swinging me up on his broad shoulders and showing me off around the district.

Jamaicans have an insatiable appetite for travel, always yearning for an escape to greener pastures. Many deserted the land for Colon and Panama when the canal was being

built, returning with possessions they would otherwise
never have had. Those who didn't go seemed to wait for
the opportunity to make a song of the returnees: 'Who does
not know one, two three, four, Colon man a come wid 'im
gold chain a lick 'im belly, bim, bim, bim. When 'im want
to know the time 'in look upon the sun, wid 'im gold chain
a lick 'im belly, bim, bim, bim.'

Aunts, uncles and other relatives were always around.
Mother was confined to the home and its vicinity, engaged
in never-ending washing, cooking, ironing, looking after
the chickens, collecting eggs, planting her herb garden and
seeing to the baby. She always seemed to have an infant at
her side; after all, there were nine of us.

Children were given chores; they had to obey not only
their parents but all adults, not to mention teachers, who
were sacred. I'm almost tempted to add the forbidden word
c—, especially when they resorted to thrashing the
daylights out of anyone who was not or apparently not
paying attention. Respect and manners were expected and
scrupulously enforced. I used to slice up coconut to feed
the chickens from a very early age and I don't remember
ever cutting my finger. From that, I graduated to tending
the goats and eventually to milking the cows. By then, I
could ride the donkey and the horse.

I started school at seven, the statutory age at the time,
but before then I was taught by my aunt Esther to read. I
remember having difficulty with the letter E, but she said
it's like the crow flying, and this registered. My
grandmother took me to the Baptist church, a journey
which took us near to the beach where the fishing boats
were moored but not as far as St Mark's church at Boston
where my father was the churchwarden; only when I was
nine did my father say it was time for me to accompany
him to the Church of England, which I did. On one of

these occasions, walking back home in the blazing sun when he was on his horse and I was trying to keep up with the pace, I asked him why I had to walk three miles to this church instead of the half a mile to the Baptist church. He explained that when I grew up I would need the minister of the Church of England to sign my apprenticeship form because the authorities would be unlikely to take much notice if it were signed by the Baptist minister. This I found incredible, young though I was.

My first day at school was daunting, compounded by an incident which took place on our way in from recess, as we used to call it. I happened to step on someone's toe – a toe without a shoe, that is. It had hardly occurred before there was a swing and a punch landed in my eye. No way could I retaliate, as I had been told that under no circumstances should I be involved in any fight at school. I therefore went to the teacher, who did nothing because I went to her shouting, more bawling than anything else. News got around to my older cousins, who declared that no one messed with the Kings and got away with it, so there was going to be a battle on the way home. However, the walk home involved passing through Black Rock, my assailant's village, and, to complicate matters, his sister Lurlene and my sister Murdella were best friends and the friendship between his father and my father went back to the time when they were both in the same workmen's barracks in Cuba. Thus, the big fight which everyone was looking forward to was called off. The combatants Vidal De Zonie and myself became best friends until this day; we both ended up in the Royal Air Force in England.

On the whole, my parents were pleased with my school work but my father, dextrous and adept when it came to anything pertaining to farming, thought I was backward and lacking in common sense: inept at handling animals and naïve in my knowledge of plants, the soil, and nature in general. After all, I was the first boy, and as such should be geared to farming, ready to take over and run Harmony and administrate the extended family's property of Egg Hill. Thus, he set about rectifying these deficiencies. I remember him drawing my attention to the crowing cock and to how this could be used to tell the time. Sure enough, at 5 a.m., just before daybreak, the cock crowed, but what if one was in the field and there was no cock? Well, the guango tree was never very far off: its leaves closed up at 4 p.m. Observe the clouds and see the direction in which the wind is blowing. When the clouds were blackening and the wind was blowing from Morant Bay, rain was on the way. These meteorological tips, together with my natural ability to obey and conform, combined favourably to make the relationship with my parents a sparkling one, me more confident and my work manageable. While still at school, I could be relied on to supervise the women shelling the pimento and pad the donkey's back with layers of cloth to make a saddle, taking the foodstuff home a mile and a half away. I could feed and check the pigs for any health problems, milk the cows and turn them out to pasture before and after school.

Putting these skills into practice was exciting for me and I looked forward to the challenge daily. I remember one big nanny goat gave birth to two lovely kids but the rainy season and the subsequent stagnant pools produced an abundance of bluebottle flies which laid eggs in the navel of one of the kids. Now I had to put my veterinary skill in practice. I used Jeyes disinfectant to kill the maggots but in so doing the Jeyes touched the tail, whereupon the mother goat would have nothing to do with the poor creature. I washed the tail, daubed it with milk and rubbed it against the mother but all to no avail. She would not let him suckle; she butted him away. No one had time for one kid so in the end, it was killed, salted and fed to the dog.

One day, as my father and I were observing the cows in the pen, there were about ten two to three year olds among them and he asked me which should be sold to the butchers. It took me a few minutes to make a decision, but then I pointed to a red Mysore bullkin. He agreed, but went on to say that a steer was like some people: stubborn in character, a misfit and to be disposed of. Even now I cannot figure out how one equates this trait with the need to be 'disposed of', but at the time my duty was to learn and not to argue.

Up to now one perhaps gets the impression that it was all work in the village and no play. Far be that from the truth; there were endless opportunities for leisure activities of all sorts for young and old, especially during the school holidays. For the children, there were the woodlands in which to roam, the trees to climb, the discoveries of unfamiliar insects and animals, the rivers for swimming and fishing and of course the wide blue sea for further adventures and exploits.

I cannot forget the day my mother allowed my brother Wilton and me to accompany our cousin George on an errand to pick coconuts. The permission was granted on condition that we stayed clear of the river which was then in spate from the recent heavy rains. We had no intention of disobeying, but having picked the coconuts in record time and with George bragging about his swimming ability, we thought that a quick splash would not be found out, so off came the clothes and in we waded. As we got in the deep, we could see that George was in desperate trouble. Wilton was a strong swimmer and he made a dash for him with me following in the rescue mission. Frightened we were, but we did not panic. We got to George but had a problem holding on as he was naked and slippery. The heavens must have helped us: we managed to pull him to the bank where there was an overhanging branch waiting to offer assistance. The disaster was averted and we vacated the offending place as fast as we could, gathered the nuts and returned home heroic but never breathing a word.

It was the sea that held the greatest attraction for the clique of boys in Islington, a small area of Priestman's River, because the beach near by was not rough and there was no one around most times, so we could be as adventurous as much as we liked. There was one huge rock from which we would jump into the water. At the base of this rock was the 'fish pot' but one ran the risk of being dashed against it when the sea was in ebullient mood. This must have been the case when Vivian McKenzie took his mule for a wash one day. Vivian really loved that mule and he was most attentive to her. She was his pride and joy and he kept her well groomed and clean, but that day he took her down for her weekly bath, Vivian never returned. His body was later found and, until this day how he was drowned remains a mystery. The saddest and most heart-rending part was when I was asked to be one of the pall-bearers.

Toys were not bought, they were made. Our creativity was manifest in the variety of products we were able to turn out at different times of the year. There was a season for every kind of game or activity. Tops, (gigs), catapults, marbles and cricket were reserved for the dry season while trucks, slides and other pursuits were year-round pastimes. The highlight of the weekend was cricket, when even the adult males would stop by to give some coaching. Sam Patterson, the grandfather of Patrick Patterson who plays for the West Indies, was the most helpful and knowledgeable. He not only advised on the mechanics of the game but was keen that we were good sportsmen whether we won or lost. His presence was always welcome.

The grown-ups on occasions indulged the community in a match with a visiting team. This was exciting; even the ladies would grace the grounds with their presence, usually for commercial gain rather than for enjoyment, but whatever the reason there was a noticeable atmosphere as they were jolly and comical. They would bring along patties, fritters, coconut drops, journey cakes, grater cake and *pone* (pudding). There would always be the ice cream man around, but his ice cream was made in a special bucket with the ice and salt packed around the tube containing the liquid mixture. It had a cranking system which was turned manually until the ice cream was ready.

The cricket was played with gusto and enthusiasm while the crowd provided the stimulus. Whenever there was a dull moment there would be a chorus of mixed voices in a sort of Mexican wave manner. The one I liked best was, 'Captain, captain, what's for dinner?' Then the reply would come, 'Salt fish tail and monkey liver, play, buddy boy, play.'

My father had a double-barrelled shotgun and together with his friends used to go shooting at Egg Hill at weekends. They shot wild pigs, conies and birds mainly lapwing, ballplate, pigeon and parakeet. That gun, I may add, was to see and not touch for us children and we adhered to that. He was also skilful at playing the guitar which he had bought and learned in Cuba. As the only one in the area with a portable instrument, he provided the music at the local dances on Saturday nights, something to which my mother was totally opposed on the grounds that it was time-consuming and, above all, too worldly for a man of the church. Consequently, he disposed of the guitar. That was regrettable and devastating for us as it had added so much flavour and prestige to the home.

My mother did not, however, object to him organising the biannual half-mile horse race at Boston, where the Flynns gave permission for the event. The races were advertised in the *Daily Gleaner* and by word of mouth, resulting in it being a real crowd-puller, with spectators coming from as far afield as Kingston and the surrounding towns. My father's horse, called Hotwater, was a three year old stallion who never lost a race. As a stud, he was fed on corn, crabgrass, a pint of stout and an egg a day, at the expense of us children who were not given an egg a day.

The Caribs and the Arawaks had used dugout canoes before Columbus arrived, and those who followed improved on the craft as time went by. When bananas were being shipped from the mouth of Priestman's River, longboats were used to transport the fruit from the shore to the ship because of the narrow draught and treacherous rocks on the left bank of the channel. For a boat, a large wild cotton tree would be felled, roughly shaped and pulled anything up to three miles to the shore to be finished by skilled craftsmen. Fishermen used these boats but this time there was going to be something more spectacular; there was going to be a boat race.

The message went out that the Allens, a fishing and boat-building family, wanted everyone to help with the pulling of the roughed-out boat which began life at Ginger Piece by the quiet stream where the cotton tree had grown to an enormous height and girth over the years. Cut down and shaped, it had to be taken to the seaside via the village, and this required as many people as possible. Even the help of schoolboys was solicited to move the rollers forward. This was a marathon task, especially as it involved negotiating their way across the furrows along the path, but both the men and boys were determined to see it through so there was a high level of cooperation. As the adrenaline flowed, the tedium and exhaustion were alleviated by the rhythmic, singing of 'Hill and gully ride oh hill and gully'. We negotiated the hill with ease and coasted down to the seaside where the boat, the Blue Bird was going to be made ready for the sea.

On the beach was an assembly of young and middle-aged women with their beautiful frocks shimmering and lifting in the late afternoon sun and breeze, waiting to welcome their intrepid and strong menfolk who could not believe what they saw. It was the time of year, late September, when breadfruit was plentiful and mangoes were still around and when the fishermen came in from Morant Cays with so much fish that they were almost giving them away. The women sprang a surprise and greeted the men with the most elaborate and sumptuous spread of curried goat and rice, roasted fish, corn and breadfruit dumplings, and all served in calabash and washed down with lemonade made with wet sugar and fresh line. For good measure there was even ice cream, home-made right there on the beach in a bucket with ice and salt packed round a jug containing the ice cream mixture. Attached to the bucket was an arm which was continuously turned, the result of this cranking being the most delicious ice cream. After gorging ourselves, we all dispersed. I was fit for nothing but my bed.

Azie Allen and his assistants finished the boat in less than two months. She was christened officially as Blue Bird and ready to show herself as queen of the sea. A beautiful bird in flight was strategically painted looking towards the bow, half way up the watermark.

The Wilsons, who were esteemed as the best boat builders, were by this time quietly working on their boat without much help from the community who regarded them as niggardly, aggressive and boastful, not that they were desperate for assistance as there were three robust and experienced brothers working with their father. From this family of Wilsons came the footballer who wore the number seven shirt for Tottenham. It has to be said though, that when their boat Tiger Shark was completed and embellished, painted and decked out with a shield bearing a tiger shark with open jaws, it was a sight to behold.

The wise man of the village, Cyrus Byran, planned the grand boat race for the Saturday before Christmas. As soon as the date was fixed punters began to take bets, but in a peasant farming community where a shilling was hard to come by, the vast majority of the men staked their bets against a drink of rum. The general feeling was that Blue Bird was going to be the winner, and this was confirmed by the fishermen who observed her on her maiden run from the fishing ground and how she skimmed the water and rode the waves.

The entire community with others from near and far swelled the crowd, with hundreds lining the seashore on the day of the final contest between the Wilsons and the Allens. The Baptist minister blessed both the crews. By the toss of a coin, Tiger Shark had the technically shorter route – the Black Rock side of the channel. Blue Bird had to settle for the Pete side but Martell Panton, the skipper would have chosen that side anyway. They were escorted a mile out, and in the distance Blue Bird and Tiger Shark could be seen bobbing up and down on the crest of the waves until the white ensign of the starter boat was up and the shout of 'They're off!' from the deafening crowd re-echoed far and wide. Half a mile into the race the Wilsons were leading; then, when a large wave took them up, Martell instructed his crew to let her run, and at about a chain from the protruding rock, Martell shouted for the crew to dip heavy to the left while he braced her with the strength of a demon. Blue Bird's bow almost came out of the water in time to fly on the coming wave straight into the sand, safe on shore. Heaven heard the spontaneous, tumultuous shout as the people went wild with excitement. Many jumped, clothes and shoes on, into the sea and on to the victorious Blue Bird.

> For what are men better than sheep or goats,
> That nourish a blind life within the brain,
> If, knowing God, they lift not hands of prayer
> Both for themselves and those who call them friends?

Living in a community such as Priestman's River and contiguous areas was not without its vicissitudes. Feuds, accidents, sickness, deaths and natural disasters there were, but these were handled in the most satisfactory and practical way. Quarrels and disputes were usually sorted out by the older and more respectable residents. Sometimes, before the quarrels, disputes and/ or malcontentedness were pacified, tempers would fray, resulting in fist fights but on the whole, the strong helped the weak; sharing of ideas, time and possessions was the norm.

I remember my parents were forever giving or lending money, clothes iron, food and even salt. These acts of undiluted kindness, thoughtfulness and magnanimity were considered in a positive way and served to mould us into citizens willing to respond to any call at the drop of a hat. Mother used to say Jesus first, yourself last and others in between, and another of her quotes was, 'Who steals my purse steals trash, but he who robs me of my good name robs me of some thing great and makes me poor indeed.' Mark you, she was not an educated person, but was marvellous and perceptive. She was not too worried about the boys but was keen to have her girls educated because then they shouldn't feel they have to say 'yes' to the first man who came along.

Children were incorporated and initiated in all aspects of these close-knit and cohesive societies where we did not live in a moral and spiritual vacuum. Not everyone lived up to all the ideals, but the basic harmony and tranquillity were not disturbed.

One school holiday, breaking pimento at Harmony, I heard the faint sound of the abeng, an instrument made from cow horn and used either to make music or to communicate. The Maroons invented it as a secret means of keeping in touch with one another over a great distance, warning of the approach of any enemies. It had come to symbolise freedom and was still in use in my boyhood to summon attention, but the Maroons also blew it on ceremonial occasions. From where I was, I could see the boats a mile out from the shore and the sound I caught on the wind came from the fishermen with their catch of grouper. Nothing could hold back the women shelling the pimento; I had to let them go for the rest of the day. I, too, wended my way home. My father enquired as to why I was so early, so I told him of the abeng, whereupon he asked what was the pattern of the sound. I said it was three long blasts. He replied that if I should ever hear one long, one short and one long in succession, it was a distress call, and wherever I was and whatever I was doing, I should stop and go home.

About three months after, late one evening, I again heard the abeng: a long, a short and a long. Within minutes, the whole village came out and the message was relayed from one to another that cousin Maude Ingleton was missing. The story was that she had been seen mid-morning with a basket on her head going to her husband's field at Mug Green, approximately two miles into the bush, but never arrived. A search was called and scores of people went out with lanterns and bottle lamps, but there was no trace of cousin Maude. The search was called off for the night, to be resumed the following morning under the directorship of George Carr who was known for his foresight and wit. George established that Maude did get to her husband's field, did pick some green guango peas and did walk back. He noticed that pods of peas had been dropped to within one yard of a sink-hole.

All kinds of informal strategic councils, consisting of boys, men, girls and women at various rendezvous, were held. The revival preacher with his flock offered prayers; even the obeah man presumed to know the whereabouts of Maude. This was now the third day; George went back over the track and was beaten again one yard from the sink-hole which was almost obscured by the thick guinea grass which showed no sign of anyone having set foot on it. George sat down under a manchineel tree in the early morning, when the grass was still wet with dew, determined to solve this mystery. He noticed a solitary crow circling high overhead. His dog was set to work but there was no answer from his trusted friend. Suddenly he had a presentiment so off he went for help. Two men were engaged to descend into the hole tethered to ropes. Sure enough, the body of Maude was at the bottom of the hole, many feet down. It was retrieved, wrapped in canvas and taken home. The doctor and police appeared and carried out an autopsy which showed that Maude had died as a result of a broken neck. There are but few people who have not been startled into belief of the supernatural, and indeed I know of no similar occurrence producing so general and so intense an effect. For weeks, discussions revolved around this absorbing theme: the absence of any clue, no elucidation, nothing elicited which could lead to a suspect. The earth was not trampled nor the bushes broken; all evidence stopped ten yards from the hole. Did she jump? Such was the mystery of Maude.

Whenever there was a death, the bereaved could count on the moral and financial support of one and all. My first experience of this was when my father's uncle died in Kingston and had to be brought back to the district for burial in the family plot. My father was informed of his death by telegram and he was the one called to preside over the funeral arrangements. That night he called the young Kings together and told us the history of Uncle Topsy. Topsy was the last of eleven sons and was born double-jointed. As a boy he couldn't stand his brothers bossing him, so he would retaliate, fighting them physically and mentally until he was old enough to leave home. Topsy went to Kingston and into the boxing ring, doing well by the time he was forty – marrying a society lady and buying several properties. His downfall came when he could not fight any more. With an insatiable appetite for money, he resorted to boxing in questionable arenas, bending the law here and there, the defiance and futility of which cost him dearly in terms of money and friendships. The end result was high blood pressure caused by worry and alcohol.

The body arrived accompanied by a busload of people. The grave was not ready because the grave diggers had struck rock which had to be blasted out, but in the end everything came right through the sheer goodwill and perseverance of the family and workmen. Topsy was laid to rest, but my father was embittered at the pernicious and prodigious life he had lived. He squandered all he had and died a relatively young man of forty and almost penniless.

My father used this story to lecture his sons on the need to be honest, hard-working and frugal. He himself possessed these qualities, something recognised by the inhabitants and by the government which entrusted him with managing the funds for the upkeep of the parochial roads. He made a good job of it. In a place where relations looked for special favours, there was no favouritism in allotting the work. In times of calamity such as hurricanes and flooding, it was to him that supplies of food and tools would be sent for distribution. Although our family would have its share of misfortune, my father never took as much as a pound of rice or a few nails. His idea was that if we looked we would find a few breadfruit, some coconuts and some sweet potatoes; besides, he was never completely broke. He was an honourable man, beloved and trusted. It was to him people went for advice. In fact, he was like a magistrate.

Chapter Two

I was blessed with some desirable qualities, and a good physique was one of them. I also had a propensity for going by the book, and with my good health and constitution I believe I was effective in commanding the respect and admiration of my siblings and friends. On reflection, I can remember only one occasion when I was really ill. I was about eight years old when I was stricken with a very high and roasting fever which had my mother in a twist. It may have been dengue, but this was not confirmed. No amount of coaxing could get me to eat, not even my grandmother's rich and delicious pea soup. Various home remedies were tried, including the famous fever grass bath. This did not work either so I was taken to the doctor who prescribed 666 – a liquid substance thought to be the panacea for all illnesses. It was as bitter as gall so I was held down and had this offending thing forced down my throat, but bingo – by the following day I was on my feet. The fever had vanished. By and large, the family enjoyed excellent health as would be expected in a place abounding in fruits. There were no additives in our food as most things eaten were home-grown. I remember the large heads of cabbage, cucumbers and pumpkins, to mention but a few.

I was touching fifteen when my father began to complain about a nagging pain in his stomach. This continued until it began to affect his ability for sustainable, effective and efficient work at Harmony and Happy Hill, to which he usually rode. He started to lose weight and to feel generally unwell, but neglect of the properties on which mixed farming was done would certainly mean a delegation of his responsibility to feed his six children and wife. Our whole life revolved around the farm and what it produced. Who would now see to the animals and supervise the planting of the corn and the ground provisions? Who would manage the gathering of the pimento which was second only to bananas as the major source of our livelihood.

We could realise up to fifteen crocus bags of pimento weighing a total of five hundred pounds, sold at two shillings and six pence per pound. At present the price is one pound per pound. It was this harvest that gave my father the most concern. Reaping involved climbing and carefully breaking off just those parts of the branches with the clustered berries. If too much of the tree was torn off, the yield the following year would be affected. Reaping had also to be done as soon as the fruit was fully mature and very green, just before the grains begin to ripen, otherwise the birds would be the beneficiaries. Then there was the shelling: the separation of the grains from the branch. This aspect of the work was done by women under the trees unless there is rain in which case the branches had to be taken into the farm house for shelling to continue.

The next stage was the drying. The pimento was spread thinly on a large concreted or board floor called a barbecue where it received the full force of the sun for a few days. Precautions had to be taken, however, so that it did not get wet, else the whole crop would be lost, so one had to study the elements and not wait even for the first drop to appear – heap it up, cover it up or take up every grain. The easiest and most pleasant part was the selling of it. Pimento was harvested once a year from August to early October but the bananas were perennial. With the pigs, goats and cows, these provided the basis for the family's financial security and pride. Who would assume the administrative role now that my father was physically unfit? I was now fifteen, the eldest son and with enough knowledge of each of these areas of worry, but to be responsible for organising the labour force was daunting to contemplate.

Attendance at school became very irregular, owing to the fact that I had to take control of the animals above all else. The cows had to be milked, the pigs fed and any sores that any of them may have had dressed, and this all before school. There were a few members of the family, cousins mainly, who offered assistance, but my father insisted that I be in charge. At weekends, my younger brother accompanied me to the fields and the pastures but there was little that he was able to do, notwithstanding his willingness to learn and to do what was asked.

One evening we sat on the verandah, my father and I, just as the sun was going down beyond the hill in the far distance. The birds could be seen racing away to their nesting ground and already the chickens were making their way to their roost on the tree behind the house before darkness fell. My father looked downcast, then said to me, 'Sam, will you take over for a while? I will be in the background to advise. As things are we stand to lose a lot if you don't.' I hesitated, then said I would. The animals were no problem but at the back of my mind was the thought of my overseeing people more than twice my age. Father could see the discomfort but reassured me that all would be right. But this didn't stop me feeling inadequate. How would I cope with employees who stopped working just to laugh and talk, to have a rest, to climb the coconut tree for jellies to drink or to roast breadfruit, corn and yam or to eat a few joints of sugar cane? Suddenly this cowardly feeling dissolved. I resolved to be optimistic and display some mettle.

The following day I got on the horse and was on my way to Harmony. The first few days were very encouraging; I pitched in with those assigned to the pimento because that was the most urgent task. I ran up a tree and dislodged the laden limbs, came down and up another and carried on untiringly while the ladies admired my dexterity and verve. This set the pace and they shelled like mad to keep up with the bundles I was throwing down. Confidence rose and soon I was in mine own with them, meaning I didn't have to say, 'I'm going to tell my father that... ' because they knew that any adverse news to him would backfire: a bob or two would be docked from their pay. My father dropped in a few times unannounced and was pleased with what he saw. The workers were also satisfied, especially as they were allowed to finish early and to help themselves to firewood and food for the family. They knew, too, that I didn't tell my father that most days they were late for work.

One day I mounted the big black mare and decided to canter, a very silly thing to have done because the road, or rather track, was full of potholes and in part had some smooth flat stones concealed by mud. As the horse trotted along she slipped on one of those stones and I went flying over her neck, landing in the slush. Fortunately unhurt I quickly jumped up, glanced round and mounted and this time made sure she walked home.

I had now left school as my father's illness persisted. He consulted the doctor but the diagnosis was always negative. Nothing was found to merit alarm but since my father kept pestering him the doctor decided to try another medicine. After a couple of doses, to his amazement and shock, out came a creature, a tape worm eight inches long and one inch in circumference which had taken up residence in his intestine. Mother was always giving us worm medicines but never to my father; these were for children who ate unwashed fruit and walked barefoot. After this horrible experience, my father was back to being the successful farmer he always was.

School had a magnetic charm, despite the lashings. We got the message from day one that we were there to learn, and this was reiterated by parents. The three Rs were first and foremost. Woe betide the one who did not pay attention to that ball frame (abacus) and did not have the stones ready for doing the sums which followed. The times tables from two to twelve were committed to memory and recited every day in a sing-song manner, and for testing, there was mental arithmetic for half an hour after lunch. Reading and spelling were similarly conducted, and the dictation of a passage was a weekly exercise. Any mistakes made had to be rewritten two or three times over. The class stood as the teacher listened to individual reading, which had to be done observing the punctuation marks and demonstrating the expression evoked by the word, phrase or sentence. There were also lessons in grammar: the parts and figures of speech, analysing and parsing. All this for me was abstruse but I did enjoy the poetry – the recitation, as it was called; perhaps it was the way it was taught and appreciated, using words which were fresh, strong and concrete with absolute clarity to make the poem come to life. 'The Charge of the Light Brigade', 'The Psalm of Life', 'Elegy Written in a Country Churchyard' are some that come to mind as I write. Every year there was an elocution contest among the local schools, held at Manchioneal, an all-age school by the sea.

Manchioneal, in addition to being an important banana port six miles from Fair Prospect, was the location of some of the scenes in *Tom Cringle's Log*, written by Michael Scott way back in the nineteenth century. The school had a large playing field and it was this that attracted the boys rather than the contest. In fact, the girls were better at reciting but the boys were delighted to go along to meet with the schools from Long Road, Boston and Rural Hill. Foreign languages were not taught in elementary schools such as Fair Prospect; this was for the privileged who had the opportunity of attending high school.

The content of history lessons was mainly British but was enlightening, interesting and relevant to Jamaica. The voyages of John Hawkins, Francis Drake, the Sea Dogs, Admiral Pen, and General Venables who jointly took Jamaica from the Spaniards in 1655, and the Arawaks and Caribs were fascinating lessons; so also were the lives of those champions who played a prominent role in the abolition of slavery. Geography was mainly about the rivers, mountains, soil and climatic regions of the world in general and of Jamaica and Britain in particular. Of science there was very little, and that was on the basic practical and commonsensical level with which I was already conversant. The growing of crops and the mating of animals, insects and birds were my everyday experiences although the names of the skeletal and other parts of the body held my attention. There was also a school garden where pupils planted seeds and made notes of the progress of their growth. Scripture involved learning virtually all the main Bible stories of the Old and New Testaments, the parables and miracles. Select passages were learnt by heart. Rote learning in all subjects was essential, as there were no books available to pupils apart from a reading book bought by parents.

There was an assembly morning and evening when all the old hymns were vigorously sung. 'New every morning is Thy love', 'Oh for a faith that will not shrink', 'Oh God our help in ages past', 'Now the day is over'; these were some of my favourites. This was followed by a reading and moral exposition. The 23rd Psalm and the Lord's Prayer marked the close of the school day.

Teachers were not overly pedantic; they expected academic achievements but they also encouraged and exposed pupils to the arts: drawing, craft, singing, country dancing (which I didn't like because it meant pairing off with girls), acting and PE, i.e. drilling, running, rounders and cricket. Mr Marcus Barrett, the head teacher, was very keen on his pupils extending their knowledge beyond the shores of Jamaica, and he did everything to encourage and motivate us to read widely. There was only one newspaper then, the *Daily Gleaner*, but it was very informative.

At the outbreak of war I remember he abruptly brought the school to a halt with a loud bang on his table with the cane, *Gleaner* in hand. All the other teachers gathered round. This only took a few minutes as it was an open plan school, the blackboards being the lines of demarcation. Silence claimed, Mr Barrett went on to inform the school of the declaration of war and what it meant for the Empire. We were then sent home to tell our parents. Every day he read something of the happenings overseas so that we were kept abreast. When there was good news he was delighted and there would be a ring of the hand bell kept on his table which meant that everything stopped for some announcement or lecture. The map was unfurled to indicate where the actions occurred, as in the case of the Battle of the Plate after Britain sunk the German pocket battleship, the *Graf Spee* off Montevideo in South America. There followed a whole lesson on submarines which had all eyes glued to this diminutive figure with a round face, receding hair and a row of beautiful white teeth.

He instilled in us the need for good manners, behaviour and industry. His quote, 'The heights by great men reached and kept / Were not attained by sudden flight / But they, while their companions slept, / Were toiling upward in the night', was repeated whenever there was a hint of indolence on our part.

One day, Mr Barrett told us the story of his humble beginnings. He was the son of a small farmer who laboured every day just to be able to afford the two shillings and sixpence per month for the boy's evening lessons. Before Marcus took the first year's exam, his father died, but his mother went picking coffee so that he could continue his studies. He didn't disappoint her, passing the first and second year Jamaica Local Examinations at the first attempt and going on to the third year. Conceit struck; he thought he was bright and did not need to work hard. He began to spend his time playing cricket, which he was good at, becoming the captain of his team. He took the next exam but when the results came out Marcus had failed. His mother was very disappointed, and when he saw her crying he realised how much faith she had in him. How could he have let her down? 'No,' he said, 'I will never allow my mother to pick coffee and wash other people's clothes all the days of her life.' In this frame of mind he planted some potatoes and sold them and the following year he borrowed all the books that were available and went back to evening classes. He took the exam – consisting of eight subjects – and obtained a first-class pass at the age of eighteen. He was now eligible for entrance to Mico Teacher Training College where he spent the next three years graduating as a qualified teacher. Upon graduation he taught in Mandeville, and married before taking up the headship at Fair Prospect.

Mr Barrett, with his strong sense of vocation, did not confine himself to school. He made every effort to promote goodwill and cooperation in the community as was expected. Teachers and ministers were not there only to teach and preach; they were also advisors, JPs, speech-makers and will writers.

He made the residents aware of the importance of education by frequently calling them to meetings and outlining his plans and wishes for the children, then proceeded to establish a partnership whereby the better-off sponsored the children for evening classes. Because of his interest and concern for the welfare of the community as a whole, he had no problem enlisting people's wholehearted support in every matter concerning the school. Men were willing to forego a day's work in order to mend the leaks on the roof of the school, to repair the desks and benches and to chop away the withies and bushes around the perimeter fence. The children, likewise, played their part in obeying the rules and doing well, outshining children from other schools around.

A new era had began for the school until there was a severe drought and many farmers lost their crops. Another disaster was waiting to happen when the rains came: too much water for the drying season ruined what remained of the peas, beans, corn and some root crops. Bananas were not doing too well in the export market, either. Coconut oil replaced kerosene oil for light, as the latter was beyond most people's reach. Men made fire by striking flint and catching the sparks on paper. Farmers were bewildered and frustrated, and once again Mr Barrett stepped into the breach. In 1933, he met in conference with Rev. Binger, James Afflick, Blackwood and my father, and together they raised five pounds which were kept securely in the vicar's office. Loans from this were made available in five-shilling amounts. Borrowers handed over their land titles until the loan was repaid with a small interest which went to swell the principal. So much accumulated that in a few years the Long Bay Cooperative Bank was established giving more loans to more people. By 1944 it had become a thriving bank with its own building and a staff of two.

Mr Barrett flinched from nothing. He gave endlessly of his mental and physical energies to making Priestman's River a better place. It is no wonder his children did exceptionally well in life. Who was to predict that after many years his daughter would attend my wife at her home-delivery of my daughter in London and that one of his sons with an engineering degree would be employed by NASA. So much have I forgotten in many years but I still remember another of his quotes: 'Lives of great men all remind us that we can make our lives sublime, and, departing, leave behind us footprints on the sands of time.' My teacher was an inspiration who taught ex gratia.

I left school at the statutory age of fifteen and succumbed to my father's plea to join him as a full-time farmer. This meant the end of my ambition to continue my studies in the evenings. For years there had been a book about the First World War on the shelf. Reflecting on what Mr Barrett advised, I picked it up and began to read. In no time, I was so engrossed in it that it was difficult for me to do anything else in my spare time. It baffled and stretched my imagination and, with the war on, I was all the more preoccupied with the idea of fighting. When not reading, I was listening to the men discussing and giving their views about what was happening in Europe. It was all they seemed to talk about.

One day I overheard someone saying to my father that the Germans could not win the war on their own after the battle of Stalingrad. They reckoned that bananas would be in demand so proposed to put their savings into planting bananas on the fertile and virgin land at Mandingo River at the foot of the Blue Mountain. They did, and within nine to ten months, large purple buds began to appear under the thick sheaves of overlapping leaves and in quick succession fingers of bananas clustered together, several of these hands on one stem making a bunch. Some of these bunches were up to twelve hands, as was expected of this species, known as Gros Mitchel but to the locals 'Go Yark', meaning that they were the best for export, mainly to New York. The war continued, shipment was curtailed and the markets as far afield as Kingston were saturated. The result was that acres upon acres of the food of the wise lay rotting in the fields. When I rode Doris through the field and saw the sight of flocks of noisy birds pecking away and the rustle of mongooses and rats gnawing the ripe fruit, my heart sank. There were bananas to stone dogs. I decided then that such misfortune would be difficult for me to bear as a farmer and therefore I'd better be looking for a way out, but until then I had to stand by my father whose resolve and determination I came to admire. Export did pick up only to find that Gros Mitchel proved susceptible to Panama Disease, but hardy new varieties were introduced, the Lacatan and Robosta. Farmers were delighted with these but it was a laborious task to replant, mulch and wait almost a year for fruiting.

Not yet eighteen, I was contemplating joining the men who were leaving by the score to widen the Panama Canal to accommodate large warships transferring to and from the Atlantic and Pacific theatres of war, but that would be treading on father's toes. Other able-bodied men were also being enlisted for the armed services while some were on their way to the factories and farms of America. The depletion of men was particularly felt by the women who now had to more than plough the fields and scatter the good seed on the land; they also had to get the firewood, reap, trade in the market and fend for themselves in other ways that some bright spark observed and highlighted in the song 'Woman a capture man'.

At seventeen years of age, a young man was expected to have a girlfriend. I definitely had the urge but did not know how to make the approach, so I confided in my friend Nattle and expressed my desire. His words were, 'Come wid mi, mek mi show yu someting man'. Gleefully, I went along to his sick friend. He was a young man but looked thirty. What met my eyes completely obliterated the thought of girls from my mind. The left part of his groin had an inflamed swelling which had burst ejecting corruption, a bloody pus so offensive that I nearly puked. Nattie turned to me and said that rushing into a relationship can have devastating results; what I had seen was the effect of venereal disease. I left the scene dumbfounded.

I must say, I was fastidious, and girls did not bewitch me, perhaps because among the five sisters in my home were two of the most demanding girls and one domineering one from whose presence I was always fleeing to find refuge in mother. At school, one girl made it a habit of going into my shorts pocket for pennies and farthings to buy mint balls and paradise plums so I used to avoid her, without much success. What should I do to stop this intrusion? One day, I was leaning against the wall at ease. Glancing out of the corner of my eye, I saw her creep up by the side coming towards me. I nearly laughed but somehow managed to reserve it for later and allowed her to dip her hand deep into my pocket. This time, she didn't skip off with a sneering grin but let out a scream which had all heads in the playground turning in our direction to witness a lovely fat, green caterpillar fall from her hand. The laughter this generated was electric. She never as much as came near me, let alone put her hand in my pocket again.

The war was having its effects on every sphere of life in Jamaica. Petrol was rationed, thus making the already deplorable transport system worse. Private cars were non-existent for miles around and the few commercial vehicles were death traps. Horse and donkey carts were about the safest and most reliable. My vehicle, a second-hand bicycle which I acquired for two pounds (the money realised, selling an eighteen month old pig) made me mobile and gave me a sense of freedom cycling to Port Antonio and around the village. For going to Harmony, I would ride the horse or walk.

One Sunday in September 1944, I got up a little earlier than usual, 5 a.m., dressed, took my cutlass, the milk pan and a rope wrapped around my shoulders like a South American banderillero, and headed for Harmony to milk the cows. Pigs were grunting, fowls were flying off to their roosts, cocks were crowing – the village was alive. I had a couple of mangoes fallen from overhanging trees. On arrival, I lost no time washing the udders, milking the cows and hurrying back, stropping only at my grandmother's and an aunt's to deliver their supply of milk. This was because there was a warning that a hurricane was heading for Jamaica and would hit that day. The wind was now blowing fiercely and the driving rain was beating against my face. I hastened home and delivered the milk to my mother, occupied in the kitchen with preparing the breakfast. The children were getting restless and jittery, the dog was cringing and whining, and someone said an owl was heard that night. This was not a good omen, but my mind was on the breakfast.

Breakfast in our house was always sumptuous, especially on Sundays: ackee and salt fish, or fried fresh fish which could be silver kingfish, jack, snapper, cutlass fish or grunt. Barracuda was never on the menu as mother was not convinced that it was not poisonous. But the wind was now visibly approaching hurricane strength, and the young ones were clinging to mother's frock and following her around. I picked up my breakfast of a mug of hot, rich chocolate tea with the fat floating on top, fried dumplings (journey cakes), fried fish and fried ripe plantain and disappeared downstairs, a basement made possible by the fact that the house was erected on a slope. I was almost through when I heard crashing sounds outside, and when I looked out I could see the trees swaying in the wind; the coconut tree in front was just bowing and resisting till it snapped like a matchstick. Roofs were lifting off, and sheets of zinc were floating through the air like dry leaves. I thought the house was going to come down so I dashed out to the leeward side against the wind to join the others upstairs. I felt the earth move and there I was, struggling to hold my balance. It was an earthquake which didn't last more than a few seconds, but was frightening. I staggered to the front door and my father shouted for me to come in, shut the door and bolt it. It was scary. My little brothers and sisters were competing with one another for the arms and lap of mother who was praying and calling upon God to have mercy. Eventually the wind blew itself out, the rain stopped and there was calm.

My father and I went firstly to inspect the house for structural damage. Fortunately for us there was none, but three-quarters of the other houses around were either flattened or severely damaged. Three families moved into the basement of our house and stayed until repairs were done on theirs. As for the trees, only the odd ones here and there were left standing. Needless to say, as we surveyed the land all the fruit and nuts were on the ground, together with a few dead pigs and donkeys.

My brother and I were dispatched to our grandmothers' homes to check on their whereabouts and then to spread the word that all men were needed and should report the following morning, Monday, bright and early, to clear the blocked road so that emergency and essential supplies could come in. Father was in charge. At daybreak, sure enough, there was a noisy crowd outside our gate, some leaning on the verandah, some sitting on the barbecue, all ready for gang work. Not all would be employed on the same scale, but my father, astute as he was, managed to stretch it and be as equitable as possible, compromising here and there, as they settled for a day, half a day or a week or two as the case may be, but none went away dissatisfied or suspicious of favouritism.

While this was going on, Wilton and I were on another mission to see what had befallen the animals and plantation at Harmony. This was fun, as we picked our way through fallen trees, mangoes, coconuts, oranges and grapefruit, eating some and kicking some as we trudged through the mangled bits of what was once houses, singing:

> Me t'row piece-deal board, me t'row piece a deal board, me t'row piece a deal board, 'Pon de broad dutty water,
> Woy-oh, a how you come over?
> Me jump so, me jump so (three times)...
> Me rock so, me rock so...
> An a-so me come over.

On arrival, what met our eyes could not be imagined. We were flabbergasted. The trees had borne the brunt of the storm, and some were torn to shreds. The pimento and breadfruit hardly had any branches, but as these species are sturdy and deep-rooted the trunks were left standing, naked and bare, like streakers. The coconuts were all down. Surprisingly, the cows were either lying down chewing their cud placidly or suckling their calves who were equally oblivious to what had passed a few hours before. The pigs, however, seemed unsettled and perturbed as they huddled together in a corner of the sty. But as soon as they caught sight of us, all their fears evaporated and they grunted and trotted towards the perimeter, switching their tails and interested in nothing but their food. The gruntings became continuous squeals. Wilton made the fire and put on the kerosene pan and water while I quickly got the cocoa, breadfruit and bananas to boil for those impatient pigs. This took about half an hour, and then we fed them. We stood there, admiring how ravenously they were devouring the warm food.

For many people, as for the pigs, it was a question of feast today, famine tomorrow, so the abundance of windfalls was gathered up and preserved for coming days. Government supplies of rice, cornmeal, flour and corned beef were sent to my father for distribution, firstly to those with children and the aged, then to others according to needs. He took nothing for his own family lest any one accuse him of 'tiefing' or being miserly. One man came to lodge a complaint against a boy and to demand his arrest for having stolen his breadfruit. As the agricultural policeman, my father tried to dissuade him on the ground that the boy had not been seen picking the fruit, but he insisted. Just then the boy was seen passing the gate. 'See 'im de,' the man said. My father sprung from the verandah and with an athletic thrust, made a dash for the boy. All the little boys joined in the chase but the felon just showed them the dust, jumped over Auntie Kit's fence and disappeared in the bushes. We older ones, with our hands in our pockets, looked on and laughed to our hearts' content. My father returned from the pursuit breathless but satisfied that he had made an effort.

Two weeks before the cyclonic destruction, I was out one evening before dusk and came upon the Pentecostal preacher behaving in an unusual manner. With his head tilted back, he was facing a coconut tree by the side of the road. As I approached him I heard a muttering which became clearer as I got nearer. He was saying, 'Yu see all de wickedness, but your time is at han'.' Now preacher White was regarded as possessing legendary powers of institution, but when I told my father that I saw him in his white flowing robe talking to the tree, his comments did not show any credulity. He said, 'Papa White is mad – leave him alone, poor man.' Mother did not agree; she said he was prophesying and one should take heed.

This was not the only strange omen. Living next door to us was a cousin who kept pigs. The sow had a fine litter and was tied to the barbed wire fence. I was picking some oranges one day when I stopped to admire the beautiful piglets as they rooted around the mother, leapt on her, sucked and played. The sow got up and strutted around, but then suddenly there was a sea change. She made an aggressive lunge at one of the piglets, sending the other three screaming and scampering in all directions, and caught it on its hind leg and pulled it backwards. She threshed it against the hard earth while the defenceless little creature yelled and wailed until there was silence. I watched as the mother with her flabby underbelly squatted and began tearing into the soft flesh, devouring it. All that remained were a few bones and some black hair. When I asked daddy what he deduced from this repulsive and monstrous act, he said, 'Bwoy, the sow smell a rat; p'haps it was a water carrier and would be dead anyway.' My mother just sat there, biting on the inside of her bottom lip, a sign of contemplation, then she said, 'You remember that story in the Bible when there was such a famine that mothers ate their children?' I rest my case.

I saw myself now as getting 'big': eighteen years old and needing to be taking some initiative in improving my status. This was not going to be through farming, though the government was now offering grants for the purpose. It was too painful to see one's labour go down the drain and one's hopes turn to despair with no guarantee of compensation or redemption. I was too vulnerable to the uncertainties surrounding farming.

I had been trying to measure up to the educational standard of my sisters at least, but stopped short when it came to mathematics. My war book and a few historical accounts of the British Empire were my main preoccupations. I was obsessed with learning these facts at the time when the war was at its height. There was no radio in my home. The *Gleaner* provided information which was more or less passed on word of mouth, but by the time it got to the individual it was distorted beyond recognition, becoming a fairy tale. One was informed of the momentous battles being fought in Europe and of Great Britain being the conquerors, confirming what I was reading that the British people were intrepid not only as explorers and adventurers but as fighters.

As I read on, I made further discoveries that Britain, like the other European nations, took part in the rape of the Asian, African and American nations, resulting in the enslavement of millions of people, and that after many centuries cracks had begun to appear, with the old order changing and yielding to the new, such as the Dominions of Canada and Australia and New Zealand which were now granted their independence. America had long fought and won this. Now things began to fall in place. I was absolutely mesmerised by the amount of information I was accumulating and I felt imbued with enlightenment and knowledge.

Chapter Three

Many men from the Empire had been conscripted for the First World War, but for the Second World War the method of recruitment was voluntary; therefore, when the Macedonian call was made, young men and women from the colonies were ready, without compunction, to fight for the Mother Country.

It was four years into the war when I heard the appeal for men and I had no hesitation in responding. At the time, I was faced with two choices: a job in a factory or farm in the United States or to enlist for active service in Britain. I was in a quandary, but, having a mother as discerning as mine, I consulted her. In her own words she said, 'My son, the Mother Country is at war; go, and if you survive you will not regret it.' I had had my decision confirmed, so I answered the advertisement in the *Gleaner*. The reply was prompt – received on the very day I was instructed to attend at the Titchfield High School in Port Antonio, twelve miles away. My bike was decrepit and could not stand up to the journey. I would be late if I rode it, so I sprinted down the road with the hope of catching the bus which I spotted leaving the stop as I straightened up round the bend. As it was taking the hill, belching out smoke, I held on to the half-opened door, heaved myself in and got to Port Antonio with fifteen minutes to spare.

There were about three hundred of us, eagerly awaiting the selection procedure. We were given two sets of written tests. Having taken the first, we were given a break while the papers were marked. The excitement and chattering continued even at the end of the interval, when only those whose names were called could go on to the second test. My heart was pounding and I was apparently temporarily deaf because someone nudged me and said, 'Answer to your name, man.' I was not too surprised, as the test was general knowledge, basic arithmetic and English, all of which was easy enough. The second test was more difficult, but the success of the first gave me the confidence and steady nerves to tackle the multifarious papers which I also passed. I was in seventh heaven. I could hardly contain myself. I rushed home to break the news to the family who were waiting with bated breath, some with reservations. My siblings weren't too happy about my going to war, and nor was my grandmother, yet there was rejoicing when the facts were known.

That night, I lay awake imagining what was ahead, what good or ill may be reserved for me. I was filled with anticipation of how I was going to come in contact with the machine guns, the planes and the brave men as my war book *The Nations at War* described. I had flashbacks, too, of war poems like 'The Battle of the Baltic' by Thomas Campbell, when the price of all the land, (speaking of Nelson) leads them on:

> Hearts of oak! our captain cried,
> When each gun from its adamantine lips
> Spread a death-shad round the ships
> Like the hurricane eclipse
> Of the sun.

Soon the news was over the whole village – 'Sam is going to war' – and it was going to be expeditious. This was going to be my first experience of leaving home, so there was a mixture of apprehension, anticipation, joy and a sorrow, but there wasn't time to be preoccupied with these emotions. The list of personal belongings had to be packed: toothbrush, comb, towels, clothes and footwear. The four of us from the village were to report to Port Antonio for a warrant to board the troop train for Kingston.

The intervening days slipped by and soon it was Saturday, the last full day with my family. Excitement rose to fever pitch, and fear jostled to captivate my heart. My head was buzzing with reminiscences and expectations. I had mixed feelings about Harmony, the work and the ticks but there were also memories of the times when my brothers and I (unknown to my father) used to ride the boar hog, the ram goat and the cow, which tickled me. Recollections of my fellow men singing the songs of the stone breakers: 'Godung a Manuel Road gal an' bwoy, fi go bruck rock stone, bruck dem one by one, gal an' bwoy' bore a tinge of sympathy and pity. I reflected on the game I used to watch my sisters play – 'Little Sally Water', 'Jane and Louisa will soon come home', 'When you see Aa pretty girl' – and knew that those days were past. Gone, too, were the family gatherings on the verandah at the cool of the day to listen to Anancy stories and stories from the Bible before retiring to bed. I thought of when at moonlight we made 'moonshine darling' i.e. a member of the group would lie on the ground and the body would be outlined by bits of broken crockery. The person would be lifted up leaving the shiny duppy to frighten adults at night. If you could imagine a branch wrenched off by a storm and smashed into bits of fragments, what you would see with your mind's eye would resemble me on that last day in my father's house. These memories washed away all but the froth of my past years and almost enfeebled me.

Expectations were more defined by what I thought war should be: fighting with real guns, seeing numerous dead and wounded, or being one of either. No, I mustn't be morbid: 'Our ingress into the world was naked and bare, out progress through the world is trouble and care, out egress from the world will be, nobody knows where, but if we do well here, we shall do well there.'

Relatives and friends were coming and going, wishing me God's speed, safe journey and offering a word of prayer. For all this I was thankful but sad. The dinner was like the Passover meal. It was the regular Saturday one: rich beef soup with breadfruit, yam dumpling and cocoa, my favourite dish to which I couldn't do justice even with much coaxing. Conversations for the rest of the evening were subdued and singularly confined – very careful and sensible. I rechecked all the listed items, as I had to leave for the early and the only bus for the day and to spend the night in Port Antonio ready for the train on Monday. The night passed with hardly a wink. Sunday was the day of the final goodbye. After I had had a mug of milk and a piece of bread, my mother gave her last homily, my father his last set of advice and the children their last tears. We embraced and kissed. I picked up my grip with my few belongings intact and left the house. At the gate I paused and turned for a last look. I felt empty, so with a bowed head, I whispered something to my Father in heaven; my fears evaporated and I knew I would be all right. Family and friends followed me with their eyes until I was out of sight. Parting is such sweet sorrow.

As I boarded the bus and sat down, a man looked across and said, 'You are George King, son,' to which I replied in the affirmative. He was the Public Works Officer to whom my father was answerable for road works. We chatted and he commended me for my bravery in wanting to go to war. So impressed was he that he invited me to his home for the rest of the day and night. During the day, Ganger, as he was called, took me out for a drink which was Coca-Cola for me, but I bought a cream soda on my way back for his wife who prepared rice and peas and chicken for Sunday dinner.

At the crack of dawn on that Monday in September, 1944, I was ready to leave my kind and thoughtful hosts for the railway station. Having complied with the instruction to obtain a warrant and to check in, I boarded the steam train together with others. At the appointed time it pulled out at the blast of a whistle which reverberated in the silent hills. Using the only language it knew, carriages snaked their way to the first stop: Buff Bay, then Anatto Bay, Highgate and Spanish Town, admitting only volunteers in whose presence I could now relax. I even began to feel liberated and independent.

Military officials met us at the terminus, Kingston, and spared no time in loading us into jeeps and escorting us to the army camp at Mona where we were to undergo intensive training for one month before the journey to the final destination: England. Upon arrival, nearly two thousand of us were massed into a large hall for the roll-call, the briefing as to the domestic arrangements, and, more importantly, to be told in no uncertain terms the reason for us being there. We were assigned to huts – fifty in each, with no more than eighteen inches of space between the folding beds and a sort of biscuit mattress. Schedules for each day were explained, and having understood and digested all this information, we were dismissed for the night.

The grounds were extensive, and a high and solid brick wall, topped with a bed of mortar and barbed wire, encompassed the while. This was the limit of our domain except on occasions when training required us to leave this prison-like rampart. The part for parading and exercising was level and covered with fine gravel.

For the first few days of mobilisation we were taught the rudiments of army life. At the end of the first week, the sergeant gave the command for us to be ready for a run which we all thought was going to take place within the grounds. It turned out to be the run of my life, from Mona to Papine, covering a distance of five miles. Men fainted in the soaring heat of ninety degrees Fahrenheit. As if that wasn't enough, in a couple of days we were told to prepare for a repeat with full kit. The training became more and more demanding and exhausting, but by the end of the four weeks it had achieved its intended consequence of an integrated and disciplined, well-adjusted squad: a unit oozing with exuberance and motivation transformed into a sharp, alert, rational and pertinacious group, but it was the most taxing and austere time of my life.

In the regimes, the officers, from the colonel down through the ranks to the warrant officer, sergeant major sergeant and corporal, were like mullahs. What they said was law; it was not ours to reason why. The sergeant in charge of my group, all six feet of him, moved with an overweening air of superiority and self-confidence, earning him the name of Swagger Stick Black Swan. Despite all this, the officers made sure we were well fed.

The long-expected instruction went out one day that all volunteers should be ready for departure the following day and that we could leave the camp for four hours. The frantic packing, which was not very much, began in earnest, and in such a confined space it was pretty hectic. It was then that I had to display a measure of calm when one man with a quick sleight of hand swapped my clean shirt for his dirty one. This was resolved when another of my friends asked if he were aware of my boxing skills.

The night was marred by a loud bawling. Upon investigation it was discovered that a young man was in so much anguish and foreboding that he had lost his nerve and was crying for his mother. The experts tried, with little success, to calm him down. For reasons unknown to me I was summoned to help.

Remembering the New Testament my mother had slipped in my case, I took it, proceeded to console and counsel this unfortunate youngster, then read a Psalm. He did listen and he stopped crying, but in the morning when we all assembled for the roll-call he was not there. He must have been of sound mind to pass the tight security on the compound and escape without being shot.

We left the camp as we came in, in a convoy of military vehicles that morning in October 1944, and were escorted to the SS *Cuba* awaiting us in Kingston harbour. As was expected, friends and relatives were there in their thousands to have a last look at us embarking on a long, hazardous and precipitous journey. They knew that ships were being sunk in Atlantic waters perhaps more than anywhere else but there was no turning back. We waved and they waved and hallooed words which were lost in the gentle breeze. The gangplank lifted, the siren sounded and the ship eased out to deeper and deeper waters while we gazed on Jamaica getting smaller and fainter until there was none of her at all. As darkness fell and the Caribbean enveloped the liner, I struggled to control my lachrymal gland, but it was irrepressible and I gave way. The commanding officer, putting a stop to self-pity or signs of femininity and indulgence, ordered us to the lower deck where, after evidence of our legitimacy to be on board was checked, bunkers were allotted and the schedule to be observed for the next four weeks was posted up; we were allowed to move freely until next mealtime, after which we dispersed to the bunkers for overdue rest.

Days into the sailing, it was comforting to note that we were not alone on the high seas; in fact, we had been in a convoy of US and British troop and merchant ships, and tankers and a battle ship could be seen at all times on the horizon. The SS *Queen Mary* joined the convoy in New York but soon steamed ahead. The SS *Cuba* was a French troop ship with a French crew. The physical environment left much to be desired, being as dirty and smelly as the fish we were fed with and could not stomach. The food was so bad that at night we sneaked out to the bakery to buy illicitly sold rolls.

We seemed to have sailed close to the coastline of America – up to Newfoundland – before cutting across to the British Isles, to minimise the risk of being torpedoed by German submarines. Having the protection of the battleship, we got complacent until at about 2.30 a.m. we heard one night, 'Now hear this, all hands on deck, get your life jackets.' We leapt out of bed and proceeded to our designated areas to wait for further instruction. Half an hour later the announcement was 'all hands below deck'. There were sighs of relief all round.

We had evaded the German submarines but could not escape the weather conditions which were hair-raising, with the wide expanse of the deep blue ocean surging and chopping, heaving, beating, gyrating and rearing high against the monstrous grey ship, lashing it with ungovernable flurry. As the ship plunged and rose with the immense sweeps and swells of the whirls, the current of the North Atlantic Drift, moving in our direction, gave an extra nudge to the speed. Unlike the ship, passengers experiencing such turbulence of the stomach were left weak from the ejection of its contents. Those of us with little experience of the sea thought the gap was closing between time and eternity. There were, however, periods of tranquillity when there were war films, talks on the need for personal hygiene practices at all times and literature on various situations and conditions which required common sense and vigilance.

Chapter Four

Christopher Columbus, on his first voyage to the New World, escaped the mutiny of his marauding men only by their sighting land. At the beginning, our expedition was novel but with minimal recreational facilities coupled with emphasis on theoretical and contrived exercises, there was evidence of flagging. As young active men, however, we passed the leisure time in socialising, especially with those from the other West Indian islands who had been transferred to Jamaica to join us. One sometimes had to take to one's bunk, being sick and dizzy, but it was an opportunity for one to reflect not only on how magnificent a thing a liner is but also on how wonderful is the manifestation of God's power: the power of the ocean in this case.

Land, at last. The SS *Cuba* made a sharp turn in the choppy sea, slowly glided into harbour and dropped anchor. We were in Greenock on the Clyde near Glasgow; it was November 1944. Silence and attention having been demanded, a stammering message was heard on the wireless welcoming all volunteers to the shores of Great Britain. It was the voice of King George VI. He had scarcely finished when we were given a short lecture, then ordered to get in the pre-arranged groups and march to the train waiting in the station. At first, I was much too disoriented to observe anything accurately until self-possession was restored. My gaze fell instinctively downwards then outwards, and what a sight! It was beautiful white snow.

'Oh, though your sins be as scarlet, they shall be as white as snow.' The sergeant disturbed these elevated thoughts and called out for a 'quick march' to the train. In store for us on the train was the hospitality of the Salvation Army serving much-appreciated cups of tea and buns, accompanied by kind words, while we were whizzed to the place from where military lorries would convey us to the military camp at Filey in Yorkshire to begin training. The wind was biting, cutting through to the bones. It was not easy to endure after coming from the tropics with temperatures of eighty or ninety degrees. We jumped off the vehicles into snow up to the ankle, and for good measure there was sleet which stung like the red ants back home.

The squadron leader gave a brief welcome, then it was on to business assigning us to billets, twelve to a billet. Other relevant information was given, including the programme for the following day, starting with a parade at 6 a.m. After the interval, we were called to the mess hall for the first British meal – mashed potato, cabbage and a piece of meat. We glanced around, meeting the rolling eyes of our comrades as if to say, 'Wha' dis man, no dumpling, no rice and peas an' chicken.' We had it, and anyway, we would eat anything. What was more pressing was sleep, so off we went to the billets. As was expected, the Tannoy went and we were on our feet, not sufficiently recovered from the fatigue of the journey but obey we must. Bearing our mess tin, utensils and a mug we trooped to the mess hall for breakfast followed by a parade. It was then that I felt a sense of pride, and all nostalgia evaporated.

The training was more technical now, involving aircraft recognition, gun handling, grenade throwing, map reading and, most disturbing, detection and avoidance of poison gas to which one had to come in contact to be acquainted with the effects. Test and gradings went hand in hand with the training, culminating in a grilling one at the end. I remember how disappointed I was in my performance for aircraft recognition, having been awarded seventy per cent, but the sergeant instructor said not to worry when I heard: the German Messer Schmitt would recognise it. He was right.

The greatest problem was coping with the cold. We from the tropics used to bung up every crevasse. One night the sergeant made a visit to our billet and felt the warmth. In his commanding voice he called out, 'Open up – you need fresh air.' I woke next morning under a frozen blanket, and the result was a shocking cold.

After three months, our togetherness terminated with us splitting up into categories for ground crew trade training as aircraft engineers, wireless operators, instrument restorers, cooks, clerks and such like. I was posted to the fighter station, RAF Hawkinge near Folkestone, for general duties which was a godsend – an escape from the extreme cold in Filey.

While travelling south on the train, I could not help but notice the beautifully laid out farms, the green wheat fields, the apple orchards and the expanse of green grasslands in the countryside. One was to move from this arresting sight to the view of a low grey mist hanging over London in the early morning, barely revealing the black, dull chimneys like sculptured mummies. As the train moved cautiously along to Kings Cross station en route to London Bridge, I saw the bombed sites and recognised that the buildings were enormous, their remains silhouetted against the skyline. While awaiting the train for Hawkinge, we were taken to a deep air raid shelter at London Bridge. I had never been this far underground, and with it being poorly lit it was scary.

My observation, as I went along, was that most of the Kent coast had gone to seed: houses were bombed, shops deserted, lawns and open spaces overgrown and weedy – a picture of the nation at war.

Hawkinge was the nearest aerodrome to occupied Europe and had a history of persistent attacks on the utilities around resulting in hardship and danger for the locals. They were, however, proud of their town and resolved to do whatever it took to defend it from the enemy – so much so that although it was inconvenient they did not object to the closure of the road leading west out of the village. The road was used as a landing strip for Spitfires. On landing these were pushed into the woods or into bunkers against enemy raids. We, too, were domiciled in billets erected in the woods because the Germans were bombing the camps. When I learned of this fact, innumerable apprehensions and uncertainties filled my gloomy mind but were dispelled both by the glorious green shoots and flowers of spring and by the lines of Joseph Addison:

Amidst all the evils that threaten me, I will look up to Him for help and question not, for He will either avert them or turn them to my advantage. Though I know neither the time nor the manner of death I am to die, I am not at all solicitous about it because I am sure that He knows them both and that He will not fail to comfort and support me under them.

The tempo was a little more relaxed here at Hawkinge. On the first Sunday, at dinner in the mess, I allowed myself to engender a sense of pride in being a volunteer to the Royal Air Force in company of men from Australia, Burma, Canada, New Zealand, South Africa and others of the

British Empire, with JAMAICA emblazoned on the shoulder of my smart uniform. In the billets, with the exception of the South Africans, we all warmed to each other, going out together on evenings off to Canterbury. Big Tom Bozart, a South African whom nature did not design to live in a thicket, was nearly seven feet tall and did not find it easy to negotiate his way along the path under the thick low overhanging branches. After a few months, he was walking with a slight stoop.

The residents of Hawkinge got to know the military personnel, were very sociable and made every effort to make us feel at home. The Hawkinge and District Young Farmers' Association asked Ben Williams, a Jamaican, to give a talk on farming in Jamaica with special emphasis on the cultivation of bananas. Ben accepted the invitation, then, realising that he had never planted a banana sucker and scarcely been in a banana field, he came looking for the 'peasant'. Ben was about thirty years old, carrying a brown oval face with a carefree expression, and at a height of two inches under six feet, he looked like a full-grown bull. He could be aggressive, as I was to suffer one morning when I was late for breakfast and rushed to the mess hall with hair uncombed and buttons unpolished. Ben vented his wrath and reminded me of the unwritten rules of the older West Indian air crew colleagues: play the game, look respectable, behave civilly in public, be British. Ben now solicited my help in this dilemma: could I speak the following Saturday evening to the young farmers? I was the only country boy in the camp.

I tried every trick in the book to avoid speaking. 'In my area in Portland,' I said, 'apart from visiting some irrigated fields, I—' but he interjected, 'Say yes or no'. I hesitated, then said yes. There and then he gave me the instructions how to get to the hall which was used as a school, a chapel, a storehouse for equipment and as a meeting house for all public occasions in the area. It was hidden among the trees and isolated; Junkers 88 pilots did not like targets like these.

It was going to be my first public speech so I went to the library for help on the subject, but there was not much. However, from one book I made notes for my introduction on the general geography of Jamaica, the population and produce; the rest would come from my previous knowledge, common sense and experience.

The day I dreaded arrived, and in my best uniform, accompanied by my mates, I made my way to the hall. Ben had informed the secretary that Sam King would be the speaker. Sure enough, there was my name on the notice board to speak on Jamaican farming alongside government notices, banns of marriage and announcements of where to obtain various items. The hall was fairly big, and the door opened directly into it. The blackout curtains were drawn and I could see in the shaded light that there were about eighty people sitting among the many bags, crates, and farm implements. Ben, having introduced me to the chairman, took his seat in the audience while I was escorted to the platform. The chairman stood, made some remarks and called upon me to speak.

Knees almost buckling, I managed to compose myself in the face of the curious crowd, and responded in the usual manner, wishing everyone a good evening and thanking them for the invitation. Placing my notes on my left, I started by giving a description of the geographic position and exports of the island. Glancing at my airman's watch I saw that I had taken ten minutes of the scheduled time. My father, before I had left, had planted two acres of bananas in the virgin foothills of the Blue Mountains and I had helped, so I just talked about the lowland planting still fresh in my mind: my last farming job.

I talked of suckering and how to ascertain a continuous crop, then went on to show how labour-intensive the cultivation of bananas can be: the need to keep the trees from weeds and parasitic plants, to support the trees with heavy bunches, spraying – the lack of which can result in a whole plantation being lost to disease and insects – and reaping, which is a specialised job as the trees can attain a height of ten or fifteen feet and a bunch can weigh up to forty pounds.

I dealt with the need for gentle and careful handling of the fruit in reaping and with the difficulty farmers face in transporting the bananas from the fields to the buying station where they are thoroughly scrutinised for any signs of bruising and immaturity. It is at this stage of grading that farmers hold their breath, as the rejection of even one stem of bananas means less money for his dependants waiting anxiously at home. I spoke of the spin-offs in the banana industry in terms of it providing jobs not only in the fields but at the station where clerks are employed for checking and recording and for packers and loaders on the Canadian, American, British and European vessels.

Having dismissed this part with ease I began to wax bolder. My eyes were no longer fixed before me; my whole body, until now stony and rigid, relaxed, and a smile quivered from my lips. I was confident that I had a captive audience, and became expansive. I launched out into sugar cane growing and the distilling of rum, then moved on to cocoa, coffee, coconut, citrus fruits and lastly cash crops, e.g. vegetables. In my concluding remarks, I touched on the subject of marketing and what an insurance to farmers was the preferential tariff promoted by Britain, thanked the audience for their patience and sat down, thinking that all was over.

The chairman, after a loud and prolonged applause, simply invited questions from the floor indicating that I would be happy to answer them. A little red-headed boy of about seven raised his hand and asked, 'What does a banana look like?' I tried my best to explain that it looked like a small cucumber: green, then turning yellow when ripe and ready for eating, sweet and pleasant to the taste and recommended for its food value. There was also a question on the percentage of farmlands ploughed by tractors. This I couldn't answer precisely, saving to say that most ploughing was done manually using a fork and in a few cases, animals. On the question on chickens I was at home.

There were refreshments laid out for all. A blue-eyed maid with an outdoor freshness about her brought me a cup of tea and a cake, and after a brief period of socialising it was time to return to the billet three-quarters of a mile away, convinced that it was a success.

We were held in esteem and with affection by the locals in and around the village. Some days later Ben brought a quantity of fruits on his service bike and a message to say there was plenty more where they came from. A couple of days hence, the Education Officer met me and thereupon recommended that we at the camp make use of the educational facilities. But just when I was loving the place and had adjusted myself to the bullish disposition of the flight sergeant, I was promoted and given forty-eight hours' notice to report to movements control at RAF Cranfield in Bedfordshire. In that time, relevant signatures had to be obtained and all my belongings had to be assembled. Regrettably, I was unable to say goodbye to those young farmers.

Once again, I had to pass through London and had the chance of seeing it in the clear light of day. I was not impressed, and in fact was eager to get out for fear of the

German V1 and V2 rocket attacks. Alighting from the train at Cranfield, I was encompassed by a crowd of inquisitive and smiling children to whom I had to give assent because of their insistence in taking my luggage and accompanying me to the bus which was to transport me to the camp. On arrival I was cleared for a specific duty smack in the middle of the airfield in a radar van working on my own linked by telephone and electrical wires to a large box of electrical instruments.

In preparing me for the post, the Canadian officer in charge confined me to camp for memorising top secret codes within seven days. I had always had a flair for facts and details so I set to work designing the best way to master it and meet the deadline. Within five days, I reported that the assignment was completed and that I was ready for the test. The radar officer was delighted. I was expecting him to reward me with two days leave when I would go into town; instead, he told me to go to sleep. I was not allowed to leave the camp for a month.

It was horrible night work aiding Mosquitoes in landing. I loved the place but hated the work, partly because of the tremendous boom and partly because of the possibility of an accident. I almost got paranoid thinking the planes would one day land on my head. Fortunately, in a matter of months I was shifted to RAF Locking in Somerset near Weston-Super-Mare to be trained as an aircraft engineer. There I met Al Gibson and Andy Brown who had both been apprentice engineers at the Innswood sugar factory in Jamaica and were now on the same course as myself. More than a few airmen of Polish origin were at Locking. They had run away and joined the service. The stories they used to tell were incredibly sad, gory and macabre – how the Russians had liberated their country from the Germans but put a Draconian regime in place; we sarcastically retorted, 'Why didn't your country try and join the British Empire?'

It was while I was at Locking in May 1945 that Churchill made the victory announcement of the end of the war in Europe. There were lavish outbursts, almost pandemonium, but exigent duties still had to be done. I was in charge of locking the hanger and of the safe-keeping of the keys, and by the time I had done the necessary and had run to the cookhouse, everyone had gone. I hastily dressed in my best suit and headed for Weston-Super-Mare. As I alighted from the bus a woman ran out of the Black Bull towards me, and on seeing my epaulette, grabbed me, saying, 'You are Jamaican', took me in the pub and bought me a drink. It was rum, and before I could tell her that although I may have helped to produce the stuff, I do not drink it, the glass was at my lips. I had to be civil and make the effort and join in the carousing, the merrymaking and the wild excitement until I quietly and unobtrusively slipped away.

The following morning, we were reminded that there was a war and the Japanese were still to be beaten, so it was back to duties. Al, Andy and I tackled the training with zest and pride and upon completion were posted to Swannington, Norfolk, where the cold winds from the North Sea never seemed to cease blowing. If man's ingratitude was compared to them we should shun the very semblance of thought from which it emanates. After a couple of weeks we learned of our entitlement to two weeks' leave and were put in touch with a service hostel on London Road in Manchester. People were very open and generous to servicemen; there were invitations to the cinema, church parties and the like. We attended a courtroom trial which was very informative and interesting, but at the end of the first week, I felt that to spend two weeks in this way was pointless, whereupon I travelled to London, stayed at the Union Jack and found a back-breaking temporary job at the Mann-Crossman & Pauline brewery unloading and packing beer, thereby supplementing the meagre air man's allowance out of which there were compulsory deductions made for next of kin – in my case, my mother.

Everywhere we were posted we found that the people had one thing in common, and that was their capacity for kindness and consideration. We had numerous invitations to cold homes but warm hearts in Swannington. Although we were always aware of the transience of our stay in any one place, it was always met with some regret at having to leave: more so at Swannington, because it was there that we united with the rapturous and uninhibited community in the celebration of victory in Europe. The Ward family comes to mind. Mr Ward, together with his eldest daughter, worked for the local council in Swannington and they had invited the three of us to their home in Nottingham when they learned that we were to leave for another assignment in Rivenhall, Essex.

Relationships with colleagues cemented as we moved from place to place. At Rivenhall I worked with gliders, in a quieter atmosphere, unlike the windy Norfolk where working outside on camouflaging Mosquitoes could be murder. Here, we had time and opportunity for outdoor activities and to be involved with the locals. Of my colleagues, Al Gibson was small in stature, no more than five foot six, twenty-two years old and walked with a slight draw in the left foot, but he had a cool, calculated manner. Andy Brown was the dead opposite – tall, all Jamaican boy who spent his spare time weight training from which he derived a beautiful body in shape and form. By nature he was arrogant, always referring to his privileged background and showing off his muscles.

None of these peculiarities were sufficient to mar our work or deportment at the camp. In fact the adjutant was very pleased not only with our military performance but with our ability to contribute to the ethos of the camp and the well-being of the community. Al was a stylish opening bat for the cricket team, David Petgrave could show some academic achievements from his evening studies at the Chelmsford Adult Education Department, and I was the assistant sports instructor and the boxing champion in the welterweight class.

I was trained in boxing for the RAF Cup by Ron Peeling, a Belgian professional boxer, and my opponent was the former Egyptian champion. Peeling instructed me to use the left jab and parry. I did that in the first round, and for the second he said to mix it with the right. Halfway through the round the Egyptian got in close and gave me a pounding in the chest and stomach. When I returned to my corner, Peeling was not pleased with me for letting him in. 'Keep him at a distance with the jab and watch for a gap, then go in with a long right to the head. Always look under the sheep's clothing: it may only be a sheep.' I did just that; a mighty right struck him on the chin and he fell – more he was put in hospital. Having won the cup, I was elated and sent it to my parents. My mother replied, congratulating me but strongly advising that I quit boxing. I never boxed again and the cup is on my sister's bookshelf in Hope Bay.

At Rivenhall, I met Fred Seagraves who took me home to his parents in Bulwell, Nottingham. They were to become my 'English parents' – Mam and Pap – and I was their black son. The Seagraves had a shop, and whenever I visited them on my days off, my job was to weigh parcels of sugar, rice and flour or make the fire until they arrived from the shop. Because I felt the cold so much, Mam used to put a brick in the coal fire, wrap it in a towel or newspapers and place it between the covers.

The camp was a wartime one and was closing down. All the West Indian boys were called together, about twelve of us, and the adjutant, in appreciation of our commitment and conduct, had a drink with us. We were to be on the march again, this time to Desborough near Kettering.

Beautiful and verdant was the countryside around Desborough. It was a long distance – covered by bicycle – from the camp to the hangers but it was a journey made pleasant as I flashed my eyes right and left to capture the charm of the herbage, enabling divestment and disentanglement of fruitless thoughts and allowing peace and calm to pervade my being. It was a panorama no human imagination can conceive. The only obstacle was Market Harborough Hill – one mile long -- which, at first, I found tedious.

I was the senior aircraft finisher and was in charge of some twenty prisoners of war, one of whom willingly interpreted for me. 'Fünf Minuten für fünf' was the signal for the men to stop work and wash their hands. Another was a POW captured from a German submarine in the Caribbean by the Americans and once sent to work on a plantation in Jamaica. Fritz was his name. When he set eyes on me he shouted, 'Scheisser, scheisser.' I didn't know a word of German, but from his countenance I detected that he was being resentful so I proceeded to add insult to injury by instructing him to clean the hanger and the trucks. No, he was not going to take orders from an ignoramus black Jamaican. Confrontation was never my style but nor was cowardice, so I had a word with my interpreting POW who in turn told the offending brat that King would lock him up and feed him on bread and water until his papers were processed. Fritz was the one who showed the white feather: he backed down and obeyed then and always. To my surprise, just before I left that camp Fritz presented me with a silver ring he had made, apologised and credited me with being fair to prisoners of war. In acceptance, I gave him five shillings, as officers should not receive gifts.

Hitch-hiking to the Seagraves in Bulwell continued; the family could not do enough for me who had nothing but my service to give in return. How Mam would make delicious puddings when she was expecting me and encouraged me to eat up although there was rationing! In addition to the household chores I used to lop the trees when they were no longer required for camouflage. In the course of time, Mam's close relatives died: grandma, Uncle Jim and Pap, leaving her alone in the little terraced house. Fred, her son was away in the RAF. Mam could more than afford a better place, but, in her own words, she said, for over forty years her family and friends had come and gone using the same door and she wasn't going to change that. The rapport I had with Mam was firmly established and nursed until her death twenty-one years later. The servicemen's popularity with the locals continued to flourish. Families frequently made a special effort to have us in their homes for Sunday lunch, for which we were always grateful.

One day at Desborough, three of us were given the job of clearing out an empty disused billet. One of them proposed that I tell stories of Jamaica while they did the work. At first I thought this was a joke, but they insisted it was not, so I assented. Sitting on a pile of bedding I tried my best to entertain them with stories of village life: the farm, school, food, storms, earthquakes, games and fun, the catapults we made, the birds we shot and the subsequent cook-out in the fields. Anancy duppy stories which they relished though they could not have understood, being city boys.

One of these young men, Harry Challis, was to become one of my best friends to this day. Harry was a mother's boy, a fine young man of twenty-three who did not like the service food, something which probably accounted for him looking pale. His eye strain, I believe, was due to his love of reading and the low wartime light. He was the sort of person on whom one could depend, and I was delighted when he was included in the next move to Dishforth, Ripon.

It was now back to Yorkshire – the place where I had been so uncomfortable in the freezing cold which never seemed to abate. Ripon was a tiny cathedral city, sparsely populated and connected by road to the vast sprawling camp at Dishforth.

As the assistant to the corporal, I worked eagerly outside or in an open hanger but there was no diversion from the labour which entailed de-icing, repainting, repairing and generally making the large York transport planes suitable presumably for warmer climates; we were not supposed to know their destination. It was exasperating. I remember in one team our united endeavours could not prevent the paint thinner from freezing, so we used de-icer and it worked.

Dishforth was my worst camp. I had previously heard the word prejudice but racism was not in vogue. I was, however, to have a taste of it, but thank God, not from my associates. A tall blond officer entered the billet one night and after a quick sweep, his eyes with intolerable horror rested on me in the bed. In an arrogant, strident, ridiculously pompous South African drawl, he pointed a finger in my direction and, with his head ninety degrees to the others, said, 'And what is he doing in here? He can't sleep here.' The apparent dismay was intense. A moment lapsed, then my friend Harry, bless him, stepped forward, burning with impetuous fury, looked him in the face and said, 'I don't know where you come from or where you've been, but he is Sam, a volunteer to the war from Jamaica. He is sleeping right where he is.' An alteration took place in the South African's strange demeanour, and like a dog with his tail between his legs, he walked out of the billet. Since then, my repugnance for racism, hinted or insinuated, has gained strength as I grow in years.

Harry and Al had similar interests; both attended evening classes in engineering and it was Al that Harry invited to his home, but Al would be found nowhere else but on the dance floor when he was on leave. The invitation was therefore passed to me to meet his mother living in Putney, London, to stay for the weekend. Apart from the Union Jack and Lyons corner shop where I washed dishes to boost my earnings I knew very little about London, so I was delighted. It was a long journey by train – four hours, arriving late on the Friday. I was greeted warmly, had a chat and was shown my room.

The weekend passed with only a stroll around the area. I was confined to bed partly because I was exhausted and partly because I was oppressed by a thousand conflicting thoughts concerning my future. The war with the Japanese was won. There was still work to be done at Dishforth, but that would be short-term, after which we were to be sent to Coventry, literally, for civilian trade training in preparation for civilian life. My experience of life outside the military in Britain was minimal. The options before me were whether to go straight back to Jamaica and sign on for a career in the Royal Air Force or finish my apprenticeship in England. After much deliberation and observation, I came to the conclusion that, given the stability of the country, the facilities and opportunities for acquisition of knowledge and the comparative wealth, it would be more advantageous to settle for the latter. All falterings of the mind were now under control. I had already begun a correspondence course in plumbing and would continue. But on my return to camp and subsequently to Coventry I was refused a place on the plumbing course. The only one available was carpentry, and I registered.

Dishforth was the parting of the way for most airmen: addresses were exchanged and the dispersal was set in motion, some to their homes in Britain and abroad and some suitable employment elsewhere. Few chose trade training camps. Comradeship came to an end, but no one can erase the vivid and cherished memories of friends and acquaintances. It is from this reservoir that I draw sensory impressions of some who displayed commendable courage and prudence, some who could be obstreperous given the chance, some the opposite – excessively reserved, some facetious and some with a sense of humour.

In the latter category, the first who comes to mind is Samuda, alias Saboteur. He often had us aching with laughter, even in adversity. Samuda's humour was not only in words but in deeds, depending on the particular flash of inspiration. He was an avid reader and was always saying he was going to do something spectacular which would make us wonder. That kept us guessing. One day, an unauthorised Spitfire took off, flew round the camp and landed. When the pilot vacated the plane, it was Samuda. We didn't have to wonder; we were amazed, because he had never been instructed in the art of flying. He was in big trouble, and got locked up and tried. Surprisingly, his punishment amounted to no more than a slap on the wrist. Incidents like this helped to brighten the closed community in which we lived, slept, worked and ate. We shared in almost everything, including hopes and fears.

At times we mingled our voices together in folk songs of all sorts, when some were brave enough to offer a solo and endure more than a subsequent chuckle. The man I defeated in the boxing ring had been trained by a Belgian. Remembering the song my mother had taught me, I raised my voice and sang. Since then, the boys were always requesting that I sing to them the Belgian song: 'When the war broke out in Belgium, And the Germans on their way, There was a cry from a Belgian woman, "Our boy's going to fight today, Send down your army and your navy, Send them in rank and file, Send down Americans, send down Canadians, send down Jamaicans but for God's sake, don't send me."' Upon hearing this the six Belgians present had just shrugged a polite and amused shoulder. It could be said that we all were self-controlled, cordial and urbane. Pranks were taken amicably and no one was contemptuous of anyone.

Those who went on to Coventry for training in 1947 were housed in huts in the woods. The German saturation bombing had destroyed the city centre and surrounding areas, not sparing the cathedral, leaving a picture of insufferable gloom, of a country ravaged, of people depressed and dreary from the effects, of tattered draperies swaying to and fro in the remains of what had been imposing monuments. Coventry was sombre, black as night. One could not help but breathe an atmosphere of deep melancholy at the sight of the obnoxious and dreadful destruction of so beautiful a city. How can such poignant memories be forgotten?

The carpentry course at the Tilehill training centre, involving theory and practice, lasted six months. As servicemen, we had to comply with the discipline imposed and an examination at the end, which I duly passed. The first wedding I attended was in Coventry. It was that of a Ukrainian girl who had walked from the Ukraine to France and boarded a refugee ship to Dover with nothing but the frock she was wearing and a gold bangle welded to her ankle by her father. She had gone from pillar to post and hitch-hiked until she had arrived in Coventry. Having no desire to return or to live in Europe, she had been delighted when a Trinidadian serviceman had proposed and married her. They now live in Trinidad.

The authorities has made sure that servicemen seconded from the forces for training were not on paid holiday. We were entitled to ration cards and '1250' identifications by which we obtained meals and access to the facilities at the centre. We had bicycles, so we took advantage on the lovely spring evenings to ride through the pleasant and luscious countryside, away from the dilapidated bomb sites of the city.

In celebration of our success on the course, two friends and I acquired travel warrants and went on tours to Glasgow, then continued by train to Holyhead where we caught the ferry to Dublin. We stayed at the YMCA opposite the famous Phoenix Park which featured in the Irish rebellion. The Irish Red Cross, on learning that we were from the colonies, escorted us to various places of interest, among which were Dublin Castle and the Guinness brewery where it was 'drink as much as you like'. I had never seen a place so green. Food was not rationed in Ireland. All meals were served sumptuously for the week spent there – I remember the real porridge and thick slices of bacon we polished off at breakfast.

On returning to Britain refreshed and rested, I collected my well-earned certificate, said farewell to the old and new friends of various nationalities, including

Poles and Russians, and reported to my old camp in Nottinghamshire.

I was now able to see much more of the Seagraves, and I also kept in touch with the Challis family in Mitcham. On one of my visits, I came across a man standing by the service hostel. He approached and introduced himself as Stan Petgrave, a serviceman who had been taking stock of me. He was about twenty-six years old, a bit shorter than me and beefy. His small head did not fit his thick neck, but what struck me most were his mackerel eyes which seemed to penetrate me as I spoke. He was from a small land-owning family in the 'garden parish' of Jamaica, but had actually been a civil servant when he volunteered. He spoke eloquently, gesticulating when a point was being made or a statement emphasised, referring authoritatively to historical events that showed how education should take precedence in order to divest people of the dependence mentality. The idea wasn't new; it was only confirming what I had held dear, long before I left Jamaica. Petgrave then went on to tell me of the formation of a secret organisation aiming to fight for the independence of Jamaica on our return. I stood impassive, then threw some questions, and when he assured me that he meant verbal pressure and demonstrations within the law, not the destructive use of guns, and sticks for that matter, I paid my five shillings to join. Blythe Alex, whom I met at the trade fair was of a different character. He was tall and elegant and was more interested in dressing up to impress. When I bought a suit at Burton's for six pounds, he laughed and showed me his one, bought for sixteen guineas because according to him, he wanted to look good on the dance floor where he spent his weekends. It was on the dance floor that he met his glassy-eyed Peachy Richards. She was a beautiful land girl from a middle-class family. Together they spent many happy hours in the library. Peachy was desperate for Blythe to meet her parents, but he was too shy. It took much persuasion, but he eventually went. When he saw her home, complete with servant, and the quality of life enjoyed by her parents, he realised that he would be incapable of maintaining her to that standard and therefore broke off the relationship which he had nursed with exemplary behaviour. We all thought it was noble of Blythe. He returned to Jamaica, but a few demobilised men had found jobs in the police force, Post Office, prisons and elsewhere. So what prospect was there for me?

I was twenty-one, seen as an attractive, strapping, tall, dark and handsome uniformed young man, a description not excessively flattering as I was always a prime target for women of leisure and pleasure, but I am by nature reticent and therefore found it easy to ignore or to decline. There were some beautiful girls with fine eyes, rosy cheeks and agreeable dispositions whose company gave me a delectable sense of freedom, but there were the odd ones who flaunted with fluency and in pleasant but cultivated tones, their desires. These I was wary of.

There was one, however, who swept me off my feet. She was Betty Drury who I met in the Barley Mow pub, High Pavement, Nottingham. She was short and petite with full eyes, shoulder-length dark hair, and spoke in a soft, almost apologetic voice, a real Nottingham beauty. Betty worked in the Player's cigarette factory.

Betty and I developed a close friendship, attending the cinema whenever we could. On one of these visits, Betty told me that she was unhappy at home and that the only way out was to be married, and then she just said, 'Will you marry me?' By this time I knew that my days in Britain were numbered, so I had to say I couldn't, given the uncertainty. She was sad and we terminated our relationship down by the River Trent.

A few weeks later we met and this time Betty was much less preoccupied, even happy. She told me of meeting a corporal and of him asking for her hand in marriage, but wanted me to give my impression of his physical appearance. This would be possible when she accompanied him to Nottingham Victoria railway station on his return to his Guildford regiment. They arrived at the station as agreed and there I was leaning on a telegraph pole with the Nottingham Evening News disguising my face while I scrutinised the man. He had a limp on his left foot as a result of a war wound. The corporal left, and Betty and I were face to face, whereupon I gave her my advice – marry him.

It had been my intention to remain in the RAF but this was not possible since I had not married an English woman or been selected from Jamaica in the first place for higher education. Having come to terms with the disappointment, I made a farewell visit to Mam and Pap. This was a solemn and grave occasion. Thinking they'd never see their son again, we embraced. Mam threw her arms around me and was profusely tearful. It was unfortunate that because of distance and subsequent cost my leave of the Seagraves had to be by letter. Together with others in a similar position, I was transferred to a transit camp – West Kirby, near Blackpool – in readiness for the voyage back to Jamaica.

During the one week allowed for preparation, we handed back our best blue uniform with heavy overcoat in return for a brown khaki tropical uniform. All my memorabilia accumulated over the years was carefully and securely packed. This included two miniature silver aircraft, one a Spitfire banking mounted on an ash tray; a Vulcan bomber in perspex mounted on a square stand; some thick

bullet-proof perspex extracted from shotdown German
Junkers 88 bombers; one damaged German Luger pistol;
the silver ring given to me by the German prisoner of war
Fritz; a small dictionary; a few books; a stone about four
ounces in weight taken from the battlement at Ashby de la
Zouch where, according to Sir Walter Scott, Ivanhoe
fought; a piece of oak about ten inches by two from the oak
tree in Sherwood Forest where Robin Hood was supposed
to have hidden from the men of Nottingham. Also packed
were a shirt for my father and my Burton's tweed suit.

Chapter Five

Everything was now in place for the train to Southampton where the troop ship, the SS *Almanzora* was in port waiting to embark on the five thousand miles of ocean across to Jamaica via Mexico. Armed with my few belongings, not much more than what they were on arrival three years ago, and with the princely sum of forty pounds I had managed to save, I took up position in the queue musing on the settled conviction that I should return. I was not embittered for not being permitted to stay, but disillusioned and apprehensive, yes.

First class passengers boarded, followed by immigrants and refugees on their way to Mexico, then servicemen numbering around two hundred and fifty. On the grey November morning in 1947, the *Almanzora* slipped out to sea and we assembled on deck to observe the disappearing coastline and the last bit of England, apparelled in the threatening clouds and mist. The order in which we boarded was also the order in which we were fed throughout the journey; consequently, there was no socialising outside the group, not even a peep to see what the first class cabin was like. Conditions on board for the serviceman were spartan. The food was bland, tasteless, monotonous and insipid, only making us belch. Water and tea were served but anything further was at a cost we could not afford. My friends and I clubbed together and bought a tin of peaches which we combined with a tin of condensed milk on deck in the evenings.

A few days into the voyage, one settled into a routine and we were happy to devise various intrigues for passing the time. There was housey-housey – a bingo game and card games which I wasn't good at playing but nevertheless loved to watch because of how smoothly and confidently the cards would be shuffled: cutting the pack in half then inserting the corners of one half into those of the other half and with a click send them falling in waves together. Ingenious. The best one was the much-loved, tension-releasing game of dominoes. Every drop of frustration or aggression went into the slamming down of a piece and the accompanying comments, raucous laughs and a final unrestrained and obstreperous glee announcing a win.

As a diversion from the close atmosphere, we would find ourselves on deck viewing the emptiness of the deep blue sea, which at this time was unbelievably calm. The performing art of the fishes jumping, frolicking and splashing was as entertaining as a circus, one group replacing another as they swam alongside the ship. At nightfall we would resort to the library for a brief while, but the atmosphere was not conducive to that sort of exercise. We held discussions varying from our experiences in the forces and the use one could make of them in Jamaica to our individual future aims and plans. The 'secret organisation' surfaced again because the instigator, Stan, was aboard, but there was also Jimmy James, aged twenty-five, of average build but looking and acting intelligently and coming over as the real leader. Jimmy was a loner. In the discussions he kept quiet and listened and analysed every idea put forward up to the point where he got restless and on tenterhooks; here he would interject, 'Fools rush in where angels fear to tread,' and on to lecture the group about political and historical realities and how our concern should be the creation of jobs. Jamaica, he pointed out, was by now internally self-governed and the political system the organisation was formed to fight was defunct. Our prime duty was to support the government elected by adult suffrage. My impression of Jimmy was that he was half lion and half fox.

The *Almanzora* ploughed on through a boisterous stretch in the Caribbean Sea on its approach to Jamaica. At long last the Blue Mountain came into sight early one Sunday morning. It was good for our souls. As the ship glided into warm crystal-clear waters, we were met a few yards from docking by boys swimming towards the ship diving for coins that the first class passengers were throwing into the water. The ship eased gently forward and docked.

While the civilian first class passengers disembarked, the servicemen got into position for an orderly and disciplined military style exit. The captain took charge and the band of the First Jamaican Battalion played us off. The band did well but I wondered then what they would do if a Junkers 88 paid them a visit. Lorries from the British Regiment, now called the Jamaica Defence Force, escorted us to Up Park Camp which was established in the late eighteenth century. We passed through the southern gate, known as Duppy Gate. Legend has it that the West Indian Regiment, keeping guard, were regularly visited by an officer dressed in old-fashioned clothing with a sword slapping against his legs. The guards would present themselves for inspection but the officer would just vanish. There at the camp was the Governor, dressed in his regalia, who reserved the highest praise for us. He thanked us for participating in the war effort and wished us well for the future. This he did with panache. We were assured of the next two months' pay, then given our discharge papers. We were now fully demobilised.

There was a cool silence, a silence which spoke louder than words. What was uppermost was the thought of us returning to a jobless situation. For some more than others, it was a predicament one would rather not contemplate. Some at least had land and home but for the majority the outlook was bleak.

Army trucks drove us to the rail and bus stations as we dispersed. I discovered that all transport to Portland had either already gone or was not running, so I booked in for the night at the Salvation Army hostel nearby. I was not anxious nor excited to get home; my thoughts were occupied on how to catch the first available tide back to England. It was a night of trepidation and serious thinking. Early in the morning, I went out in search of a photographer. I had some pictures taken, and while they were being processed I hurried to the Immigration Department, filled in the necessary form and, together with the pictures, applied in person for a British passport which I obtained after a mild rebuke to the effect that I had not tested the waters before making what might be a mistake. All this was done with just enough time to get on the 'Eastern Tiger' bound for Port Antonio via Priestman's River.

I took advantage of the window seat, to view the recent developments but after clearing the city, my attention was diverted to the manner in which the chauffeur was driving. My heart was in my mouth as the driver seldom applied his brakes as he swung round those winding roads. When he took the corner at See-me-no-more – which, as the name suggests, is like a ragged semicircle with trees bound with parasitic plants and withies – the bus was almost on its side. He drove with gusto, careering rights and left depending on the terrain. The concept of 'keep left' didn't seem to enter into his calculation: down the hill, over the boulders, into the potholes, all in the same gear. It was a relief when I arrived at Priestman's River in one piece. I did manage to notice that the countryside, especially around St Thomas with its banana and coconut areas, had not fully recovered from the worst hurricane to have come out of heaven in 1944.

Strangely, I was not excited or anxious to be home. For the time that I had been away, I had without fail written to my parents twice per month but they had not been informed of my leaving England. However, a little bird, Mam, had let the cat out of the bag, unknown to me, although the precise time was not given.

When I alighted from the bus there was no one to meet me, but I was not expecting anyone. Up came a boy of about fourteen and asked if I were Sam. I responded in the affirmative, and without introduction he grabbed my case and preceded me up the hill of nearly half a mile and deposited it by the gate of my house. The first thing came to mind was that my prayers had been answered: I was back at my father's house in peace.

As I approached the gate the dog came out barking and would not let me in. He did not know me: the very opposite of Ulysses when he returned from the Trojan War and it was only the dog that recognised him. On hearing the racket, my sister came out and commanded the bitch to sit. It was late evening, already dark, and the family would be indoors. I opened the door and came face to face with my mother sitting in her rocking chair. 'Oh my God, who is this?' She flung herself at me, hugging and kissing me and crying. My father couldn't believe his eyes either. He jumped up and embraced me with the words, 'My son, oh my son.' By this time, all my sisters and brothers, giggling, were holding on to my hands, my legs and my waist, just about any part that could be grasped. My ninety-eight year old grandmother was patiently waiting her turn in the corner. Every one was accounted for except Dena, my eldest sister, who was a resident nurse some miles away. I had difficulty sorting out my third and fourth sisters as the latter was now taller than the former. When all the din and excitement had died down, my ever-alert mother brought her rocker to stop and asked me whether I had been shot in my left leg. I said no but that the leg in question had been frost-bitten at RAF Filey in Yorkshire. She replied, 'I detected that there was something slightly wrong, I know the footsteps of all my children and yours were not forgotten.'

By morning, the whole village had heard the news and before I was out of bed they were at the gate and on the verandah to see 'soldier boy' and the 'war man'. Had they known, they would have killed the fatted calf or goat, flags would be waving and I would have been treated as a hero, which I was not. The routine at home was almost the same as before. I did not leave the home for two days. Mother thought I had changed and was unhappy. On the third day, I gathered enough impetus to go through the village to pay my respects and to see how things were. Many of the senior citizens, as would be expected, had died, but there were many new and better buildings as a result of the government scheme after the hurricane of 1944. All the children had grown out of sight; some I did not know and others I could not recognise.

The following day, I saddled the horse and cantered up to Harmony. As I opened the gate and went in I had a pleasant reverie of how Wilton and I used to race round to the pond next to Patterson's, now Errol Flynn's property; we used to go like the wind. I dismounted. The dew was still on the grass. I knew because I remember hearing the horse cutting the thick, rich crabgrass. I walked along the ridge of the hill to the farmhouse and the barbecue, a distance of about four cricket pitches, to the pig pen. It was empty and I was dejected. It was in that sty that two of my four six month old pigs had died just before I left for the war, and to add insult to injury, my father had attributed the blame to me; according to him, I had not cleaned the pen properly.

Further on, in the lower pasture, there were the donkeys, but I could only identify Sugar Foot; the others were new. They all stopped cropping the grass and looked up; one or two brayed, reminding me of the proverb: 'Every time Jackass bray, him 'menber something.' Delighted at the sight of Sugar Foot, I took a few steps towards her and rested my hand on her shoulder. To my surprise, she resented it, pulling back her ears and giving me her back as if to say I was an intruder.

The sun was now waxing hot, about eighty degrees in the mid-morning, and I was thirsty. The solution was a coconut, so I struggled up a tree and dislodged a few. As I sat in the shade, I could see the village three hundred feet below, alive, echoing with the chattering, the laughing, the chopping of wood and the noises of animals bouncing off the hills around. There were the lit fires 'wafting their blue-black smoke to sapphire skies'. The first wave of the Flynn cattle, mooing, munching and moaning, could be seen descending to lower pastures, and in the distance, two miles as the crow flies, was an enormous white steamer slowly making its way to the resorts on the north coast. The mist had evaporated and the velvety, emerald Blue Mountain was clearly visible five miles away. It was from here my father taught me to 'read the wind', that is, to take cognisance of its direction, whether it bounced off or attacked the mountainside. One's prediction of rain or no rain depended on the bearing of the wind.

Keeping to the shade, I went through the pimento walk and saw the poor reaping of the last crop. There was such a waste; at least five percent more could have been added to the yield. On my way to the cows I came upon the goats which were looking healthy and beautiful and were frightened at the sight of me. What reaction would I get from the cows? They were oblivious to anyone around until I got nearer and whistled two longs and one short – the signal for them to come – but they only looked up and stared, saliva dripping from their mouths. In my boyhood days that would have started them on their way to their enclosure. I wasn't too disappointed. I was a stranger.

Wearied from the walk and from the exposure to the sun, I sat under a large spreading guango tree, my clothes wet and clingy with perspiration, and had another drink and a sandwich at leisure. Apart from the animals, there was no distracting sound. This was Harmony, a fruitful place with an abundance of everything and trees which not only yielded but beautified. The guango tree under which I took my rest was known as the rain tree and was over fifty feet high. Superstition was attached to it because the grass beneath the tree was greener than the grass around it. The pink-tufted flowers were beautiful but soon gave way to black pods containing a sweet pulp avidly eaten by cattle. The wood made attractive and durable furniture. This was the land of my father. I should be able to identify with the thought expressed in Pope's verse:

Happy the man, whose wish and care
A few paternal acres bound,
Content to breathe his native air
In his own ground.

But I had reservations with the words 'Happy' and 'Content'. Musing upon this, I felt a presence which was disturbed by the whistle of farmer Jones in his field. I had a stroll around, picking and eating some succulent guavas, feeling free as a bird. As I retraced my steps I noticed the Flynns' herd of cows one behind the other, lowing as they moved lethargically and turned the corner at the foot of the hill by the number eleven tree to their night meadow. It was time for home.

It was twilight, and the crows began to fly back to the hills from their day's scavenging at the seaside. Men and donkeys with loaded hampers were on their way home before dark. I led the horse to the pond for the last drink of the night, then mounted so I too was going home. I remember, listening to the sounds of the insects and small animals as I rode along the bridle track, sounds I had taken for granted and disregarded before, like the 'peenie wallie' which is one of the fifty or so species of firefly found in Jamaica. It cannot be mistaken or ignored because of its luminous and clicking characteristics. The lights turn on and off, giving a glow. The flashing lights are for courtship purposes. The dark also brings out the bats known as 'rat bats' in Jamaica. Some live in caves, but there are the tree-dwelling ones prevalent in the bushes which can be heard as they search for food.

Grandma Mary lived on this road, and as soon as I called in she brought out home-made lemonade and cake, quizzing me about England as I ate. Grandma Mary lived alone in a small thatched cottage; she was poor but very independent. She would never live with any of her children. The next stop was at my other grandmother, my favourite, Auntie Kit. Her cake shop was already closed and she had retired to her small three-roomed shingle house. It was to her I would run when I was threatened with a smacking. She took a long time to be convinced that I had not had a hard time in England among those 'wicked' people.

I tried to calm my restless mind, looking at various schemes to which I could apply myself, but they all turned out shadowy and vague. I could not see myself making headway socially or financially in Priestman's River, or in Jamaica for that matter. Banana cultivation, still not yet recovered from the hurricane and the subsequent Panama disease, was proving to be a non-starter. Coconuts, although one of, if not the most useful trees, producing food and drink, oil for soap, cosmetics and cooking as well as other novelties such as hats, had been virtually wiped out by lethal yellowing disease. It was possible to start again. There was the land, plenty of it, but not the money to invest in making it economically viable in the long or short term.

The following day I took the relevant documents, i.e. my pay book and release document, to the officer in charge of the welfare of ex-servicemen in Port Antonio to collect my resettlement entitlement of fifty pounds with which to buy tools. I was interviewed but was not given the money; instead, I was asked to make a list of all the tools required with their prices and signed by a builder or a reputable hardware store. I was later to discover that what the officer had said was irrelevant and that what he had wanted was a bribe of five pounds, without which he would not release the money. I decided on principle that I would rather deny myself that fifty pounds than be involved in anything dishonest and corrupt. That was my day of decision. The die was definitely cast and marked ENGLAND, sealed and settled. I would never return for my fifty pounds.

On my way home I stopped at my cousin Millicent who was more than pleased to see me. I was not in the best of moods, however, due to the disappointment, but I had the opportunity of unburdening myself. Millicent was twenty-four years old and five foot seven inches tall. Hearing of her achievements brightened up my countenance. She had won the all-island needlework competition and had been offered a job at Government House which she had turned down as the wage quoted was 'sweetie money'. Her main interest was to find out whether I had an English girlfriend.

I had always remembered Millicent for her sardonic humour, and she hadn't changed. She was bright. Millicent kept chickens and offered to sell me half a dozen of her prized leghorns to start a chicken business, a suggestion I would not have entertained even if I had received the fifty pounds for my resettlement.

I was a haunted and shattered man trying to come to grips with various possibilities. The recommendations and ideas I was getting so far were half-baked, ill-considered and impracticable, coming from people with inadequate knowledge of the changing world. I needed to pull together the many strands of thought, to analyse each idea and to bring about a cohesive and stabilising plan for the future. I was impatient and eager, I grant you, but I felt that time was running out.

One day, I did decide to escape from the family and the endless stream of relations and friends and take a walk to the cooperative property, Egg Hill, just to assess my feelings and to cogitate. It was peaceful there, with a silence not as deep as death but broken only by the numerous inhabitants of the vegetation. As I looked around the vast acreage, unperturbed, I was tempted to identify with Alexander Selkirk in Cowper's poem: 'I am monarch of all I survey, my right there is none to dispute;' but then I recollected that it only partly belonged to the family, although there would be enough for me to make a decent living if there were adequate funds and expertise. It was encouraging, notwithstanding, to see that things were better there. Farmers had switched to Lacatan and Robusta bananas, less susceptible to Panama Disease, and with government funds for spraying they were looking good. The coconut trees were laden: cotton trees silhouetted to the sky and pimento trees recuperating from the careless breaking a few months prior to my arrival. I sat on a large boulder and allowed myself to be lost in admiration and wonder at the greenness, the luxuriance and verdure of such a beautiful place.

There were animals about; goats and cows with enormous udders taking big bites of grass and switching their tails at the flies while their offsprings pranced and gallivanted; a few donkeys unenthusiastically and lazily cropping the sweet grass – all amicably intermingling. The mongooses dashed for cover and the birds were nearly as cautious. They twittered and flew from limb to limb and I thought of the days when they would never dare remain that close. The catapult would be in operation. In the animal world there is always conflict, as was evident as I watched the tree lizards, some brown, some green, chasing and gulping down insects. The male lizard displays his throat fan when chasing or when attacked. If provoked, the green ones change to near black, like chameleon. When I was a child, I used to be told the story of the galliwasp, a large lizard now extinct in Jamaica. It was harmless, but its bite was considered fatal. The belief, traditionally from Africa and propagated by the slaves, was that if one was bitten by the galliwasp, one should outrun the creature, who would be running too, to get to water first; if not, the victim would not survive.

There were at least one hundred and sixteen species of butterfly in Jamaica, but the most spectacular is the giant yellowtail with its striking yellow and black colouring, found only in Jamaica and, more specifically, around the eastern end of the Blue Mountain. Egg Hill was the main habitat. There were swarms of these gorgeous creatures flitting at low levels. The metamorphosis from a lowly caterpillar to something so energetic puzzles me.

I walked onto Miller Hole, which is not a hole but a river, in the vicinity of which there was a mill where the proprietor made cane sugar. The quiet murmur of the river could be heard as it cascaded over the smooth stones spreading out and following the path it had made years before. The undergrowth was thick; the great trees – mahoe, ebony, cedar, mahogany – stood majestic in the well-watered area. The water was pure and cool, almost cold. This was truly the land of wood and water. I thought of the days when we used to jump in Miller Hole to catch fish with our bare hands. They just seemed to laugh and disappear under the crags. Later we devised an ingenious and effective method using the ribs of the coconut leaves; that was before we discovered how to make fish pots to trap the crayfish.

At the river's edge there were great big bullfrogs. In the flat area, water used to settle during the rainy season and the frogs spawned in these little mini ponds. After a while, little tadpoles would arrive and we would harass them; if we stayed away, when we returned there would be these amphibious monsters leaping about. It was our childish pleasure to batter them to death, but before that they would inflate themselves and spit out a milky cuckoo spit. At this stage we would run away as the story was that if that stuff got in one's eye the result would be blindness.

It was arranged that there should be a thanksgiving service for all the sons of war at St Mark's Anglican church, where my father was the warden. Four of us went from

Priestman's River, but unfortunately my friend from school never returned; he was killed in action.

Returning to that church brought back many happy memories. The structure is unique, built from stones and put together by slave labour. It stands against the most violent of hurricanes, and not even the earthquakes do more than minor damages. It sits on a hill overlooking the sea and Fairy Hill, a new village in the making.

The packed church was in buoyant mood. The choir sang, and when it came to welcoming me, they really drew the long bow. At the end, the young people crowded around, blocking out the older folk. I was chuffed when my eyes met Barbara Burke's. She was now nineteen and had grown to almost six foot with an athletic, feminine body, lovely face and pug nose. I remembered her as a placid girl, quick to see a joke and laughing a lot. Barbara was now preparing for the Teachers' Training College. Listening to her mother, I deduced that a special service in her honour would not be for a long time, not even for Errol Flynn, 'the Master of Ballantre'. The church was hoping that I would be the one to take charge of the young people, to be a role model, a mentor, but I was not prepared to fulfil that role, at least not yet.

Chapter Six

My problem was to find a way of telling my parents what I intended to do in the near future. I had been experimenting with various projects. For instance, with my camera I took pictures, made perspex hearts, put them on a chain and sold them. I had enough orders for two months, then it dried up. I carried on rearing animals, helping on the farm and repairing beds. I was pleased with the work I did on the last bed for five pounds for a relative, only to be told that he could only pay two pounds now and the remainder after the next year's harvest. There was no wisdom in doing these jobs; the people simply could not afford such luxuries.

It was after one Sunday dinner that I plucked up enough courage to disclose my plans to my parents. At first there was silence, then my mother said, 'I figured that out long ago; you are not happy and you won't return if you go.' My father's words were, 'Stand on your own two feet when you go!'

Centrifugal and centripetal forces were at work. Economic conditions in the island were shocking, and workers were flexing their muscles calling for strikes while the unemployed had become restless, causing a few disturbances in Kingston. The government, under the new constitution of 1944, was in the hands of the charismatic Alexander Bustamante, who was seen as the champion of the poor and oppressed. He had fought a long battle for organised labour and challenged the colonial authorities by attacking the social and political conditions of colonial Jamaica. The government, therefore, had long-term measures for unemployment, but these were promises I wasn't prepared to believe or to wait for.

It was now Christmas, with all the traditional celebrations, but these meant nothing to me. Normally I would have been out to view the *Jonkonnu* (John Canoe), that is, a band of masqueraders donning cows' heads, horses' heads, pitch-fork devils, kings and queens, accompanied by musicians playing the fife, drums, rattles, horns and conch shells, all drawing the crowds as they moved along the road. I could have gone to a garden party complete with dancing in the open: jigs, polka and reel quadrilles to the music of the rumba box, guitar, banjo, shakers and even graters and combs. There was also the Christmas fair consisting of raffles, maypole dancing, merry-go-round, egg and spoon races, donkey races and all sorts. And if village entertainments were not enough, I could have taken the bus to Manchioneal where the Bruckins party would be in full swing. This was a lively dance party performed by two rival groups trying to outdance each other. During the interval the show bread was brought out, and at the end, the *yabba* of jerk pork, tureen of manish water and bird pepper patties in the main were served.

As a young man susceptible to vanity, one would expect me to have attended one or other of these venues, the scene of pretty girls tastily and attractively dressed. During this festive season, in temperatures of seventy or eighty degrees, one of my delights was a trip to the beach. There was the enticing Blue Hole called the Blue Lagoon, a beauty spot one did not ignore, very deep and popular with divers and swimmers. Also within walking distance was Boston Beach where the best jerk pork was seasoned and grilled right there on the seashore. But for all these I did not leave the 'yard'. Not going to the fair where there was something for all, young and old, was beyond comprehension. Three girls were dispatched to get me, but they left empty-handed. I went nowhere apart from the Christmas service.

I had kept in touch with my English friends in both Bulwell and in Mitcham. In fact, I had sent a parcel of tea and rum to Pap and Mam who appreciated the gesture, but Pap was not too happy about the duty the customs charged.

A friend in need is a friend indeed. There is a friend who sticks closer than a brother. Both these expressions could be applied to my dearest friend Harry. In reply to my letter, Harry informed me of a troop ship on its way to Jamaica. On the receipt of that letter, I started making tentative preparations. My passport was in order, so was my medical certificate. The problem was money, so my father sold three cows and handed me the proceeds. My parents knew I was not joking when I turned over my duties at Harmony to my younger brother. Three weeks later, an advertisement appeared in the *Daily Gleaner* stating that there would be limited accommodation on board the MV *Empire Windrush* sailing for England on 24th May, 1948 – Empire Day. That was a good omen! – and that booking would commence the following day.

Chapter Seven

I was first at the bus stop for the late evening Eastern Tiger, to Kingston, nearly sixty miles away, staying overnight with my uncle to make sure of a place. When I got to the Royal Mail Line, Kingston Wharf, I was in front of over two hundred people but also behind the same number. Everyone was tense, sweat dripping as we stood patiently in the scorching sun. The lollipop and snowball men did a roaring trade that day. Hours passed and we crawled forward until at last I stepped inside. My papers were meticulously scrutinised, and after a few carefully worded questions, I paid the grand sum of twenty-eight pounds ten shillings and tax of five shillings in return for a ticket entitling me to a troop deck place on the MV *Empire Windrush* to England the following week.

I returned home in a triumphant and exuberant mood, although sorry I could not help my friend Blythe who had asked for a loan for his passage. I immediately posted a letter to Harry, went on to see my sister and stayed overnight, going over family affairs.

My mother doted on me and we were very close, so it was heartbreaking to see her cry. Auntie Kit was more understanding, and even complimented me. 'Sam,' she said, 'knows to say yes when that is the right answer. He will do well in England.' Having missed out when I had first gone, my father was determined this time to have a gathering of the family and friends. That meant the whole village, so once again I refused to be drawn in. As far as I was concerned, I was facing an uncertain future, but my reluctance perhaps was misconstrued. I did, however, attend the school fair and went around the village thanking everyone and bidding goodbye to them all.

I had become an expert at packing at short notice, but my mother assumed that responsibility – not a big one. The few belongings were assembled for a kit bag and a suitcase. My mother made sure to darn the socks and replace the buttons on the shirts. She washed the soles of my shoes, polished them and provided me with clean handkerchiefs. My brothers and sisters were particularly obsequious and attentive in every way, giving me first place at the table, in the games, to the bathroom. I did not find the parting as daunting and bewildering as the first time; war meant death and I was going to die – so we all thought – but now it was only that I wasn't going to return. There were tears, however.

When all but a few had boarded, there was a big commotion outside and the cry of 'Tief, tief' from a man on the gang plank. The police were called and he reported that his passport, receipt and other documents had been stolen. An investigation ensued, and on checking the records against all the receipts of payments, this man's name could not be found. He was lucky to get away with just a caution and a swift removal from the quayside. His stunt did not work. He should have consulted with the more subtle and shrewd, the kind that undermined the most elaborate and well-organised security, as we were to discover in mid-Atlantic.

And so the *Windrush* floated out on the evening tide with four hundred and ninety-two pioneers on board. The MV *Empire Windrush*, a 14,414 ton (gross) German troop ship with two funnels, was taken by the British Navy after the Germans surrendered. It was beautifully laid out, well organised, German-built, well rigged, painted sea green and very clean, unlike the *Almanzora* or even the SS *Cuba*. Fixtures still bore German SS markings. After the war it had the added charge of being used as an immigrant ship; therefore, when it arrived in Jamaica on its circuitous route from Australia, there were a number of European immigrants on board.

The men from the RAF returning from leave boarded in Jamaica, but the attention was on the four hundred and ninety-two independent-minded panthers who, from all over the island and with an average age of twenty-four and in accord with the same aim and steely determination, were leaving the Rock to seek an honest living in the Motherland. We dubbed ourselves the pioneers on the second *Mayflower*. Mention must also be made of the additional unlicensed, unauthorised 'barracudas' who surfaced later in the voyage. The sea was no stranger to more than three-quarters of us. Some had already travelled to Panama, United States and England and were familiar with foul and fair conditions, the food, the berths and seasickness.

The first leg of the journey took us to Mexico, where stopping was just for a few hours, and so we were not allowed off the ship. One of our number, however, spotted a handcart man with some watermelons by the quayside. He sneaked off, returning with an armful of melons. A treat for us, we thought, so we all gathered round him. The man set about cutting them in pieces and selling them to us. He was thereafter known as Columbus, a name to which he answers to this day in Brixton Market.

The next brief stop was Havana, Cuba, where another batch of Europeans disembarked in calm waters to the small and beautiful island of Bermuda. In Havana, it was alleged that there was mechanical trouble which would take some days to rectify; therefore we were permitted to leave the ship and go ashore. Of course, this was a thrill. For three days we enjoyed the hospitality of the islanders as we toured the island through and through, even participating in a game of cricket. We felt at home in this very clean, peaceful place. The buildings were painted white and with meshes to keep out the flies and mosquitoes; there were no cars, if my memory serves me right – only a fire engine and an ambulance. Horse and buggy were the means of transport. Only the Americans, however, could afford to holiday there.

While we were having such a stupendous time, a rumour was being circulated in Jamaica that the *Windrush* had gone down. But we resumed for the long haul on her demanding course due north-east. The *Windrush* glided away from the shores of Bermuda, escorted by the seagulls far out to sea, then stood firm in the waters and rode the ebbs and flows of the waves like a child on the wooden horse in the fairground, so unlike the first time I crossed the Atlantic when it was almost impossible to maintain a footing on the deck.

All along, we were mindful of the 'barracudas' who had to lie low and could not make use of the opportunity to touch land. They would be detected because their clothes told the story; shirt necks were the give-away and so was the odour. It was decided that clothes should be lent. Fortunately, there were officially twenty women passengers, so the lone female stowaway was put in their care. Meals were smuggled out to them or unused meal tickets passed on. We were served typical English meals as the crew was English: cereal and tea for breakfast, a drink and something to snack on at midday and fish and chips for dinner was the norm.

The three weeks on the wild sea went quickly. People were generally affable and jolly despite the apprehension about the future, but we weren't going to cross any bridges before we got to them. There was a briefing session for those whose knowledge of British customs, manners and laws was not up-to-date and who would not have known of the paperwork to be done on arrival. There was a willingness to hold conversation upon any topic, whether of minor or major importance.

In my estimation the women aboard were on average twenty-four or twenty-five years old. Listening and talking to them, one gathered that nature, with minimum help from their parents, enabled them to survive along with good health and basic education. As things were, the scales were tipped against Jamaican women; their place was definitely in the home to bear as many children to lecherous men as their fecundity allowed. With an inadequate income, these children would have a two per cent chance of their ability and personality developing to the full. Most of these women had begun life in the rural areas but at the first opportunity had deserted the country and moved to the city to acquire skills mainly in dressmaking or as nursemaids to the better-off or as domestic servants. The ones I met on the *Windrush* were optimistic, adventurous, creative. One would not have thought they were bound for a strange land.

The women travelled as cabin passengers and did not have much contact with the main group except in the organised activities when they dolled themselves up for the cinema and dancing. They would also join in the games of cards and dominoes, and some attended the boxing matches. All in all they displayed agreeable behaviour and were very alluring. I well remember the comradeship that developed and the good humour, as well as the fears and aspirations in which everyone shared.

The peace abruptly came to an end when there was news that there had been consternation in the House of Commons when members had been informed of the number of immigrants aboard, and that the ship had been ordered to turn back. Many were distressed, despondent and forlorn, and some were overcome with grief. I took charge when I saw a man crying like a baby, and arranged for a couple of domino players to stay close by, listen to the wireless broadcast and report anything adverse, while I went around calming the situation and appealing for patience and tolerance towards one another.

The disturbing situation was compounded by the voice on the Tannoy of the stern and inflexible Lieutenant from Sierra Leone, J.H. Smythe. He was the welfare officer seconded from the Colonial Office to Jamaica, and was on board. His message was to strike discouragement and perhaps fear into the already distraught passengers, and to drive the last nail in the coffin he had a message typed, distributed and pinned up on the notice board. It said, 'I could not honestly paint a very rosy picture of your future; conditions in England are not as favourable as you may think. Various reports you have heard about shortage of labour is not general. Unless you are highly skilled, your chances of finding a job are none too good. Hard work [as if we didn't know] is the order of the day in Britain, and if you think you cannot pull your weight you might as well decide to return to Jamaica even if you have to swim the Atlantic.'

With us in such close proximity for three weeks the ship became a hotbed of frayed nerves and loss of temper but there were no fights. The operative command was no disturbance, peace and love whatever the matter. Behaviour remained impeccable. I was beginning to feel relieved and cool when an announcement supervened. One day at around 9 p.m.: the *Windrush* would be docking in a few hours' time. This sent the passengers wild with awakened excitement and happiness which went on all night as we kept a watchful eye on the clock and an open ear for the next public call for attention. The hours ticked away and it wasn't until towards daylight that we could feel the MV *Empire Windrush* diminishing her pace until she emerged from the dark and desolate waters and approached Tilbury harbour on the Thames, in a chilly prevailing wind, on the 22nd June, 1948.

We were never to hear of the MV *Empire Windrush* again until 1953, when it sank in the Mediterranean on its way from the Far East. Four of the crew lost their lives fighting a fire in the engine room, but the twelve hundred troops were evacuated. One could see this as a portent, pointing to the eventual loss of the Empire.

Chapter Eight

We disembarked and dispersed. All the men without accommodation or prior arrangements were taken to the Clapham Deep Shelter, which was an underground railway siding used during the war as an air raid shelter and for holding prisoners of war. After the war, it became a home for students on a short term basis. Sections of it were empty by 1948, but the bunkers remained.

Some immigrants went to addresses in the industrial Midland, and the RAF ex-servicemen to friends in other parts of the country; the boxers made for Liverpool where it was easy to get bouts and accommodation. The women took a similar course. The predicament of the female stowaway was put right by fellow passengers clubbing together and paying her fare, and she was taken care of by the Salvation Army hostel. A few ex-servicemen who knew the area found work in the Gedling colliery in Nottingham, where they were able to obtain furnished rooms.

We had liberated ourselves from an economically depressed island where there were only a few large- and small-scale industries and where tens of thousands of man-hours' work on the land brought hardly any financial reward. Some had earned a living from small workshops, woodworking and furniture, shoes or clothing. This had made us tough, even if poorly educated. Coming from a situation where chattering was more important than the job in hand, most immigrants now had to get used to working to schedule.

Because Jamaica was comparatively backward, it was subject to influences from outside and its situation was entirely dependent upon what happened and what was decided outside. This gave the inhabitants, by and large, a feeling of inferiority and a clumsiness when it came to expressing themselves, but it did not mean that they were simple-minded.

Coming to England was the chance of a lifetime and for those who had had the opportunity of working in the United States and on the Panama Canal it was a second chance. It was fortuitous. The imperative of the hour was not to wait and see or wait and do nothing; in fact, it was hard to accept the normal content of the day and hour. There was a passion for constructive experience of work. A sense of inadequacy did not arise as far as I was aware. The new arrivals proceeded with the business of living undaunted, not allowing themselves to be governed by fearful sensibilities. Endurance was fundamentally far more important than happiness. This was a realistic view to counter indifference and discouragement. Our very survival depended on this attitude to life and work, and we soon discovered that the capabilities were there but were underdeveloped. Therefore, given time, people were to discover what was inhibiting, depriving and diminishing this potential. Talk of 'the bad old days' of the war certainly encouraged a belief in progress and general and personal expectation of better days ahead; this stimulus speeded up the individual's application to the new environment and the desire to rise above an underprivileged existence. The work ethic became obsessive for those who recognised the need for fraternity and whose intention was therefore to open the way for those of their relatives who were just as earnest and were awaiting the call to join the fortunate ones in the land of hope and glory.

The interplay of the push and pull scenario was much in evidence in the years following the *Windrush*. As soon as immigrants settled and found employment and lodgings, families and friends would be sponsored. There was a recruitment drive in Barbados, Trinidad and Jamaica to fill vacancies in various areas such as London Transport. South London was the hub for activities: ships were busy in and out of the docklands and the supporting industries grew accordingly; as these were labour-intensive, there was demand for manual labour. Men and women were needed for the buses and trains, hospitals, clothing and construction. Factories which used to produce for the arsenals were in some cases converting to manufacturing goods for civilian purposes. At the same time, British people were emigrating to the greener pastures of Australia, New Zealand, Canada, South Africa and the United States, resulting in this acute shortage of skilled and unskilled labour. This situation offered new hope and was attractive for people who had been constantly threatened with floodings, hurricanes, earthquakes and the consequences of these disasters. Immigrants would go anywhere at any time and take any job, whereas the natives would pick and choose.

Ten years after the *Windrush*, it is estimated that the number of entrants of working age from the West Indies was one hundred and twenty-five thousand. They were all British citizens, welcomed even by government Minister of State Enoch Powell at the time. They had come by sea and air with their grips, dressed in their felt hats and raincoats clutching their passports stamped 'British Citizen' and carefully wrapped in handkerchiefs or even in newspaper. It was colonisation in reverse, and Louise Bennett, the genius of a creator and entertainer of Jamaican folklore, picked this theme up in her poem:

Wat a joyful new, Miss Mattie,
I feel like me heart gwine burs'
Jamaica people colonizin'
Englan' in reverse.

By de hundred, by de t'ousan
From country and from town,
By de shipload, by de plane load
Jamaica is Englan' boun'.

Dem a pour out a Jamaica,
Everybaddy future plan
Is fe' get a big time jab
An' settle in de madda lan'.

Wat a islan'! wat a people!
Man an woman, ol'an young
Jusa pack dem bag an' baggage
An' tun history upside dung.

Oonoo see how life is funny
Oonoo see de tunabout,
Jamaica live fe' box bread
Outa English people mout'.

Most West Indians on their arrival had given themselves
five to ten years in Britain. They will say now that although
they are tired and cold they can't go back but would like to
die in Britain anyhow.

In 1948 it was common for an immigrant to be offered a
choice of jobs from the Labour Exchange. These were,
however, low paid, strenuous, monotonous and rejected by
the indigenous population – no wonder the local council

thought the newcomers were a godsend. On learning of the new residents in the Deep Shelter, the mayor of Lambeth gave a tea party as a gesture of goodwill while the staff of the Cooperative Labour Exchange and the area's large lodging houses and landladies put away their suspicions and fears and helped in their own ways.

Most of the immigrants could take care of themselves. Although they were not as refined as one may have liked, they were independent to the point of arrogance and had something that the locals admired. The immigrants had come to work; they went to church, played the national game – cricket – and they could understand the English language, though their accent and vernacular were not always understood. This was no barrier to obtaining jobs, which all had within a few weeks of arrival. It took a longer time to get government documents completed than to find work. Time was lost in the bureaucratic system filling in forms and finding one's way in and around London. People were aware of how much had to be learned in this vast metropolis, but, orderliness, civil behaviour and good transport facilitated this process of learning and adaptation.

Job security meant that the those in the Deep Shelter were able gradually to move to better – so they thought – accommodation. The hostel in Gordon Road, Peckham, is an example. Refugees were housed in these hostels but so were the mentally confused, tramps and thieves. Sanitation and basic hygiene were practically non-existent, but lice and vermin abound. This was not a situation that even the poorest Jamaican would tolerate.

While the *Windrush* was still on the high seas, the *Daily Dispatch* had carried an offensive about coloured immigrants coming to England. It made my English friend Harry Challis so worried that he sent a telegram saying WELCOME HOME SAM. As I set ashore, Harry and his seven year old son were on the dockside, waving. He shouted that there was a letter with the shipping company awaiting me. From his usual pleasant, courteous smile and firm grip of the hand, I felt I was truly welcomed. The letter was to say that there was room for me at his home, just as before. Remembering the words of my father about standing on my own two feet, though, I declined the offer.

We met the following day and Harry accompanied me to the local labour exchange, which was packed with applicants. I was called for an interview, and when I gave carpentry as my skill the clerk audaciously pronounced that the standard of the Jamaican carpenter was not up to that of the English when it came to flats and high buildings. Upon hearing this, Harry, who was always speaking up for me, interjected and asked that I show my certificate, then went on to say that this man was in the Royal Air Force. I produced the certificate stamped 'Coventry, England'. The clerk not only apologised, but offered me a choice of five jobs. I said, 'Thank you, I am going to rejoin the RAF.' I went straight to Mam and Pap in Bulwell. They were ecstatic, and Pap set about finding me a job. Pap had a wholesale and retail grocery in Mansfield and his friend had a garage nearby. He had a word with him and I was employed to spray cars. This friend was a kindly whimsical man with a head for business. His family, he said, had lived in that area since before Prince John started oppressing the serfs.

Chapter Nine

The young men who stowed away to America eventually reached a cultural and economic standard they would otherwise not have achieved in their lifetime in Jamaica. Stowing away was chosen chiefly by stevedores who saw little reward for their labour, who, if uneducated, could not join the army. Working on a shipping company provided an excellent opportunity for this venture. Tim Malcolm, alias Baltimore, usually repeated his story at functions when he had had a few drinks. He had no qualms when he told of how he spoke to the Baltimore police on patrol with the same confidence and pride as if he were on his native shore. If he had been cowardly he would surely be in Yankee hands in Ellis Island. Stowaways were not looked upon as criminals, but did best to try to redeem the situation by marrying and by keeping out of trouble. They had broken the law, but the real guilty ones in their eyes were the immigration laws and the political system.

When I spoke to Eva Buckley, the woman stowaway, she let me in on the secret of her life story. Her mother had died leaving her father to look after the children. Encouraged by a friend as soon as she was old enough, she left for the city where she became a seamstress, bought a Singer machine and opened a dressmaking shop doing good business at Christmas time. When she heard of the ship sailing to England, she sold her old machine and the odd bits of furniture she possessed and went to book her passage, only to be told that women had to find fifty pounds and not twenty-eight pounds ten shilling as did the men. She was distraught, but was determined to be on that ship by hook or by crook. After racking her brain she had to conclude that stowing away was the only way to get off the Rock.

Eva wore a beautiful frilly dress designed by herself and carried a grip like any of the other ladies. She went to the back of the queue and got to the table where the checking was taking place. Not having the yellow card for the immigration officer, she pretended to have left something and turned back. A tall young officer saw her struggling with her case and went to her assistance. She came clean and told him of her intention and the reason for it. The officer said nothing, but when he vacated his position for a second Eva crept under the rope bypassing the checking officer and lost herself among the other ladies. She assessed her new surroundings and attached herself to Lin Speed, a country lass who was all at sea about everything and constantly being seasick. Eva moved in with Lin, who turned out to be dishonest, stealing Eva's money. From a boxing exhibition, raffles and a singing contest, enough was realised to pay Eva's debt. She landed in England with the necessary documents and no entry was made against her. Eva was successful in getting a job as a machinist in a Polish firm, was very independent, and within four years was able to make a deposit on a leasehold house in Camden Town. From a romantic point of view, she did find fulfilment in her voyage through life. She was married and later emigrated to the USA (this time she did not have to stow away) and became an established landlady in New York, living in a splendid house in Mount Vernon.

A similar story was told by a young man who had tried to make an honest living, was beaten by the social system, but would not accept defeat. He had not lost the will to try, but this effort would be made in a foreign land; for this, he was prepared to be the ship's human rat and a detective's running dog. That epic voyage created a permanent bonding of *Windrush* people which is still maintained and nurtured by regular contact. We were the magnificent five hundred.

The brotherhood consisted chiefly of the volunteers for the war who had been compulsorily dismissed and dispatched to Jamaica and had reconvened in that big reunion on the *Empire Windrush*. Now without government constraint, we were taking the bull by the horns, climbing up the rough side of the mountain. As always happens to mortal men in the assent, some indeed have toppled off the slippery crags and cliffs and suffered broken body and soul, while others have soft-landed and have been able to reason themselves into sufficient courage to take stock and set off again to the promised land, encountering the hideous barren rocks and whirlwinds. Unfortunately for a few, after fifty years the summit is still out of sight, but the fruitless struggle continues. At times as one would expect, persistence is lacking, cold feet sets in and a right about turn seems to be the best course, but beckoning to a helping hand from one who is securely lashed to the promontory averts a disaster.

Bradley Badham and four of his friends who went down the colliery in Nottingham did so mainly because there was availability of overtime. Badham organised a saving scheme among the fifteen Jamaicans living in the area, with each depositing five pounds a week. The system allowed members to take it in turns to draw the entire amount each week with no interest and repay the loan within fifteen weeks. This method of saving was the quickest and most successful way of accumulating enough in a short time to deposit on a house or to make other purchases. A house was the main aim, as the average immigrant was finding lodgings difficult to get. Ex-servicemen were the avant-garde of a method of saving which was to be adopted by early immigrants whose main intention was to buy a house and which they more often than not achieved within three years of arrival.

Badham was twenty-five years old, nearly six feet tall, with a good physique and a handsome face. He was on his own hunting ground because he had spent his leave from the RAF in Nottingham. His girlfriend Becky was a lovely person but the fire in the romance had been dampened by the attitude of her father, who worked with the local council as a carpenter. Her mother and sisters, however, liked Badham. On Becky's birthday, Badham took her a box of multicoloured threads and unexpectedly the father returned for lunch. Becky's mother hid him in the coal cellar but Badham found this degrading and the romance, which did not have much fire in it, was now broken off. Some time after, Badham encouraged one of his friends from school to take up nursing in England. She came, and Badham bought his house in Hyson Green and got married. Both Becky and her father attended the wedding and her father was honest enough to say that Badham was trustworthy and decent. They were able to accommodate the newly arrivals and Badham changed his social habits, no longer going to the Barley Mow pub.

Sonny Kelley was a boy Jamaicans would call regular. His father drove a delivery van for Johnson & Sons and so he was able to educate Sonny at the fee-paying High School. Much to the displeasure of his father, having finished school he contracted to work on a farm and factory in the USA for three years, leaving his half-Indian girl friend in Annotto Bay. He was astute and thrifty, returning to Jamaica with a good balance in Barclays Bank. Troops were stationed at Wag WaterVale and venereal disease was common among the men, and when he found out that his girlfriend had been attending the clinic he was shattered. Most of his money was gone, leaving him with just enough to book his passage on the *Windrush*. As an experienced traveller at twenty-four, he took things in his stride and humbly went to Clapham Deep Shelter.

Conditions in the shelter, compared with those in the field and factory barracks in the United States and at home in Jamaica, left much to be desired. Sonny took his leave and booked in a hotel in Kennington only to find it too expensive, so it was to a hostel he had to take up residence. Facilities were just one notch above that of the shelter, but far below the Californian standard. He stayed long enough to earn his fare back to his native land where he was fortunate to obtain a job at Gray's Inn sugar factory. At the end of the harvest, however, Sonny was found to be sympathetic to some workers whose honesty was called into question. Investigation failed to absolve him, and this led to the loss of his job.

Sonny was deterred. He went into Kingston, bought a second-hand car for fifty pounds and set up a taxi service in the tourist area of Montego Back at just the right time after the war, when the Americans were flocking to Jamaica. Demand was beyond his wildest dream; he purchased another car and another until he had a fleet. When I saw him years after, he quoted, '"There is a tide in the affairs of men / Which, taken at the flood, leads on to fortune; / Omitted, all the voyages of their life / Is bound in shadows and in miseries. / On such a sea are we now afloat, / And we must take the current when it serves, / Or lose our ventures." I learned that at school,' he said. Nothing is more endearing to him than to take tourists around, especially to his home town of Annotto Bay where the unique Baptist chapel, a national monument designed by the Scottish minister Charles Barron, gives prominence. It is believed that the minister himself cut the glass, fitted them in the frames and decorated the walls of the church with verses of Scripture.

Wally Jackson, of European mix, was qualified as a motor mechanic at Kingston Technical School when he volunteered to work in an ammunition factory in the US. Having a very rosy picture of the Motherland, he was easily persuaded to accept a transfer to England. On arrival he was sent to Leeds and although he was disappointed at the conditions under which he had to live and work, he could accept it, but the cold, damp climate, the air raids, blackouts and deaths were too frightening for comfort. To chicken out, however, did not appeal to him especially when he saw the women unflinchingly facing up to the demands of war. He made a particular effort to perform to the best of his ability but dreamt of the time when the war would come to an end and he would be free to return home. He began to read the Communist *Daily Worker*, convinced that the Russians were operating in his favour by emphasising equality.

At the end of the war, Wally was on his way home. He was thirty, with very progressive political views, but Jamaica under Bustamante's colonial government was not the place to be a communist or to be sympathetic to that ideology. So now Wally was on the *Windrush* heading once more for Leeds, England, the place he detested. But things had changed for the better in Leeds: people were planting flowers in front of their houses instead of potatoes and beans, and it was not hard to find a reasonably well-paid job.

Mrs Cohen, whom he had known before, had been a war widow since the Battle of the Bulge in 1944. She was thirty and had a beautiful nine year old daughter with long hair. Mrs Cohen had sold her house in Chapeltown and bought another one; a move to start life afresh. She was receiving a war widow's pension. With hardly any alternative, Wally asked for lodgings and was given a room. When the Germans had informed the Red Cross of David Maine's death, the people who knew him remarked that they had to be one jump ahead to kill him.

The next time I visited Wally, I was delighted to see the transformation of the place. The muddy patch in front of the house had paving stones, a green and beautifully manicured lawn at the back and fruit trees dotted round. By 1950, the house was the talk of the town. The neighbours now realised that Wally was a credit and not a liability, even if he was coloured. Mrs Cohen began to believe that they were meant for each other and married Wally, thus putting a stop to the tittle-tattle and nasty comments.

One Saturday afternoon, Wally and his friends were at a football match when there was a knock at his door. His wife, thinking it was one of the neighbours, tidied her hair, wiped the corner of her mouth and opened the door. She nearly fainted. It was David, all five foot six inches of him, with receding hair and a stone lighter. She attempted to scream in fright and joy but held her mouth with both hands. She took hold of him and led him inside the house he did not know, and sat him down on the large settee. She sat beside him, fidgeting, then came out with, 'I thought you were dead.' His story was that he had changed identity disc, clothing and every necessary thing with a dead comrade when he had realised that the Germans had overrun their position and that worst of all, they were SS storm troopers. He had later found himself in a German hospital with a head wound. They chatted over a cup of tea, then David said, 'I hear that you have married a bloody nigger.' Wally himself was completely caught off balance. The minister was called in for a conference and Wally agreed that Mrs Cohen should go back to David, but David refused to have her back.

In contrast was Alti Townsend who also returned on the *Windrush* with his wife and two sons to join him in Cheshire. He rejoined the RAF and served for ten years in Germany, Malaya and Cyprus, leaving Penny, his wife, with the boys, who were at school. In his absence, the family was subjected to endless abuse from racists resulting in Penny being sent to a mental institution. On learning of this he asked to leave the service, and the day he was demobilised he was on the ship to the USA. He would not live a day as a second class citizen in the country for whom he was serving. Penny stayed behind, and when the boys were on the road to higher education she joined her husband. Alti was a bright boy who learned fast and did not have any problem securing a job as a television engineer, a skill he had acquired in the RAF, returning only for the graduation of the boys from university. Both of them became lawyers. Alti was prepared to tolerate the American colour prejudice as a foreigner but not in Britain with a British Passport. Such an obstacle to his climb up the mountain was anathema.

George Brown, a reserved and quiet chap, had a similar experience. His girlfriend, who was well placed in the social bracket in Jamaica, could not come to terms with the indifference she was experiencing as a student nurse. She grinned and bore it, as the saying goes, until she was qualified as a State Registered Nurse, got married and worked at the Manchester General Hospital for a time. George had a small grocery shop in Moss Side but in his spare time was studying to be a mechanical engineer. On both being qualified, they applied for jobs in Canada and the Canadian authorities accepted them as qualified people on equal terms with the indigenous Canadians – who were also the Empire's children. They disposed of their property here and, with jobs waiting them, emigrated with their children where they bought a home on arrival. The only bother for them was the extreme cold, mitigated by holidaying in Jamaica.

Alfie Sinclair, alias Spaniard, was not a volunteer in the war but he was certainly on the *Windrush* as the 'mouse man', participating in everything possible. On the dance floor he was the pretty boy, showing off the latest style, and was all eyes at cards and dominoes. In conversation, he was very entertaining. Spaniard had vitality and was sure of himself and confident of the future, virtues he attributed to his Scottish background.

His family had land, but like most young men at the time his perception of a future on the land did not inspire. Spurred on by tales of those who had responded to wanderlust, Spaniard left for Cuba, where he spent a few years, returning to open a village shop. There were lessons to be learnt, and going to England would teach him some. With this outlook he was not to be left behind when the *Windrush* showed herself. Not having an address on exit from the ship, he joined those en route to Clapham Deep Shelter.

On his first visit to the Brixton Labour Exchange, Spaniard displayed his true colours, being most assertive at the interview. He wanted work, he said, but only with a firm with the name Sinclair because his grandmother was a Sinclair and she was from Scotland. He could afford to be bumptious because he had a little money in Barclays Bank. The clerk gave an oblique response, but when another clerk, a Scotsman, heard the story he consulted the directories, came upon a company in Shropshire and passed the address on to Spaniard. The firm was impressed with Spaniard's application and determination. A job and lodgings were offered at Sinclair & Company in Ironbridge. He was in for more surprises, when he arrived: there was a small gathering of the clan. Having worked in Cuba, he was able to cope and was an asset to the firm, and was befriended by the employees who did not show any jealousy when he was promoted over them.

All good things must come to an end. Five years after this, the lady he was to marry said 'yes', but she was living in London and could not be persuaded to reside in Ironbridge. One night he took a taxi and abruptly left the firm. When a man marries, his wife sooner or later estranges him from his old friends, and I would add from his job, if need be.

Monti Peter was not in North Africa on a holiday in 1943 – he and his men in the recovery unit were with the 8th Army as specialists in repairing tanks, anywhere, anytime. The damaged tanks in North Africa were in demand against the Fascists and Nazis. Monti was twenty-seven and tall. His broad smile revealed a gold tooth on the left side of his mouth, and the epaulette showed him as a Royal Electrical and Mechanical Engineer, a training he had begun in Jamaica. From North Africa, Monti was dispatched to Italy and remained there until the end of the war when he was demobilised. Like others, he was sent back to Jamaica for a year, living and working on and off in Montego Bay. Having lived in England, he knew that there was regular employment to be had. The *Windrush* did not put to sea without him and on arrival he went straight to Bedford where he had been stationed. At the labour exchange, work was available at the brick works. Although this was not what he had anticipated, he took it: a bird in the hand is worth a thousand in the bush, but he was amazed when those in his team spoke Italian. He had taught himself Italian but pretended not to understand; however, he could not disguise the fact when an Italian boasted of how many blacks he had killed in Ethiopia. A fight was averted only because he allowed good sense to prevail. The Italian apologised.

Surprisingly, both enemies became bosom friends and until Toni, the Italian, left, he did everything to avoid offending Monti. His ambition was to buy an ice cream van, which he later achieved.

Monti also came into his own four years after. He was employed repairing cooperation vehicles, which he enjoyed and for which he was trained. That was exactly what he had wanted in the first place. The only snag was that it involved a change of residence. Monti moved to Birmingham and lived in Handsworth. Now married, he purchased a house at the bargain price of twelve hundred pounds because it had a sitting tenant and the couple was emigrating to Rhodesia. Insults were traded, with the tenant objecting to having a black landlord. It got even worse when he was asked to give up one of his rooms to make way for Monti's relatives coming from Jamaica. It got to the point where Monti was taken to court, but the ruling went in his favour. After all, the house was offered to him first and he was a clerical officer who could afford the repayment.

The tenant then enlisted the help of the British National Party. This did not frighten Monti who had fought Fascists on their home ground. The whole episode was resolved satisfactorily when the Christian Association to which Monti belonged intervened and suggested that the tenant be given one hundred and fifty pounds on the understanding that he vacate the flat. He did. Monti was not to be diverted; his eyes, too, were fixed on the summit.

My friend Rex left the shelter to hostel in Gordon Road, Peckham, but this was jumping out of the frying pan into the fire. Sunday was usually the day for room hunting. While he was out with a friend on such a mission, Rex stopped in Queens Road where a man was outside a public house selling shellfish. They placed an order and enquired whether there were any rooms to let in the area. The trader was concerned for them and invited them home, introducing himself as Dye. The terraced house was as shabby as Dye's oversized coat. It had not had a visit from the painter for years but Rex and his friend appreciated the kindness. His wife satisfied their hungry stomachs while Dye talked endlessly about himself: how because of his chest he had been pronounced unfit for the war and how he made a living working at Billingsgate fish market. Rex and his friend became regular visitors to Dye's home, helping to mend the gate and paint the house. Rex coached their nine year old son in mathematics for which they were very pleased when his position in the class improved beyond belief. There was an empty attic which Rex cleared out and was allowed to move into to supplement the family income. It later came to light that Dye was a police informer spying on the coloured immigrants.

Chapter Ten

The acute shortage of accommodation was the biggest problem facing immigrants who were arriving in large numbers from the new Commonwealth countries. The host nation saw the influx as an imposition and became hostile. The partnership saving scheme accelerated as demand for accommodation outstripped supply. Rooms, and in some cases beds, had to be shared. The landlords became the hunters, exploiting every avenue that would lead to pecuniary rewards. Families made joint purchases and house-buying became an obsession. Some were envious of the rapid economic progress that was evident among immigrants and assumed that vice was behind it. There may have been, but not on a grand scale – immigrants were smart and quick on the uptake. They realised that the locals were not all sympathetic, perhaps out of ignorance of people coming from undeveloped countries to be confronted with the complexities of large cities and uninviting weather conditions.

West Indian immigrants were viewed as uneducated country bumpkins but they were innately resilient, with high hopes. England, for them was a symbol of goodness, of fair laws, of sound education and beliefs. When the church gave a Nelson's eye and the government of the day actually watched a few skunks eject immigrants from their neighbourhoods, the newcomers were bound to be cynical about these flags of righteousness. Admittedly, there were and still are authorities and individuals who spoke against these intolerable behaviour and attitudes.

Employment was available, and immigrants gradually moved from the low paid jobs into work that carried better status and monetary rewards. The trade unions were not supportive either. The employers whom they had fought so hard to box in now had more room to manoeuvre as the influx of job seekers continued. The latter were single minded; Germany had many immigrant labourers and was using them to great economic advantage. The immigrants learnt and moved up the employment and social scale; some went to night school after realising that in many cases their trade skills were technically well behind that of their British counterparts. The indigenous workers were at times more scathing. After the war, Marti Alfred attended the Croydon Government Trade Centre and passed out with a certificate in vehicle maintenance. A British road transport garage manager would have employed him but the shop steward strongly objected. The case was referred to the head office where it was found that Marti was more qualified than the shop steward. Marti got the job, continued with his studies and was rewarded with a promotion. The work mates' criticism was that the immigrants were being too ambitious.

A sheet metal company employing eighty people was apprehensive, but took George on for the only vacant position that no one wanted in the degreasing plant. To everyone's surprise George devised and introduced a new method which resulted in increasing production to a new level. He was given a pay rise and transferred to another section. When the manager discovered that George was studying for his National in sheet metalwork, he allowed him time off and was pleased with his ambitious coloured worker.

Hardships were widespread but it was nothing to write home about. There is always light at the end of the tunnel. The first winter, which, according to the Minister for the Colonies, the Rt Honourable Creech Jones, would send immigrants packing, did not come to pass. In fact, the first winter was a novelty. The problem was how to keep warm, but immigrants had their own contrivance of wearing two of everything from top to bottom which looked comical to the locals. Unfortunately, many immigrants lost their lives using the paraffin heaters to which they were not accustomed.

Experiences varied from region to region. The north, Manchester and Birmingham, were damp and there was accommodation but not as many jobs as in the south, especially London.

My car spraying job at Nottingham was only temporary, in view of the fact that I had already signed up to rejoin the RAF for a further four years. I would be the recipient of a fifty pounds gratuity, and at the end another fifty but until then my bank balance was showing only seven pounds ten shillings. Soon, my recall papers, a railway travel warrant arrived in Bulwell with instructions, to report to RAF Cardington, near Bedford, where there were military barrage balloons. Seven of us were kitted out and the following day we travelled to RAF Sealand near Chester, leaving behind one Irishman who spent his gratuity in the pub and was unfit to travel.

From my own gratuity I sent thirty pounds to my father to replace the three cows he had sold for my fare. He bought a horse, and I was displeased. I was given my old number – 715839 – and the same rank as leading aircraft man – LAC at 45 Maintenance Unit (45 MU) in a team spraying Bedford troop carriers, mainly for overseas. I knew that because a Bren gun hatch was on the passenger side of the cab and the craft was sprayed in jungle green camouflage.

The peacetime billet was really a house equipped with an inside shower, bath and hot and cold water for the seventy or so servicemen. It was a four star hotel compared with the billets during the war. Within a year I was made a corporal and was privileged to take parades. My asset was my thunderous voice which I had the ability to project to the last man when I took the four wing parade of five hundred men. There was a great camaraderie among the seven West Indians in the billet. We went on leave together to Manchester where many immigrants were congregating. Once, at the camp, we were permitted to use the cookhouse so we cooked a simple West Indian meal of pork and dumplings.

It was at Sealand that my friend Vic Campbell fell in love with a pretty blonde Worcester girl. Phil Bees was a very natural girl, placid with extremely lovely legs. She was pleasantly frank and could calm the handsome but irascible Vic. Her brother, however, threw her out the house because of the friendship with a black man. Vic was a mixture of Jewish, African and Colombian, with broad shoulders, long firm hands and curly hair and was six foot tall. Well, Phil moved to Chester, got a job and planned the wedding for the first Saturday in June. We at the billet were all invited to the marriage at the register office. On the big day, vows were exchanged but when the ring was called for there was no ring. It was in Vic's locker, ten miles away. Phil had the gift of being able to keep calm, and on this occasion she really did have her nerves under control. Vic rushed out, hailed a taxi and was back in less than an hour. Everyone was jubilant: they were man and wife and remain so, living a life like a picnic that never comes to an end. Her brother now accepts Vic into the family, perhaps because he plays cricket for Worcester.

Eighteen months on, my younger brother Wilton came in on the boat to Liverpool. I was not keen on him joining the Manchester scene, so after a few days with me he was sent to my sergeant friend who was willing to give him lodging in London. As soon as he was in work we agreed that landlords were too unscrupulous and money-grabbing and should be avoided at all costs, and we should consider buying a house. We lived as frugally as was possible in order to save the deposit. With me, a corporal, and Wilton, a fitter's mate at Dulwich Hospital, I applied from Sealand to Camberwell for a mortgage to purchase 9 Sears Street, London SE5.

Within a few days, the local council replied thanking me for the letter but recommending that I go back to Jamaica. My brother and I took the letter to the owner of 9 Sears Street who was taken aback that one who had fought in the war could be treated with such scant courtesy. He invited us in and said, 'Most of you people are Christians – swear on this Bible that you will repay the money in ten years.' We put our hands on the Bible and said, 'We will repay the money in ten years.' He then took us to the solicitors Meaby & Company of Camberwell Green, where we signed the appropriate legal documents and moved into the house on the following Saturday. I spent a day there and returned to Sealand leaving Wilton in the five-bedroomed house, but not for long.

I had a pleasurable surprise when I returned to Sealand. The adjutant had chosen me for a short, intensive course at Manchester University. It was interesting and profound because I had not met psychology in a structured and academic way before. Though brief, this facilitated the steady build-up of a personal growth and expertise from which I could draw in coping with people and problems. My girlfriend at the time was living in Manchester so I had the chance of visiting her. I always remember Smoky and Jack, the two Alsatians she had, and how they warmed towards me as I took them for a walk.

The Communists under Stalin were now giving trouble all over the world and were a threat to the West. Britain, as the first line of contact for the USA, leased RAF Sealand to the Americans, resulting in our transfer to RAF Kinloss, near Elgin in Scotland. It was extremely cold in winter, as anyone would imagine, and hardly any better in the summer, but it was a beautiful place. From Elgin one could see the snow on Ben Nevis. The cold, however, was no deterrent to a game of cricket, as long as it wasn't raining. On one occasion when the RAF team played the college at Inverness, I made twenty-six runs and took four wickets. I was man of the match, with my name and picture in the local paper. A fortnight after this, I was promoted to open bat to play Elgin. I proceeded to the crease and took up defence against the first ball. It was a full toss and I was bowled in front of the large crowd. I nearly cried.

At Kinloss I worked on the Hanson and Harvard propeller training planes and it was the first time I saw the Meteor jets on the ground. We were instructed never to touch them until we received the proper training. That was all right until one day when the flight sergeant was suddenly taken away ill and I, the senior NCO, was left in charge of the hanger. It started to rain and with the help of the chief engineer, the plane was rolled back inside the hangar.

With the fear of Russia, we resumed war training which included living in tents in the woods. Once we had a twenty-four hour fighting training and it was raining. We were equipped with a ground sheet and full pack. When the officer in charge of my group said 'Down' I had to relay it to the squad of twelve. He took some time to give the next command, so we all remained down. Slumber fell on my tired eyelids and my jaded body just sank in the trench of water. When the directive to move forward was given, Airman Patterson, a Scotsman, had to nudge me. He joked, 'You banana farmers are too soft, spend your leave with my father trawling in the North Sea – he sets off from Lossimouth seaport in November.'

Food was still rationed. Taffy, a corporal once asked me to take a small suitcase to his wife in Manchester on my way to London. He brought it to Elgin station and put it on the overhead rack. When I got to Crewe I had to change trains and I could hardly lift the case. At London Road station I put on a label addressed to Taffy's wife and took it to the left luggage. I did not want to have anything to do with black market food.

On the *Windrush* there had been an entertainer who played the guitar with such prodigious flair and style that everyone was mesmerised. He played and sang the calypso with the vigour educing beads of sweat from his forehead. This man was about thirty years old, slim, always attractively and elegantly dressed, walking with a spring in his step giving the idea of one stepping on hot coal. He spoke facetiously and I was able to detect from his accent that he was not Jamaican. In fact, he was a Trinidadian living and working in the islands around.

This man was Kitchener. Enough of the West Indies – Kitchener was determined to extend his horizons, so with fourteen suits and perhaps not as many pounds in his pocket after booking he had embarked on the *Windrush*. He was not for lodging in the Deep Shelter so he went elsewhere in London then found his way around Liverpool, Birmingham and Manchester. I was to meet this man again in an entirely different setting. By now he had assumed the title of Lord and wanted to be addressed as such. He was an admirer of the real Lord Kitchener of Khartoum who had been given the office of the Secretary for War.

When the West Indies cricket team arrived in the summer of 1950 for another thrashing by England – as the majority of cricket lovers thought – I organised my leave in order to attend the last two days of the Test at Lord's. The West Indies batted first, and with the three Ws, Worrell, Weeks and Walcott, who batted like Trojans, they declared at 429 for six wickets. England started well with Hutton and Washbrook as openers but the indomitable Ramadhin and Valentine cut loose and destroyed the English batting. During those two days I saw some awesome displays of audacious batting: cutting and driving, forward and backward, hooking, sweeping through mid-on and mid-off, a whole array of strokes, shots off pads, late cuts pulling off back foot. Equally entertaining and inspiring was the bowling: yorkers, in-swingers, off-breaks, prodigious spinners, with England caught and bowled and clean bowled at both hostile and medium pace. It was Valentine who effectively destroyed England, although Ramadhin was right there with him at three for 38. They were all out for 274. It was the first time West Indies had ever beaten England on their own ground.

The paltry West Indian crowd, numbering about twenty, was ecstatic. Kitchener had a sudden inspiration and started humming; humming gave way to words, each of us volunteering a word here and there with a tune – a song was in the making and you know what materialised:

Cricket, lovely cricket, at Lords where I saw it
Yardley won the toss but Goddard won the test,

With those little pals of mine, Ramadhin and
Valentine.

I can still visualise his hip-swinging and the few
enthusiastic West Indians in procession round and round
the perimeter. It was theatrical and the crowd of spectators
looked on. I was there.

On the downside, I may say that few *Windrush* people
brought with them a culture which tended to conflict with
that of mainstream Britain, but it was the overcrowding in
tenements which contributed to bad behaviour and
provided an impetus to the criminally-minded. Housing
was the priority, and with money as the driving force, the
early settlers exploited the newcomers. They established
boarding houses, unlicensed bars and gambling facilities for
a people not used to spending leisure time in public houses.
Some, indeed, sailed near to the wind, others went over the
edge and were in trouble with the law.

Overcrowding was exacerbated by the opening up of
immigration not only from the West Indies but from
Guyana, Honduras, India, Pakistan and Africa, encouraged
by news of the availability of a shortage of labour in Britain,
wages umpteen times greater than in their native land and
obtainable financial assistance. To people who were
permanently unemployed, that was good news. Without a
fixed address, immigrants were prepared to go where the
work was, which meant Wales, Midlands, and, of course,
Greater London. They would jump other hurdles when
they came to them.

Chapter Eleven

It was three and a half years since I had returned to Britain, and having a brother and a house made me more settled and optimistic than before. Now a joint landlord, I looked forward to going to Camberwell, as was the case on Fridays while on leave. I had a quick glance around and went to the communal kitchen, which I found dirty and untidy. Off came my battle dress shirt; I got some hot water and was in the process of cleaning when a young woman came in. She was exquisitely dressed, with shoulder-length hair neatly tied back, rather tall and with a sweet smile and amiable face. She said hello.

The bottom door of Sears Street was never locked. It was the policy of my brother and me to give any West Indian lodgings for two days or until a job and accommodation were found. The girl I saw did not look like one in search of either. It turned out that she was Mae, the aunt of the front room tenant, and had recently arrived to be trained as a nurse. Learning that her niece, Lus, would be taking her to the local drill hall dance on the Saturday, I held myself in readiness to attend. I was there bright and early, and sat and waited. Both arrived looking gorgeous and youthful. Turning to me with that really charming smile she asked if I had been waiting long as if she had expected me to be there. The dance got under way but these two girls were not dancing – they were just standing there chatting. That gave me the chance of having a good look at her profile. It was astonishingly beautiful, a slim and shapely figure. I approached and asked her for a dance. She sprung to her feet with obvious delight and we took to the floor. She was a pattern of decorum and discretion impressed indelibly on my mind as I returned to camp. By intuition, I knew that filly was mine but patience must be exercised.

Mae went into Queen Mary's hospital, Sidcup, Kent to be trained. Many other West Indians followed, including my sister, whose first choice was St Giles Hospital, Camberwell. I remember a couple of days after arriving I took her to St Giles for the interview, but the panel just took one look at us and said there was no vacancy. Eighteen years later, my sister entered St Giles, not as a trainee but as the Matron.

My four year contract with the RAF terminated, and I was demobbed in 1952 and given a month's paid leave. During the month I worked on the building site of Cliffe and Cooling and did painting work in Charlton, but a stable and permanent employment was my aim. I applied to the Post Office and was called for a test, which I passed, and became a postman assigned to Waterloo Office. As there was no canteen there, postmen received ten shillings more per week. I remained there for two years and was moved to the South West District Office at Victoria for background experience before being trained as a sorter. For one week I was on mail duty to Buckingham Palace. I had to be smartly dressed in my postman's uniform when I went to the Master of the Horses at the back of the Palace.

Two months later, fifteen of us were posted to the sorter's training office at Old Street. Two men were very sorry for me because they thought that being a Jamaican I was not accustomed to the geography of the United Kingdom and the place names would be too difficult for me to learn. One fellow who worked as a despatch clerk at

Harrods and had passed the two week course with three days to spare also thought it would be too hard for me. A few days into the course, I asked for a test. The instructor thought I was joking; anyway, he gave me the test of five hundred East Anglian places. I did it on time with only two mistakes when up to five were allowed. He thought I had cheated and gave me another, which I also passed convincingly.

It had been decided that positive discrimination would be applied in my case, but I did not need any favours. Still doubtful of my honesty, I was taken to the manager in charge of the training centre who gave me a brand new East Anglian pack of places involving the many market towns: Stowmarket, Market Harborough, Market Rasen, Needham Market, Newmarket, Butter Market in Ipswich, and scores of little villages. Again I applied mnemonics and threw them off in an even shorter time. Now satisfied, the boss asked how it had been done. I replied that I had composed a song using the place names. In reply, he said I'd passed. For the remaining days I was given odd jobs then I requested that I also learn Ireland and Scotland. By the last two days, I had more than a working knowledge of both these provinces.

Eastern District Office at Whitechapel was my posting as a sorter. Some of the older sorters hated newcomers to the registered enclosure. They hogged the overtime. My stay there was not one I wish to recall, saving to say had it not been for the grace of God I would have been marked failed and returned to base as a postman. But who did I see come in as sorter one day but Clarke, a panther from the *Windrush* and a comrade at RAF Sealand. He cheered me up and I was in a position to help him settle into his new environment. A nephew of one of my tenants also joined as a driver but was set upon and harassed. That he could cope with, but when he was confronted with barefaced mendacity the poor fellow was not a little out of temper. Without enquiry, he was dismissed. The real reason for all this nefariousness was because he had a Welsh wife.

Personally, I disliked east London because of the distance I had to ride from Camberwell and later from Herne Hill. When Tower Bridge was raised, I was delayed and not knowing these movements well beforehand I always made sure to leave myself ample time. During the Notting Hill Riots I was about to get onto Tower Bridge when I was chased by two thugs and before I made my escape I received a hell of a kick which, thanks to my anticipation and agility, did not unseat me as was the intention. My union only made a brief note of it. At the retirement of one of the senior staff, I gave one penny because of his treatment of me.

I remember walking along the dock area of Cable Street when I was informed that the Black Hawk was going to be at a certain night club and that I should be there. This man was a Trinidadian, about forty years old, tall and slender. He was 'the big chief' because it was believed that he was the man who had snatched Haile Selassie of Ethiopia out of the jaws of the fascist Mussolini.

The only laughter I had at Whitechapel was on the occasion when a sorter was caught with his binoculars spying on some nurses sunbathing on the top of the London Hospital. After four years I asked for a transfer, which was granted, and I was posted to South Eastern District Office, 239, Borough Hill Street, SE1. I took up my position there one Monday morning in the summer.

I was not welcomed by some; not a smile crossed the faces of those who were too busy guarding the overtime. I spoke only when necessary. One week into the post, I asked for overtime on the Irish section sorting letters beyond

Dublin to Limerick. There, my colleagues saw that I was not as green and naive as they thought. One fellow in particular was most obnoxious whenever I put in for overtime work. He made hurtful remarks and was not cooperative. Others joined in, but I was there to do a job and nothing was going to make me flounder or even show resentment. My performance was far above these petty nonentities. I held fast to my integrity.

Chapter Twelve

Forty years on I would watch a man advance towards me and as he got nearer I would make out that it was Larry, the very man who had given me grief at the borough office. He was looking frail and worn by now, with a benign expression. I had often wondered what had become of him. He was friendly now, and in his shaky voice told me of the run of misfortunes in his life: his wife had died and he was living alone in a council flat because his daughter was not in a position to have him. A wave of pity for Larry swept over me. I took him home for a meal and we talked without mentioning bygones. There was no bitterness. He was not attending a place of worship, so he was invited to the church to which I belong. He attended week after week until he became ill, was hospitalised and passed away. It was not mine to take revenge.

Back at the office, my record was good and I was proposed for a managerial position. One middle executive gave all the assistance and tutoring required for me to be sufficiently proficient and competent at my work, which required good judgement, promptness, accuracy and speed. My yearly grades were As and Bs. He was frank with me. He said he was aware that some did not like black people in executive positions and would like to downgrade me. He was right: one executive called me into his office one day and out of the blue told me of his contempt for immigrants. He had been livid when he had called County Hall and an Indian voice had been heard on the telephone. Addressing me, he said, 'If I had my way you would not even be a postman in my office.' I did not reply. Not long after, I was promoted to an executive position.

For experience, it was necessary for me to take up short-term duties in various offices. The first was Peckham. On the first morning, I walked in and the officer in charge was so sensitive that he instructed me not to speak to the men as they had not served under a black man before. I was not worried; in the forces I had been in charge of more men than were at Peckham. Hardly had I settled down when a man called out to me by name and asked what I was doing there. That defused the tense situation. He was the union representative who was really the power there. We knew each other as Labour Party and union members.

The ice was broken so it wasn't such an ordeal when I was asked to administrate at Herne Hill, Camberwell, Kennington, Walworth and lastly Rotherhithe. At the latter, the docks were closing and men were coming in in droves asking for jobs. This was compounded by the influx of immigrants from Eastern Europe, mainly the Ukraine, Poland and Hungary, as well as from Western Europe, some even from Germany. I could only take their particulars and send them on to headquarters. On the whole, there were no vacancies. In the course of my work I came across people, especially immigrants, who had no reservation in telling their sensational life stories. Some were desperate to let someone know that they were still being affected by the war. This opened my eyes to the fact that scattered on the mountain were other climbers who had set off from an entirely different base but had similarly encountered the obtrusive and obstructive precipices of the shining rocks, the furious winds and the resulting dizziness where one miscalculation could have ended in a plunge headlong into the abyss.

The story I am about to tell comes from Inge, a German girl who for the past forty years has visited her country of origin only once. She was only a girl when Nazi Germany overran France in 1940, when Adolf Hitler revealed his procedural tactics as firstly the capture of Britain and secondly to use the blacks from French and British colonies to rebuild Germany to demonstrate the superiority of the Nordic race. At the time there was also a purge of the mentally ill in Germany, of which most Germans were aware, and destruction of Jewish businesses and establishment of the concentration camps. Many Brownshirt (comparable with the Combat 18) Nazi Party members were demanding a share of the spoils taken from the Jews while the German middle class had no compunction in using Eastern European Slavs as poorly paid domestic labourers.

Inge told me of how her Papa Hezlar returned home one summer's night in 1941, clad in his Brownshirt uniform of the Solingen Section from the outskirts of Düsseldorf, and after a hearty meal of French wine and cheap Russian food proclaimed the propaganda of the Ministry of Information which was headed by Goebbels. Papa Hezlar was an employee in the local scissor-making factory. He was blond, very tall and had volunteered for the Düsseldorf SS Panzer Unit, but had been rejected on medical grounds. To his death he claimed his Jewish doctor for not curing his asthma. Papa Hezlar rated the Slavs as subhuman, like the blacks and Jews, and said they should be beaten if they disobeyed orders. He was looking forward to managing a scissors factory in Sheffield when Germany took over Britain.

Inge told me of the large and immaculate house, formerly belonging to a Jew, into which the family had moved. Papa Hezlar instructed them never to think or talk of the Jews and told them that the Nazis had the final solution now, unlike in the First World War when their men were stabbed in the back. Then Inge demonstrated how her father had gone on to say, 'We are the master race and our leader is a genius. We will attack the Bolsheviks; it will be like pushing over a rotten dam; our Panzers will be running all over the Steppes and Goering', he boasted, 'will beat Britain with the German Luftwaffe.' He admitted to liking the English because they had come from good German stock way back, but although they had ruled a quarter of the world they had become soft by communist infiltration. 'We must not be soft.' He slammed his fist on the oak table to make the point. Inge's Mama Hezlar was pleased with her husband's manly exhibition and asked the children if they had heard what Papa had said.

Six months before, Inge had met a young pilot in his Luftwaffe uniform at a Hitler Youth rally. He was a pilot in the Junkers Stuka bomber squadron. It was love at first sight. This young man was a fanatical Nazi but Inge wanted to tell him not to bomb Sheffield because she wanted to live near Papa in a big house. Inge was commanded by the Blackshirts to supervise a house with a family of eight children and two slaves, and was paid ten marks per month. She did not like the work and took it out on the Polish and Russian labourers.

On dark winter's night in 1942, Papa Hezlar arrived home subdued and did not eat. Then he shared the burden of his heart with the family: the German army had lost the battle of Stalingrad and the subhuman Asiatic horde was sweeping towards the beloved Germany accompanied by the American military; he thought they were going to be bombed into the grave. The family was moved to the air raid shelter praying that the Americans would get to them before the Russians did.

Spring did bring the flowers, but Inge had no white wedding for Papa and Mama to see, not even the grave on which to put them, because her beloved pilot friend was shot down over the English Channel. Inge was heartbroken and Papa Hezlar now smelt a rat.

Papa Hezlar's scissors factory was completely destroyed by five-hundred pounders. He now had to work long hours in an ammunition factory, but he was not totally broken as Goebbels assured workers that there were many secret weapons left to win the war. Fools believed it, but Papa Hezlar realised that the hunter had now become the hunted Nazi brutes in the eyes of the world and he began to have horrible nightmares. He imagined that his two daughters were on the receiving end, that the invaders were plundering, pillaging, raping and murdering his fair daughters. When the Western Allies invaded occupied France on the 6th June, 1944, and the tanks were advancing at their will, Hezlar had to admit that there was no master race and that nations do rise and fall.

Inge was concerned for her mother because she was so affected that sometimes her stomach churned when she heard that the Russians had broken through another defence. Papa, she said, had started to admit that the Führer Hitler had made a terrible mistake in issuing order number 45 instructing General von Paulus to stand to the last man at Stalingrad resulting in ninety-three thousand young men being captured and sent to Siberia. He knew in his heart that very few would see their mighty Germany again and even if they did, it would not be the one they left.

The Americans did come to the Hezlars' town and street. When Inge saw a black GI guarding her street she panicked and ran in the opposite direction. The GI sergeant in charge took notice of the incident and at the next opportunity spoke to her in German. She was surprised because Papa and his colleagues had always said that blacks were monkeys, couldn't cope with Nordics and could only grunt, and she had believed it. The sergeant conversed with her at length and at the end gave her some chocolate, which she had not seen for two years. When she told the family how and from whom she got the chocolates, Papa once more strongly forbade her to speak to blacks.

In 1948, when fraternisation was relaxed, Inge met and fell in love with a British soldier stationed in Germany. He was bullish and held similar views to that of her Papa, and during the Berlin airlift she married him not so much for love of the Englishman but to fulfil her dream of a big house in England. However, upon arrival she became unhappy, sharing accommodation with her in-laws in Colchester. After seven turbulent years, her husband died and she moved to London where, though unskilled, she obtained work in a factory for twenty-seven years retiring for medical reasons. That she was childless was her greatest regret. Happiness did not completely evade Inge. In the course of her employment Inge entered into a relationship with a black man, a Jamaican. They have been happily married and together for more than forty years in South East London. As Inge related her story, I could identify with her in many areas. It was the union of a German fox and a Jamaican mongoose; money was paramount. Inge has long since abandoned the views of her Brownshirt Papa and Nazi Germany, and the tyrant Hitler is long dead. In fact she has remained impervious to other such ideas. Inge has survived, chafed and roughened by exposure to the heat, rain, and cold and to the sharp edges of the rocks as she clawed her way up the rough side of the mountain, but so far, unlike many others there is no disfigurement.

The author left Jamaica in 1944 to enlist for active service in Britain during the Second World War, 1939-1945.

Left: promoted to assistant inspector at the South East District Post Office based in SE1 in 1976. *Right:* at work in 1985.

The author with his first wife, Mae, meeting the Queen at her Silver Jubilee Celebration, Rotherhithe Park, SE16, in 1978.

The author as the first black mayor of the London Borough of Southwark, 1983-84.

The author and his niece, Mayara, as mayoress, meeting Princess Anne at King's College Hospital, 1984.

The author marrying his second wife, Myrtle, October 1984.

The author standing in front of his home in Jamaica in 1991.

The author *(left)* with three of his brothers and two of his sisters, in the garden at Brockley in 1992.

The London Labour Mayors' Association-past and present mayors of the London Borough of Southwark gather in Southwark Town Hall, May 1993.

The author with Clive Lloyd, the West Indies' cricket captain, at Southwark Town Hall.

The West Indian Ex-servicemen and Women's Association at Harlow Cenotaph, 1993.

Chapter Thirteen

I had always been the guest of my friend Harry and his dear mother; therefore he was the first to be invited to see my house in Sears Street. From the experience gained in working on war-damaged buildings, I had no problem, apart from the many man-hours and sleepless nights, transforming the old house into a habitable place of abode.

Harry was delighted, but as a frank, plain-speaking person – no mealy mouth, he can call a spade a spade – he castigated me for having a house full of tenants. He thought I was a capitalist, no better than Tate and Lyle exploiting the black people in the West Indies. Unoffended, I tried in my controlled way to explain that, in view of the housing situation at the time, I was only being considerate and philanthropic to my people, otherwise they would have had to take up residence under the trees or on the pavements.

Harry and his son returned about a year later to meet my relatives and two of my ex-tenants who were now landlords. This time I had the evidence that there was no exploitation involved and let him into the secret of the partnership saving scheme which we operated among properly vetted, honest and resourceful men and women in steady employment. They were immensely impressed with the entrepreneurial acumen and the satisfaction and joy of owning a house. The advice I gave was to start off preferably with an old house, then repair, renovate, extend if desirable and sell. Then the dream house can become a reality. The door of opportunity was soon opened for the young man, and he stepped inside.

By no stretch of imagination could I have conjured up a picture of what was to greet me when a few years hence I was invited to see what my friend Mike had made of an old cottage called Journey's End in Gloucestershire.

Journey's End was the last of six Georgian cottages one mile from the village on the highway. About five miles from the British Lion, the only public house, you turned right into a narrow winding road which barely allowed for two vehicles to pass each other. On the right there was Rose Cottage, set in about half an acre of ground, then St Andresberg, perhaps with a German history. Stone Cottage indicated that local stones were used for building. Three Chimneys was the largest of the six cottages and the architecture gave the impression of the owner being a lover of botany. The three chimneys could not be seen from the front but if one went to the back one realised that the original owner had concealed a third chimney; the penultimate one was Number 14, then came the old stone building of Journey's End. The road ended in front with enough space to accommodate five cars comfortably.

Journey's End, without altering the original features, had been modernised with fitted kitchen, additional bathroom and built-in wardrobe. The old iron frame fireplace was retained; so was the monstrous Victorian grandfather clock with its long metal chain, standing in the modern dining room. It was a very spacious house. An oak-panelled staircase led one to the upstairs where there was a full view of the back garden crowded with fruit trees, a vegetable garden, a profusion of flowers bordering a beautiful lawn, a chicken run and a rabbit hutch. There was even room for a small thicket through which ran a little brook, the Little Avon. This was the part of the country where one would like to live but only in retirement. I went back to the South Eastern District Office pleased with Mike's achievement.

The Post Office was recruiting mainly ex-servicemen, providing they passed the Civil Service tests and paid the charge of five shillings to be established. It was at this office that one such serviceman, Dumi Singh, told his story of why he decided to emigrate to England. 'You are on the wrong ship; this ship is taking men to France and you should be in Egypt,' his captain had said to the diminutive twenty-four year old soldier of about nine stone. In France, Dumi Singh was given a sealed envelope and was put on the next ship back to Dover, from where he was despatched to Woolwich barracks to be re-routed to an Indian unit in the Middle East.

Singh was born in India and joined the armed service as a general fitter after leaving technical school. England was bewildering for him and when he was posted to Egypt, where he should have been three weeks before, he was delighted. He settled quickly into his new unit where he was to serve for three years in the theatre of war as a general fitter in a team of twelve specialists in different trades. His duty was giving first aid to armoured units. When the Nazis and Fascists were driven out of North Africa, Singh was shifted to Sicily and then to Italy with the 4th Indian Division before being sent back to India after the war but his fellow men accused him of being too pro-British at a time when they were struggling for the independence which India gained in 1947. He had seen England and had had a taste of a way of life far superior to that to which he was accustomed. Having read about the first batch of immigrants on the *Windrush*, Singh corresponded with an ex-serviceman and set foot on the mountain in 1949. He went to an address in Smithwick, and within forty-eight hours was working assiduously in an iron foundry. His relatives joined him by the following year.

The trickle of Indians soon became a flood, most of them finding employment in the Midlands. Later, Singh applied to the Post Office and was taken on as a willing postman, but his sights were set an higher things.

A similar story came from Ahmed Khan. The Moslems in Pakistan were killing Hindus and he had been targeted. So far, he had been spared even though he had a Hindu wife. Khan had been educated at one of the better schools in India but when his father died he had to take over the one hundred and twenty-five acre estate. The problems started when he dismissed some older Hindus who were not pulling their weight. When he got wind of their intention to kill him, he took five hundred rupees and, passing his wife at work sewing, he told her he would not be back. He tried to board a train on which there were many terrified Moslems with the same idea as himself. Armed guards were on the train to prevent disturbances, and thus he was able to cross the border into Pakistan, a foreign country. His letter to his wife instructed her not to join him in Pakistan because the people were killing Hindus and were just as mad as those in India. In return, she sent him a cutting from an old newspaper about the Jamaicans immigrating to England. There was the possibility of war between India and Pakistan and he was drafted into the armed forces, but with the help of the Pakistan authorities and his friends in London, Khan left the army and emigrated to England, the very country in which he had worked as a student to evict from India. He obtained work in a rubber factory. The estate in India was proving difficult to sell, the workers became squatters and the Indian authorities could do nothing save recommend that they claim one of the many farms left by the Indians in Pakistan.

Ahmed's wife and daughter joined him in Southall where they lived together in peace and safety, and with tight economy they had enough for a deposit on a home within two years. Someone had thrown them the chance when only the gleam of it was visible; they caught it and never let go, even when they suffered confusion of mind from the fierce snowstorms and boisterous winds on the mountainside.

Should one be stricken with insufferable gloom or unrelieved exhaustion on the journey up the mountain – look! There are footsteps permanently impressed on the rock face giving clues to where and from where other travellers have been proceeding

As a sturdy young man, I had no political ambition. My father, though in charge of the parochial roads, one of the founders of the loan bank and chairman of the local Labour Party, did not really fire me. The schooling I had had did not expose me to political thoughts. No mention was made of Booker T. Washington, very little of Paul Bogle and George Gordon, much of Drake, Hawkins and Columbus. It was not until the great strikes led by Alexander Bustamante and the formation of the People's National Party by Norman Manley that a few flimsy thoughts began to wander into my vacant mind. Thus, when I arrived in England I was naive, but by 1948 the scales had began to fall from my eyes and visibility was lengthening enough for me to scrutinise the narrow path trodden by weary and bruised feet.

I had detected many footmarks on the mountain, some faint from time, but there are some that in my estimation, will never fade. Among them are those of the Jamaican Marcus Garvey, and as I have studied them I have found much that influenced, much that encouraged and much to emulate in the ascent. 'God Almighty created men equal whether they be white, yellow or black and for any race to admit that it cannot do what others have done, is to hurl an insult at the Almighty.' These were the words of Garvey, who travelled the West Indian islands and the United States of America speaking out against injustice and oppression, highlighting the problems of black people and arousing black consciousness. He took the fight to every part of the USA: schools and colleges, religious gatherings, political institutions, the judiciary and even to prison.

Garvey was a philosopher, clever and courageous. From his research, he discovered that after the signing of the Emancipation Proclamation in the USA the white man started to think of how the problem of the Negro would be solved. The plan devised was, 'Now that America is undeveloped and we have but thirty-four million in the population [thirty million being white and four million black], a number not large enough to develop the country as we want, we will use the four million blacks until we have built up the country sufficiently and when we no longer need their labour we will throw them off and let them starve economically and die themselves or emigrate elsewhere, we care not where. Then no one can accuse us of being inhuman to the Negroes as we shall not have massacred them.'

Because of his outstanding defence of the underclasses, Garvey became the victim of conspiracies and frame-ups from selfish, jealous and wicked men. Indictment and ultimately incarceration in Atlanta was the final nail in the coffin. His successful appeal led to the commutation of his five-year sentence in December 1927 and his deportation to Jamaica as a convicted alien felon. He still had enough constitution left in him to get involved in politics, but without success. Not to be defeated, he moved his headquarters of the Universal Negro Improvement Association to London. Although Garvey did not live to see his grand design materialise, he did provide inspiration for the New World blacks who had begun to take pride in their colour: as James Brown sang, 'I'm black and I'm proud'. Garvey, who was shunned and despised by the ruling elite, was made a national hero in Jamaica and a bust of him erected in the Heroes' Park. His body was exhumed from its London grave and interred in Kingston in an impressive and elaborate ceremony. His name lives on: the Jamaican government has set up a five thousand pound Marcus Garvey Prize to be awarded to the one who has made the most significant contribution in the field of human rights. For Marcus Garvey, whether in the eyes of the whites they be octoroons, quadroons, mulattos or blacks, having as their goal the making of an nation alone is a people's racial salvation.

Others like W.E.B. Dubois, James Baldwin and Martin Luther King also scaled the mountain, but it is Claudia Jones who most had the practical and political wit to dodge the falling rocks.

It was purely coincidence I came in contact with Claudia. West Indian students had met for a meeting in Baron's Court to discuss a few matters which were causing concern in Brixton, and as a member of the Labour Party and the trade union and an upcoming activist, I attended the meeting. Claudia listened intently, and at the end her summary of the arguments was very profound. She was a 'no nonsense' person, I was to find out. Her conversations ranged widely from social and political science to jurisprudence and theology, and they were solid, instructive and interesting with the minimum of humour. The retentiveness of her memory was enviable as one listened to the anecdotes of her life.

Claudia Verna Cumberbatch was born in Trinidad, and from the age of eight she amazed her teachers with her enquiring mind. She was always asking why. A career as a teacher of religion was destined for her. Her father emigrated to the USA and the rest of the family followed shortly after to live, so she was brought up in the poor immigrant area of New York, but nothing could dampen her hunger for knowledge. She did exceptionally well in high school and upon graduation she received the Theodore Roosevelt Award for good citizenship.

Being poor, Claudia had to work her way through college in restaurant kitchens. She travelled as a journalist all over the Southern States writing about the beatings and lynchings of Negroes, the oppression under Jim Crowism, the segregation and the discrimination. Because of this she was a marked woman by the Southern Legion and the Klu Klux Klan. Eventually in 1948 she was arrested and held in jail on a charge of suspicion, but with the aid of the liberal press in the north, the coloured community and the Communist Party, she was set free on caution not to enter the South again. Claudia emerged from the prison cell a changed person mentally and physically, went into hiding for a rest and then resumed her work as Claudia Jones. She advocated the use of force and aroused the blacks to organise themselves against the oppressive system. The Klu Klux Klan was to the whites as the Gestapo was to Hitler's Nazi Germany. While Claudia was investigating a Florida lynching she was beaten and humiliated but refused to be silenced, thereupon earning another arrest under the Smith's Act, which was an extension of McCarthyism. She pleaded guilty to fifteen charges and defended herself against one by saying that if her sentence helped in any way to make the life of her people better then she was glad to plead guilty. 'If I am guilty', she said, 'under the Smith's Act of the USA and no one is guilty for the thousands of lynched Negro men, then this system is wrong in the sight of decent people and of God.' Awaiting deportation in Anderson prison, she asked to be deported to England. The request was granted and she was met by a handful of left-wing West Indian students. She landed with five hundred pounds collected from a national appeal by her friends in the USA.

This was the gist of a vibrant life that was so full of promise. As Claudia sat at meal in my house with my wife and me, her lips quivered and the tears flowed freely as she demonstrated and related her experiences in the redneck state when she was imprisoned in Little Rock where the warden was a Klan member. She thought black people were suffering from an inferiority complex because of their historical background and peasant mentality which made them slow to grasp the reality of the situation, so her mission was to educate. Within days of her arrival she organised a meeting of eighteen to twenty people whom she thought would be the forerunners in the fight. She was astoundingly confident and somewhat authoritarian, but the new immigrants needed someone with experience, drive and leadership qualities. Her unbending and uncompromising stance qualified her for such a role.

One of the spin-offs from this meeting of minds was the establishment of a company, the Coloured People's Printing Press, and the subsequent launch of the *West Indian Gazette and Afro-Asian Opinion* of which Claudia was the editor and I the circulation manager. This was the first immigrant mouthpiece and Claudia had a clear run in the field. In addition, she gave invaluable practical advice in matters pertaining to employment, health, the law and fund-raising promoting art exhibitions, dances and lectures, all with the aim of uniting immigrants in areas of high concentration where differences of religion, language and culture were putting a strain on relationships not only among themselves but also on the host population. This was most noticeable in Nottingham, Birmingham, Manchester and London when I investigated the uneasiness, but policies were put in place to alleviate this.

It was not that easy to deal with such a situation in Notting Hill, London. The skinheads, not disposed to reasoning, went on the attack rather like animals in the jungle protecting their territories. But the immigrants resisted and retaliated, resulting in a fierce and nasty riot. As expected, it was quickly contained.

I remember Mr Norman Manley, QC and Prime Minister of the colony of Jamaica arrived within days of hearing of the most disgraceful thing ever to happen in modern Britain. While touring with government personnel he stopped to speak to two black men. A police officer interposed and ordered then to 'move on'. The official guide produced his credentials and informed the ignorant constable that the gentleman was a Prime Minister, but the reply was that all must 'move on' or be arrested.

When Claudia heard she laughed – well, it was more in the manner of a tiger's sneer – and continued getting legal advice for others who were arrested. Late one night she too was picked up and taken to a West London police station on a charge of 'on suspicion of theft'. Many hours passed before she was allowed to contact a lawyer, and without charge she was released. This is what I call harassment.

When the tumult and the shouting had died down, Claudia met with us again and while brainstorming we arrived at the idea of instituting something to enhance integration and understanding: to make others aware of our contribution to the British economic recovery and that we were here to stay along with the progeny that sprang from our loins. To achieve this, as black Britons, one voice was heard to say, 'We should be thinking of ways in which we can enrich the social and political environments in which we choose to make our home and not be distracted by what the sea-hawks throw at us, the doctor birds with their iridescent plumage.'

The latter are the only birds that can fly backwards and they have a scissor tail. As the rhyme goes, 'Doctor bud, a cunny bud, hard bud fe dead', meaning it is a clever bird, not easily killed. The point was taken and a committee was formed to discuss a West Indian carnival. The committee assessed all the possible objections that could have been voiced against such an event and put in place a counterblast to every unreasonable one. Claudia and her henchman, nicknamed the Cobra, had done their homework.

It was a bright and glorious Saturday evening in August 1958 when Seymour Hall opened its doors to hundreds of people witnessing the first West Indian carnival in Britain. A multitude had to be turned away. The carnival was a success. The behaviour was impeccable, apart from two drunks who were quickly brought under control and disposed of without police intervention. We even made a profit of thirty-two pounds ten shillings, and the media gave it a good coverage. The neo-fascists, of course, were none too pleased, arguing that such things had no cultural value in England, but the Cobra did well in refuting this misconception.

A cloak-and-dagger affair began to emerge as the authorities started to take an interest in Claudia's general activities, including her letters and telephone calls. Claudia visited Russia and as an invited guest saw the atomic test explosion in China. She was admired for her brilliance and resilience; to say the least, she worked assiduously for the betterment of coloured people, but in the end her supporters, wary of her political ideology and philosophy and her unappealing communist ideas, drifted away. Claudia did have one wish, however, which was for me to meet Martin Luther King. That wish was fulfilled. I was introduced to Dr King and had the privilege of making him tea. Emotional and physical strain exacerbated her heart condition, putting an end to her dedicated and arduous life on the 29th December, 1964. She was cremated and her ashes were buried near Karl Marx in Highgate Cemetery.

Where ignorance is bliss it is not always folly to be wise. Claudia was not alone on the receiving end, encountering solid obstruction all the way. It takes strength and character not to succumb when others purport to have tangible evidence of one's movements and behaviour in order to accuse and convict. Fortunately, there are fair and all-pervasive laws which give protection from those who abuse them unjustly. In some cases, the only offence is to be in the wrong place at the wrong time.

I remember I was about to get on my bunk on the *Windrush* when I brushed against another guy in the process of mounting the top bunk. He spun round and pushed me in an aggressive manner. He was about three inches shorter than me and, without boasting, with my long arms he would be no match for me. I was just about to swing into action when someone intervened and said, 'Beard, since the English did not hang you, we have to tolerate you and live with you.' I added, 'To think that like hundreds of other West Indian servicemen I gave what I could to save your neck i.e. five shillings.'

As servicemen we used to be regulars at the public house on Oldham Road near the amusement arcade where the jukebox never seemed to stop playing 'Straighten up and fly right, cool down papa, don't blow your top.' Well, during and after the war some burly Americans from Texas used to hang around at the arcade and if they could not find the company of a girl after the pubs closed, they would beat up the black servicemen and take away their girls as they came down Oldham Road to catch the bus in Piccadilly Square in the centre of Manchester. For protection, we travelled in twos and threes and took the back streets. This also became dangerous after the boyfriend of Cheshire Cat – Bet, the tall girl from Stockport – was set upon and had to be hospitalised, so we decided that we would have to fight back if we were attacked just to survive and maintain the respect of those girls who befriended and enjoyed the company of West Indians but suffered for it at home, at work and most of all on the street. These girls were decent and fun-loving.

Truth crushed to the ground will rise again. Beard is still alive and in his right mind.

Chapter Fourteen

A year after leaving the air force, I married Mae at St Mark's church which is now home to Bishop Meade's flats and some trees on Camberwell Road. Our first child, a boy whom we named Brian, was born a year later, six months before Mae's final nursing examinations. Brian was a treasure but it was a very taxing time for both of us, especially Mae who needed all the time possible to revise. With this in mind, we got a child-minder for Brian.

One winter's night, the telephone rang, Mae answered and suddenly out came a terrific shriek. Her countenance changed, her eyes dilated and I saw her lips move but there was no sound for a minute; then she said, 'Brian is dead.' We were stunned and for a while we just froze in each other's arms. The post-mortem recorded the cause of death to have been cot death.

Mae did manage to write the exams and was successful, but the agony was too much and lingered in that house, so 9 Sears Street was sold. Jointly with my brother, we purchased 13 Castlemaine Road in Peckham. We needed a bigger place, too, as my three sisters and two brothers were now residing at the same address, but not for long, as their aspiration was the same as ours: buy your own home. My brother, partner in the house-purchasing business, got married and branched out on his own. It was the time when small estate agents were ripping off housebuyers and gazumphing was rife: some were taking deposits on one house from various people, using the deposits to buy another house for cash and selling, making huge profits. Refunds took months. We were caught out ourselves, and had to seek legal advice at Meaby & Co. When the case was outlined, a sympathetic lady solicitor showed us another house on the market that we could have instead of a cash refund. This was 8 Secretan Road, a property with eight rooms, three kitchens and three toilets, planned on three floors, a freehold and priced at nine hundred pounds, so we went to view it. The interior was gloomy, the walls were bleak and grey, the doors and window frames were suffering from many years of discoloration, fungus was spreading over the whole exterior and in some parts the masonry had fallen out. On the whole, it was in a shocking condition, with no electricity. It was, however, a firm and stable house, sound and dry. We bought the house and straight away commenced the repairs with the help of friends; we decorated and had the rewiring done and within a few weeks it was ready for letting.

We were soon blessed with another son and moved into the downstairs flat. After a few weeks with the baby, my wife returned to work and the baby was looked after by a nanny while I did the maximum amount of overtime at the Post Office. Twelve hours a day was not uncommon for me

People were still finding it extremely difficult to obtain lodgings. Instinct seemed to direct them to the houses bought by West Indians and so the knocking continued. One young woman was very persistent and would not take no for an answer, so she was invited in and shown that all the rooms were tenanted. She turned to me and said, 'Land master, you have a little room and if I can't get that I'll stay under the staircase.' It was the store room, eight feet by four feet, to which she was referring. It was filled with brooms, the pram, my tools and my bicycle. Winnie was a cleaner at the Peek Freans biscuit factory. How could I turn her away? We cleared it out and put in a folding camp bed and a chair, and she moved in at one pound per week while the others paid two pounds. On Sundays she did her cooking in one small pot on the first floor; on other days she used the firm's canteen and at night she ate broken Peek Freans biscuits without a single complaint.

Winnie began to be sick in the mornings and I suggested that she went to the doctor, but my wife with her knowledge of such things called her into the front room and had a chat. Winnie was expecting a baby. Her story was that one of the influential employees at Peak Freans had promised to get her on the assembly line where the wages were better, and this he would do for sexual favours.

Because of the lack of space, in the course of time Winnie left of her own accord. Years after, when I was acting manager of the sorting office at Highshore Road, a woman came in with a beautiful young girl, and on recognising me, she approached with a broad smile and said, 'Land master, you remember me? This is the baby that I wanted.' Winnie had her desire, and so did the employee because his wife was unable to have a child. To crown it all, the goodly gentleman helped her to acquire a small terrace house in Peckham.

Our son was four years old when we had another child, a daughter. Everything was to our desire and we were extremely happy, but as the children grew older, a warm sense of complacency was beginning to be stirred. My wife was not satisfied that the environment was right for the children, and was determined that they should not live and be schooled on 'Mud Island' near Surrey Canal, so the search was on for a residential property with conducive surroundings.

I was out delivering leaflets on Half Moon Lane when I spotted an advertisement for a house with a garage for sale in the next street. The description was compelling and it struck me as the ideal one: a detached Edwardian house on a quiet uncrowded road in Herne Hill near Dulwich Village. The agent advertising the sale was Meaby, the very one from whom I had bought most of my houses. Upon request, I was given permission for us to view the property. As we approached the house, I could detect Mae's approval and I knew it was the place for us; however, we went through just to assure ourselves. The price did not seem exorbitant either, because there was a sitting tenant who had a Rolls-Royce parked in front. Some time after, we were to learn that it was the home of Richard Church, the writer of *Over the Bridge*, *The Cave* and others. It was a five-bedroomed house in very good condition but it was the architecture that appealed to me most. The rooms were large, the windows tall with fretted vaulted ceilings. The only snag – no, two snags – the garden was small and the lack of central heating made it very cold in the winter. The tenant was offered one hundred pounds to give up his tenancy, which he gladly took and left. We did not have Chippendale furniture, Dresden china, luxurious Persian rugs or Turkish carpets but this was the house to which my wife devoted her time in making it cosy, charming and welcoming. The house is now a Grade II listed building with a blue plaque.

Just when I thought everything was in place for a good life with a happy and contented family, I was informed by the council that all the houses in Castlemaine Road would be compulsorily purchased so my property was lost. In its place is now Gloucester Grove Housing Estate. As if that wasn't enough, a few years later a compulsion order was served for Secretan Road, now Burgess Park. In the course of twelve years I lost two properties. I say lost, because all I received as compensation was the purchase price of each. These houses were not in sought-after streets. There were rows of shabby ones on these streets: badly in need of a coat of paint, with nothing in front except uncut grass or no grass and a narrow strip of pavement leading to the front door.

Things seemed topsy-turvy but at least I was left with a roof over my head when the tenants were thrown out. This time I was not able to help, but I comforted myself with this thought: 'The glories of our blood and state / Are shadows, not substantial things.'

I was particularly sorry for Mary, a Karen girl, (an ethnic minority girl from the Arakan Yuma Province of Burma), who had been brutally abused by the Japanese. She had married a British soldier whom she met in Burma and was taken to Newcastle, but was not accepted by her husband's family. She came to London, found a job and became one of my tenants. Her life changed when she fell in love with Big Tom, a Jamaican. She loved to talk and when I went to collect the rent she always engaged me in conversation and would tell me of how her Christian people had fought the Burmese Muslims and the Japanese. Mary became ill and lost a leg. Big Tom attended her like a nurse would, and when she died he buried her and took pictures of the funeral for her family. Tom also lost the will to live and returned to Jamaica as a recluse.

At this point, I should provide some explanation of the background to my increasing interest in political activity. As a boy, I just wanted to be included in the team for the cricket match and was not interested in holding a position in the club. John was captain and Vas had put himself forward as the captain but there was an objection. A band went up and someone argued that Sam should be the secretary, and I was selected unopposed. I was fourteen then, and the first time I made a public speech was in the presence of about two dozen boys and a few adults. It was no more than a few words of acknowledgement and thanks for making me the secretary of Castle Boys' Cricket Club. All this meant nothing if our team did not win the next match, so together we practised in the playground, on the beach, on the road and in the backyard, careful not to break the windows. On Empire Day 1940 we met in a twenty-over knockout and we won.

Chapter Fifteen

As I grew into manhood I began to think that there may be something more than my height of six foot, my upright carriage, my well-proportioned body and my sonorous voice as to why I was singled out to deal with difficult situations, be it in the camp or in civilian relationships. I remember when my father wanted to 'break' a horse he would get me to jump on the bare back and he would tell me to ride. You can picture what follows when a horse has never been ridden: firstly, his ears flatten and his shoulders twitch as if bitten by a horsefly, but that is just an introduction to the action to follow. He rears up, shunts backward, bolts forward, dances sideways and kicks. The worst part is when he bends his head forward. My horses were not even controlled by a proper bit and bridle, just a rope for the halter. While spectators looked on, my father would be giving directions. 'Come on, don't let him throw you, bwoy, sit down and ride.' After half an hour of this, the beast would get the message as to who was in control. He would submit, lower his ears and walk obediently to wherever he was guided. One learns not to fear; one keeps an eye on the lookout, rather like with a bull in the pasture. If a bull starts giving a low groan, snorting and digging with his front feet, you know that he is about to charge.

I also took note of how my father conducted himself in the eyes of people and at home. He was an example of patience, soberness, honesty and love of mankind and was blessed with nerves of steel although with all this, 'A brute I might have been, but would not sink the scale.' By God's grace. From those days I resolved never to run away nor to seek recognition but to do what I am asked within the confines of my limited educational ability.

I had been a member of the Labour Party but not an active one until I went to live in Herne Hill. My first assignment was to be in charge of the collection in Ruskin ward. During this time I met Robin MacDonald, a teacher from one of the comprehensive schools in the area. He was a polite and kindly man never too busy for a conversation. It was on one of these occasions he told me of his Scottish background. He used to joke that his ancestors must have welcomed Bonnie Prince Charles to the Isle of Skye when the Scots fled from the Duke of Cumberland after the battle of Culloden in 1746.

Robin's father did not follow in the sheep farming tradition but became a teacher, changing his residence to London where Rob was born. Rob always spoke of his father as an intellectual, being a professor of classics at Cambridge University and of he himself being sent to a public school. We had something in common in that he had done his national service in a Highland regiment in Fort William, Inverness, Scotland. He had risen to the rank of an officer but was annoyed that he had had to remain in Fort William while his regiment was sent to Aden in the Middle East.

When he was demobilised, he wanted to study sociology with a view to understanding anti-social behaviours and the problems facing the immigrant population. When he told the officer of his intention, the comment was that sociology was not the thing for the colonies; it was best to send missionaries then guns and administrators. Robin brushed him aside and entered Cambridge University, then, a further course at Liverpool University which was followed on by a book throwing light on the importance of one's early upbringing and the socio-economic environment. Robin thought he could serve the underprivileged better by being a full-time community worker, so he resigned from teaching and became the chairman of Cambridge House Community Centre in Camberwell. His particular concern was for youth.

I attended one of Rob's meetings and was very impressed with his ideas. As my children were born in England, were still young and were not encountering any problems at school, I was not aware of the less fortunate. Rob's argument was that children from rural, peasant backgrounds were expected on arrival to fit into an urban, complicated and modern school system when they were disoriented and lost. At the meeting he was trying to enlist the cooperation of all the voluntary organisations in the boroughs of Camberwell, Walworth and Southwark newly incorporated into what is now Southwark. He proposed that one way of helping the immigrant children in our schools was to encourage their parents and give suitable ones the chance to be governors: this would help to solve the feelings of isolation. Rob spoke with conviction. Here was a man prepared to ignore his privileged upbringing and genuinely put himself in the forefront of the battle against failure. This was applauded by the immigrants, but the professional politicians opposed it on the ground that school governors were political appointments. At the end of the meeting it was only the immigrants who forcefully supported Rob; the others were reticent and lackadaisical.

Rob and I continued to meet for discussion on various topics and when the opportunity arose for a school governor at William Penn comprehensive school, I was recommended, politically appointed and was pleased to acquiesce; although it was an added responsibility both to that of home and work, it was an area of need in which I felt obliged to serve.

Negativism only serves to depress and discourage and contributes nothing to one who needs all the physical and mental energies for climbing the rough side of the mountain. To call a halt is simply to wait for inevitable death and to look back and down is to indulge in melancholic reminiscences that hinder rather than propel, losing one's grip on the dizzy heights with results which would be folly to attempt to describe. At times one has to lie flat and wait for the calm, until the tempest, which whips up on the mountain and comes by with a sweep, passes over. It may seem strange, but sometimes when one is in the very eye of the storm, in the jaws of the fury, one is more composed than when approaching it.

In the 1950s and 60s the mountain got really crowded, hence losing one's way was a distinct possibility. Many stories and books have been told and written about this period, based on the unrealistic expectations of the West Indians in particular and on the widespread prejudicial attitudes and behaviour of the indigenous people, but I will not dwell on this aspect. I will give it a wide berth; I will not be a fish in troubled waters.

The early hostilities, arrogance and ignorance which found expressions in the riots which occurred in Robin Hood's land – Nottingham – in 1958, soon followed by ones greater in size, scope and ferocity in Moss Side, Handsworth, Chapeltown, Bristol and London were encouraged to some extent by sensational journalism. Some positive action was taken but the legislation which emanated was seen by immigrants as a clumsy measure to appease the hosts and to cool tempers. For us the laws were discriminatory, legitimising and institutionalising racism. Immigrants, however, had made their point, that the idea that they were to be seen and not heard should not apply to them. They could now turn their attention to defending themselves, with or without the assistance of the unions, at the workplace where they occupied the most menial, dangerous, dirty and ill-paid positions. Here it is much more difficult, but the second generation has found strength in examining the history of the interminable series of hazards encountered by travellers clinging to the crag with their eyes on the summit. The new generation has a living history and these are not tales told by idiots.

Two-fifths of the black people living in Britain today were born here and are fully-fledged members of British society. They may face continued racial discrimination in housing, education and employment, but among them are those who are gaining new heights in the level of educational qualifications and subsequently jobs. There is now a vibrant black businessmen and women's association, and black voices are heard on multifarious issues. This is not a call to complacency, bitterness or hatred; it is a rallying cry. I want to say to the present generation: you are not educationally subnormal, you have the intelligence and opportunity and a proud tradition. Therefore be determined, be positive, inculcate virtues not vice, love and not hate, and make your contributions.

Peter Fryer has retrieved and revealed the lost histories of some who have traversed the mountain during the last five hundred years. John Thorpe, the son of a Sierra Leone trader, studied physics and law at London University; so was John Wright, freed from Portuguese slavery, and Samuel Lewis who was called to the Bar. The first black man to be honoured by Queen Victoria was Edward Jordon; Peter Moncrieffe and Alexander Heslop, both Jamaicans, were educated at Oxford and both married

English women; the former became a judge and the latter a member of the Legislative Council and the colony's Attorney General.

Chapter Sixteen

I am a country man and yearned for the balmy air and the scenery, but more than that, I wanted the children to experience the beauty and to catch a glimpse of farming life. With this in mind, I acquired a car and once a year would take the family to the West Country. I remember one year we went to a mixed farm at Nurston near Buckfastleigh in Devon. The farmer used to transport the grain in bags to the silo and I gave him a hand, but it was harder than I thought and had to retire after a while. There was a stream there, and the youngsters loved to watch their reflections in the transparent water.

One day we drove to the vital naval base of Plymouth where we saw some of the destruction of the city brought about by the Germans. We also went to Plymouth Hoe, a park with a monument to Drake. They were fascinated with the story of how Drake was playing bowls when he was told of the sighting of the Spanish Armada but said he was finishing the game. His men were panicking but Drake knew that the tide would not turn for the next two hours which meant that the ships could not come in; in fact there was a gale, the Armada scattered and the English got between and defeated them.

My parents were eager to see the grandchildren but many years passed before I could afford to send my wife and children to Jamaica while I stayed behind for the three weeks. It was twenty-five years after the *Windrush* that I was to revisit Jamaica. Several hurricanes had swept the island

and numerous earthquake shocks had rocked the island during this time, but I was surprised to see a little prosperity here and there due mainly to the remittances from families in Britain, Canada and the USA. My parents were now on their own with one grandson, but my father was producing more than when we were all at home. The house had been upgraded with an extra bathroom upstairs; there was running water from newly laid pipes and electricity throughout. The girls had made sure mother had every necessity. They spent a fortune sending bed linen, curtains and just about everything for a modern house. One luxury she would never have was a refrigerator.

Time was short, but I did manage to get to Egg Hill which the government had leased from us. People were being paid to plant lumber trees, but with hardly any supervision they were also planting something which was more profitable in the short term. The Americans would send their light aircraft to pick up the stuff and what was left presented no problem for disposal.

My first appointment as a school governor was not without raising eyebrows at the Labour Party group meeting. When the idea was proposed and seconded, an overfed and oversized old man just managed to prize himself from his seat to oppose the notion. In his opinion, I was an inexperienced young man whereas he had been a governor of four schools. The old guard supported him and this was carried. A couple of years later, my son was now attending Dulwich Hamlet primary school and I was being more active in the Ruskin ward when out of the blue came a request for me to fill a vacancy for a school governor at William Penn, a school which holds many memories for me.

William Penn was originally the property of London Electricity Board sports ground, which was green and beautifully laid out with poplar trees on the periphery. One summer I played there with the Castle Cricket Club against the LEB Frank Bulcher and I put on one hundred and five runs – a record for the club – but soon after the Greater London Council purchased the land and the school was built. It had all the facilities and amenities required for a secondary school. The science laboratory and design technology areas were the envy of the other schools around.

It was true that I knew very little about the role and responsibilities of a governor. But I had no intention of being a charlatan, so I visited the library, spending many hours acquainting myself with the powers, procedures and duties of the governing body; there was no literature given. There were, however, relevant courses at County Hall and I attended them. In the governing body were also efficient and knowledgeable people: a professor, a medical doctor, a retired bank manager and a councillor among them. By listening and learning the art of dealing with complex issues relating to staff decision-making, budgets, the law, parents and community and health and safety, I was able to contribute to the debates, sit on the appointments' panel and to assist in the promotion of the interests and ethos of the school whose roll was over one thousand boys.

By observation and the records available, it was found that the school was falling short of expectation; the pupils were underachieving. Twenty per cent of the children were from ethnic minority backgrounds. The head was heavily involved with the union which meant frequent absences.

Approximately four years later, at the beginning of the school year, the governing body elected me as the chairman of governors. It was going to be tough with a full-time job but I accepted the position. The local administration office of the Post Office had to be notified and their approval sought as there would be times when I would have to attend school meetings in office time. It was sanctioned, but some of my colleagues made some very aggressive assertions, one being that people born in the colonies should not be governors in English schools and another that I was out of my depth to be any school governor let alone chairman.

At the next yearly general meeting of all chairman of governors at County Hall, I reported that the standard and quality of education at William Penn was unsatisfactory and below the average for the borough and that perhaps it should be reduced in size. The rocket went up, the statement was followed by an inspection of the school and it was confirmed. William Penn, now Dulwich High School, continues to be in the news, which is not good, apart from the steel band which was the idea of a teacher and to which the governors gave full support.

While I was at William Penn I was approached by the Bellenden Labour Party ward for another appointment as governor of Grove Vale Primary school, Goose Green. I accepted this as well and joined a governing board that was really committed, whose members were ardent and experienced workers. Two years on I was appointed chairman which necessitated my resigning from this position at William Penn, though I remained a governor.

The head teacher at Goose Green, Mrs Pat Cottell, was very professional. She won the hearts and cooperation of the parents. They were not kept at bay and could go in to see her at any time. She was enthusiastic and full of vigour and originality from which the school benefited. Each year, it was oversubscribed. Everything in the garden was rosy until one night in the November fog she was crossing at the roundabout in Blackheath, when she was knocked down and killed instantly.

I was to have another shock when at the interview for the headship at County Hall the acting head who had been doing a marvellous job did not get the post; instead, the selection panel was guided to appoint another woman with far less teaching experience.

In addition to these unpaid and voluntary activities, I was asked by the council whether I would serve as the community healthcare councillor at King's College Hospital and I agreed. Healthcare councillors met every fortnight with the administration to assess and plan within the budget. We could make suggestions and recommendations regarding patient care. I remember that there was a move to disband the large mental hospitals and rehouse patients in smaller units and I, rightly or wrongly, voted against it.

Mother's health had always been excellent so it was a blow when the news came that she had had a heart attack and would be needing daily medication for her to live for another five years. In 1980 there was also an outbreak of dengue fever in Jamaica, and my father was a victim. He was taken to Port Antonio Hospital, but there was a shortage of doctors and he had to be transferred to St Margaret's hospital in St Thomas. He was getting better and was about to be discharged when there was a hurricane which damaged the hospital. Father also had a heart attack and died on the 7th August, 1980.

I had already booked for my summer holiday to start on the 10th August for three weeks to see my mother. When Mae had telephoned to say she had bad news for me I had expected her to say my mother had died.

The airline was sympathetic and brought the date forward, and I flew out to bury my father. Priestman's River was looking good, with a big new bridge across the river, and I was delighted, but when I got to the gate and saw a pig in the potato field I was greatly annoyed. I remember having given a clear directive: put the pig back in the pen or shoot it. The former was duly done. Everyone was glad that there was someone to give some orders now that the man of the house was gone. My mother had aged. My first task was to have the grave dug in the family burial ground, and there my father was laid to rest after a church service at St Mark's where he had been a warden for thirty years.

Before I returned, my mother asked three things of me: that I would not take the burden of Egg Hill upon my shoulders; that I should endeavour to hold the family together; that I should think carefully before making decisions. Then she said that God had answered her prayers letting her live to see all her children holding their own in the world and she was ready to go now that her husband was not around. One morning after her breakfast of a fresh egg, bread and milk she had a wash, dressed herself and said that her mother had come for her. She went to bed and died peacefully ten years after her heart attack.

I resolved to keep the family together. One sister, who was trained as a nurse, married and went to Nigeria, was taken back after her husband died. She was the only one giving some concern.

For the local elections of 1982 I was selected as a Labour candidate for the Bellenden ward. I had to do some canvassing and from the reception I was getting on the door steps I was convinced that the voting was going my way, but I took nothing for granted. I received much help and encouragement from colleagues and well-wishers and when the voting was declared I won with an overwhelming majority. I dropped almost all my other commitments and concentrated on serving the Bellenden ward and the people of Southwark. As a newcomer to the council, I stuck to the party line and did whatever the leader prescribed.

Chapter Seventeen

I certainly would not have time for Egg Hill apart from recording and preserving its history. Errol Flynn may have acquired his property through stealth in a gambling deal with Patterson, but the men who purchased this enormous estate did so through sweat and blood in the banana fields and by catching and selling wild pigs.

The former proprietor was a Mr Orr, a slave owner who, after slavery was abolished, returned to Middlesex, England, leaving his overseer to administrate the property. This was not successful, and the property went on the market. Fourteen members of the King family, four generations back, saw the opportunity of owning land at last, combined their resources and purchased the two thousand, two hundred acres as shown on the deed, obtaining the signature of the Lord Mayor of London. When the white landowners, the Streets and the Joneses, learned of the precociousness of the fourteen ex-slaves, they were aghast and challenged the legality of the transaction, arguing that Mr Orr was sick and therefore could not make a valid decision, but the doctors in England confirmed that Mr Orr was of sound mind and that he had no intention of returning to Jamaica. Busha Genoa, the owner of Castle, was the main protagonist against black buyers, so the people in their anger tried to frighten him with Obeah – black magic, illegal in Jamaica and therefore secret – but he knew that this was hocus-pocus. One day, Busha Genoa went for his daily morning swim as was his routine, and when he did not return as expected his manservant became suspicious and went to the beach in search. He wasn't a little affrighted when he saw his master's body floating face down in the sea. The post-mortem showed death by drowning. It still remains a mystery as to how a good strong swimmer could have drowned in calm water apparently not far from the beach.

Descendants of the fourteen families have an annual meeting, which I remember vividly because my father was the chairman and from the age of twelve I had to write out the agenda and deliver copies to the heads of the families. This was only a formality as they would have attended anyway for the curried goat, rice and dumplings and coconut water laced with rum.

The men who had survived in the First World War, returned to Jamaica and were capable of working, were compensated with lands from the colonial government. There were crown lands bordering on to Egg Hill at the foot of the Blue Mountain, earmarked for distribution. The government surveyor, in his preliminary research, discovered that the new owners of Egg Hill were paying taxes only on twelve hundred acres and would now have to settle this claim retroactive to twenty years, otherwise one thousand acres would be expropriated. My father called an emergency meeting and outlined the dilemma. No way could be found to reimburse the government unless they were to borrow the money, something they were not predisposed to doing, and so Egg Hill Cooperative was beaten, regrettably losing one thousand acres. No bribes or threats would save the situation.

In the eighteenth century this would not have happened because among the inducements offered to people to settle anywhere in Portland were attractive and generous land grants, plus two barrels of beef and one of flour for each person so that he could feed himself until the crops he planted came to maturity, and freedom from taxes for several years. The Great Head area was utilised for planting bananas which were distinctively different from bananas elsewhere: heavier and verdant as opposed to the pea green of other types because of the high rainfall in the shadow of the Blue Mountain. With the instruction of my wise and beloved mother and the occasional report from relatives, this was where I left Egg Hill.

Chapter Eighteen

'The evil that men do lives after them' – how true. People never seem to forget the very trivial, nor are they prepared to alter a misconception. I remember when I visited Jamaica after twenty-five years, I went to see my ninety-eight year old aunt who asked about me every time she saw my father. At the sound of my voice she was out of her little house calling out, 'Auntie Mary's Sam.' Then she turned to my father and said, 'Auntie Mary's Sam was a bad boy, he gave me some crayfish and took them back.' The truth was that I indeed caught some crayfish and that on my way to Buckley Valley on the day in question I left her some in a calabash. Someone took them without asking or telling her; somehow she believed that I was the culprit and I could not erase that from her mind. She died at the age of one hundred and one still convinced that I took back the crayfish.

How one small incident can have consequences that are incalculable, profoundly affecting one's life forever! Knowing this, I pledged from the outset of my campaign to be elected as a councillor on the 6th May, 1982, that whatever was said or done must be reasoned and unequivocal. Firmly entrenched in my executive job at the Post Office, a health councillor, a school governor and a member of the borough deanery which coordinates the work of twenty-two churches, I was waxing in confidence. Through all these experiences and more, at the age of fifty-six, I had developed a remarkable reputation as a no-

nonsense person, a tough guy, so when the opposition sought to demolish and rubbish me, to blackmail me by innuendo and sophistry, I was unmoved and unaffected. I reflected on how, when the ship's authorities were checking and rechecking each paper thoroughly, allowing for no stowaways on the *Windrush*, a waterfront labourer sitting casually on the wall laughed and remarked, 'Man, all combinations can be broken, given time.'

My politics were grass-roots socialism answerable to all local people, not just to those who voted for me. The policies I set out were clear. I was going to influence the council and take firm action in improving the unemployment situation from which so many evils arise; housing, social amenities, leisure, healthcare and community policing were all going to be addressed. I also saw how the churches could contribute in these areas by allowing their halls to be used for activities and by sharing their buildings with others who had no place in which to worship.

Doug Moore, the councillor retiring after twenty years, gave his wholehearted support to the three candidates Ann Ward, Judy Cliffe and myself in the Bellenden ward. I had the ability to know where the cat would jump so I kept my insight to myself until I was sure I had the upper hand. A race unit was established in the council and most people assumed that I would not need any persuasion to accept the chair of that unit, but it was the opposite; I did not accept the position. I did, however, accede to being the whip of the committee.

With so much involvement in housing, both practically and academically, I made housing my area of interest. The housing stock was split into four districts and I was selected as chair of Dulwich housing with over five hundred housing stooks. I put all my knowledge and energies into visiting the areas and getting the dwellings repaired so that when the officers reported I knew where and what they were talking about. On rent, I went by the book and the collectors knew that I wanted results not words. The message that went around was that 'If you don't pay your rent, Sam King will throw you out'. It worked.

My interest in the church or anything to do with church was something I took great pleasure in doing since childhood when I used to ring the bell on a Sunday. My attendance had lapsed during the war and stayed that way to the time I got married. This was due mainly to long hours of work – twelve hours a day and one Sunday in three. I was also playing cricket for Castle Cricket Club on Saturdays. My wife was now a district nurse, with two children and the other houses to oversee we had a home help and I resigned from the Club in order to spend more time at home.

Within weeks of moving to Warmington Road, a lady across the road asked whether she could take our children Michael and Althea, then aged four and one to the local Baptist church. We agreed, and the whole family would go when we were not working. In the course of time my wife joined the women's meeting and I the men's fellowship until someone in a prominent position made a remark which I regarded as an aspersion and I was hurt. My wife also had a similar experience in the women's meeting and we decided to discontinue our attendance. However, when I became the mayor I accepted an invitation to a special event there, but insisted on full protocol, that is, that the mayor would arrive five minutes before the start of the function and that the congregation would stand. By this time there was a new minister with whom I had good rapport because he was an RAF pilot trained in Canada.

From the early 50s, immigrants were finding their presence in the established churches unwelcome; they were forming Christian house groups and this practice was spreading. Some met in church halls until, with much sacrifice and perseverance, they were able to purchase their own buildings.

One Sunday evening in 1976, I was coming from work when I came face to face with some people, Bibles in hand, in the Herne Hill and Ruskin ward area. Upon enquiry, I discovered that they were meeting in the church hall and the next Sunday I went along to the gathering of nearly a hundred people. I was happy with their style of worship: 'Amen' and 'Praise the Lord' were unbounded. At the end of the service there wasn't a rush for the door; people socialised and the pastor came off the platform and welcomed me heartily. Numbers were growing rapidly and space was limited. The proposition to buy a church building was put to the congregation and was met with delighted approval.

Months passed but no suitable place could be found in the area. The Pastor called the congregation together and suggested that we all pray just as the children of Israel did. Within a month, an empty building was spotted and upon investigation was found to be the property of the Roman Catholic Church, who were approached. Yes, it was on the market, but when the asking price was mentioned we nearly called a halt to the negotiation. Further surprise was to follow when a delegation went to make the final agreement. They were told that a furniture business had made an offer and that if we wanted it we would have to pay an extra three thousand pounds. We bargained as hard as we could, even appealing to their spiritual sensitivity that God's building should be for worship and not for trade, but they would not give ground. The situation and the size, however, were ideal for a growing church so we agreed to take it. Most members were only low wage earners, so to raise the deposit there were covenants and some of us lent what we could interest free. Nearly half the cost was paid and a twenty-year mortgage was secured for the remainder. The church moved into 7 Allardyce Street as the Church of the First Born and we paid off the mortgage and the loans within ten years. God is good.

Preaching was never my calling, but there were occasions when I had to respond to invitations to speak from pulpits other than that of the Church of the First Born. One of these was a church near Streatham Common headed by an African, Rev. Aji Bodie, to which I gave regular assistance as its secretary and as a preacher, but with added responsibilities and my wife's illness I had to relinquish this. I was the borough dean and was occupied with 'Faith in the City', documented by the Church of England, an extensive part of which identified the need to increase dialogue with minority groups and initiated a campaign for change by bringing together the institutions of the Church and the council in order to make them more responsive to the needs and aspirations of people.

The International Ministerial Council of Great Britain, a charity organisation involved in Christian participation and community development, was another avenue of service for me. IMCGB was founded in 1968 and has as its aim the unification of people of differing beliefs, races and backgrounds to work and share in practical ways to fulfil each other's needs. By this, we are aware of each other's existence and promote mutual understanding. As a voice for black Christians, IMCGB recognises the independence of each Organisation. It does not interfere in doctrinal affairs and itself has no political affiliation or attachment. Its aim is to break down barriers, to draw the attention of local and statutory bodies to community needs and to work for a better, more multiracial and multi-cultural society. As an honorary member, sworn in together with Paul Boateng and Sybil Phoenix MBE, I represented IMCGB at the British Council of Churches, of which it is an associate member. I strongly believe in rendering unto Caesar that which is Caesar's and unto God that which is God's.

Chapter Nineteen

I hadn't completed a year as councillor when a veteran Labour councillor informed me late one evening of the Labour group's intention to make me the next mayor. My first reaction was that there were bright people around – why me? I remember the haste in which I left for home to break the news to my wife. As I burst through the door without greeting her, I said, 'Mae, would you believe they are going to make me the mayor?' Her response was, 'Sam, you can be anything but you lack ambition.'

In mid-April 1983 at the Labour group meeting to select officials and chairmen for the ensuing year, the proposition was put for Sam to the mayor of Southwark. There were forty-six members present in the council room entitled to vote and three names went forward. I was most surprised when I won on the first ballot with over seventy-five per cent of the votes cast without ever contacting or asking anyone to support me. Somehow recollections of my life came flooding in, my first speech, calming the situation on the *Windrush*, taking parades, setting up saving schemes, buying houses – ha! These were training grounds for a position I never had the audacity to envisage let alone to hold. I, the first black mayor of the London Borough of Southwark would now have the responsibility for the running of the council and would be always in the public eye. I managed to summon some courage, rose to my feet and accepted the mayorship.

This was going to be a daunting experience because I had to face the role without the support of my dear wife of thirty years. She had passed away that January and I was still profoundly bereaved and sad, but she would have liked me to go ahead. She had lived for people as a State Registered Nurse, was always interested and concerned about the welfare of others, a wonderful mother, and was a source of strength to colleagues and to me.

When I was elected as a councillor, I did not possess much business ability or professional skill but was anxious to serve and help the community in which I chose to make my home. I recognised that the local authority controlled vast resources, ranging from manpower to land and material, all of which could be utilised to improve the quality of life for everyone, but how the local machinery worked was puzzling and complicated to grasp at once. This called for much fact finding and getting hold of relevant advice and sources of information. There were books and journals in the library but the most reliable were the councillor's handbook and the seminars and courses to inform one of one's roles, responsibilities and rights. A week's course was given at the finance office department, half a day when the council was decentralising the housing stocks, and a few evenings in different departments to learn about preparing for disaster. Discretion is the better part of valour and nowhere else is it more true than in a place where every word is weighed, where body language is hastily interpreted and where banana skins are strewn everywhere.

I tried to be as prudent as I could, especially in dealing with situations and issues with which I was unfamiliar. Here, policy statements and background papers were invaluable although it was almost impossible to assimilate all the masses of information involved. Having a full-time job meant that I was always pressed for time to read the agendas and supporting reports, correspondence and additional materials, so I had to refrain from too much committee work. The practicalities were learnt on visits to establishments such as housing, hospitals, schools, children's and old people's homes and clubs as well as at my once-a-week surgery held in my Bellenden ward, where the complaints and problems ranged from noisy neighbours to dogs fouling the pavements and gardens to housing.

I remember one woman reported a roofing problem but refused to allow anyone to inspect the building. I went, and after explaining that no work could be authorised without an inspection, she let me in. On making my report to the council, I was told that the family was fascist. There was another one-parent family who wanted to be rehoused and didn't want a flat but a house with a garden.

It was advisable to observe the procedures and practice, to examine the astute and adept senior councillors at work and to make an in-depth study of the items in which one was interested or had some knowledge before asking questions or making a speech. By the time I was made a mayor, I had acquired the knowledge relating to the roles of the councillor representing a ward, in committees, and the structure and working of the council on the whole. I knew that the mayor took precedence in the borough as long as it did not prejudicially affect Her Majesty's royal prerogative. The standing orders for the regulation of the proceedings and business of the council were studied and mastered as I was fully aware of the ploy of the fascists.

As soon as it was announced that Sam King was the new mayor, the media got hold of the news and it was beamed across the land. I was almost embarrassed to see the headlines the following day: THE KING OF SOUTHWARK; SAM TAKES TO HIS THRONE; KING OF THE TOWN HALL were some of the ways the media presented me, but it gave me a high profile in the community at a vital time when the fire had gone out of my belly and nothing seemed important. The opposition Conservative and Liberal councillors were particularly accommodating and supportive. Some had even attended the funeral of my wife.

There were others who were devoid of compassion and proceeded to add insult to injury. The neo-fascists with their decadent minds, slanderous towards non-whites and downright stupid to say the least, began a series of racist threats against me. Telephone calls to my home, made in all seriousness, promised to burn down my house and slit my throat if I dared to hold the position of mayor. The Saturday evening before the official robing ceremony at the Town Hall, I received a threatening telephone call so I phoned the police station, asked to speak to the officer in charge and told him the threats made to my home and life. He did not seem interested and I put the phone down. About fifteen minutes later, another call came saying the same thing. I could hear traffic in the background so I knew the call was coming from a public telephone. Again I reported it to the police. This time an officer arrived and I calmly told him what had been happening. While I was speaking, another call came. I asked the policeman to answer and he heard for himself. As a result, there was a police officer at my home day and night for weeks and I was given a police escort. My main concern was for my young niece, just out of university, who willingly stepped in as the mayoress.

It is not very often that a politician is met with favour from both the public and the critics, and although I was judged with both deliberate and instinctive precision, there was nothing adverse to report about me. The press really was kind. There were compliments for everything I did, and the people of the borough fell behind me to show solidarity when many of them otherwise did not have much interest in local government. I went about my duty as best I could without fear, and had the support of the churches and the staff, especially the chief executive with his legal advice who made sure I did not put a foot wrong.

Everything was done to shield and shelter me from the racist pigs but I was not going to allow myself to be cocooned. It brought back to mind the story of the great musician and composer Samuel Coleridge-Taylor, born in 1875. The 160-strong Samuel Coleridge-Taylor Society of Washington DC had invited him to the States to conduct a festival of his works but conveyed to him their fears of the racist insults to which he would be exposed. His reply to them was, 'As for the prejudice, I am well prepared for it. Surely that which you and many others have lived on for many years will not quite kill me. I am a great believer in my race, and I never lose an opportunity of letting my white friends here know it. Please don't make any arrangements to wrap me in cotton wool.'

In the by-election for a member of Parliament to represent Bermondsey, I was the one to announce the winner, Simon Hughes, the Liberal candidate, with the television and photographers trained on me. The nation saw a black man doing a job with military precision amidst fascist chants. The behaviour of one woman was disgraceful to the public office of the mayor, but I ignored it. The police didn't. She was arrested, charged with disturbing the peace and was found guilty and given a probation order. There were others, too, who made derisory and outrageous comments which were offensive to the aspiring spirit of a man who was only performing his duties, but nothing was going to deter me. The publicity I was attracting served to enhance my reputation. I was receiving letters of support from even Germany. I attended a function at St George's Catholic church and a South African student showed me a picture of me published in Soweto. 'Sweet are the uses of adversity, / Which like the toad, ugly and venomous, / Wears yet a precious jewel in his head; / And this our life, exempt from public haunt, / Finds tongues in trees, books in the running brooks, / Sermons in stones, and good in everything.'

Putting the year of my being mayor, 1983–4, into perspective, I would say that politically it was one of ups and downs, both at home and abroad. President Reagan had failed in his intervention in Lebanon to stop the fighting resulting from Israel's full-scale invasion of that land. Things were settling down to normality after the successful war to retake the Falkland Islands, but there was a crisis in Grenada when the government was overthrown by the pro-Communist military coup resulting in the killing of the Prime Minister Maurice Bishop and five of his supporters. It was the year when in the general election Mrs Thatcher won a landslide victory over Labour with a majority of one hundred and forty-four. The abolition of the Greater London Council and the metropolitan counties, the introduction of rate-capping and the privatisation of British Telecom all featured in the Conservative Manifesto. Admittedly, at the time inflation was low, output was high and productivity was at record levels.

My term in office was varied and gruelling, but the pressure was eased by the Post Office releasing me whenever I requested it and by the deputy mayor taking his share of a very full diary. There were school and youth functions: sports day, tournaments, swimming galas, contests, prize-givings, school leavers' ceremonies, pantomimes, formal and informal visits to social events at hospitals, churches, residential homes, fairs, fêtes, bazaars, garden parties, Christmas parties, dog shows, charity balls, walks and disabled sports and achievement awards. I was invited to the annual function of the Southwark Women's Cooperative Guild at the civic centre on the Old Kent Road and was totally surprised when at the close I was presented with fifty blankets knitted by the women for the mayor's good cause. It was very touching. They were given to the chairman of Age Concern who was present. Perhaps I should have kept one as a souvenir. The Civic Service at Southwark Cathedral was well attended that year and there was a choir of one hundred who volunteered to sing in support of the occasion which was seen as a bridge-building effort.

As would be expected, many of these invitations were to luncheons and dinners, which I favoured since I was without a wife. I was the guest of the chairman of the GLC for a Tchaikovsky evening and buffet supper and the glaziers' installation dinner. Some I attended with delight, like the luncheon with the estate governors at Alleyns because my son was a pupil there. It was followed by a presentation of *Ishkamish* by the Dulwich School of Dance and Drama. Then there was lunch with officers of the Metropolitan Police at Scotland Yard. As I sat there receiving the best of attention and courtesy, I remembered how, when I was about to leave the RAF in Kinloss, I had applied to join the police force. I had taken the academic and medical tests and had passed, but when I had gone before the selection board I had been rejected. Now that I was the mayor, the Commissioner of Police expressed his concern for the lack of applicants from minority groups and asked why. The highlight of these invitations was not the Royal National Anniversary Banquet but the Mansion House Lord Mayor's dinner, preceded by considerate pageantry. I was seated next to the Duke of Norfolk, a retired general of the British armed forces, a kingmaker and owner of Arundel Castle, where the touring cricket team of the West Indies always starts with a warm-up match. My assessment was that the Duke was more proud of the runner beans he developed in his kitchen garden in Norfolk than in the cut and thrust in the House of Lords.

Chapter Twenty

When God planted the Garden of Eden, he placed man in it to care for it and not to destroy it. One of my interests, as a peasant with a rural background, is the preservation and upkeep of the physical environment, and as a mayor, invitations to anything ecological were always welcomed. I was there with the councillor and the people in the Kings Grove area in their fight to deter the council from building houses in a vacant lot. The need was to allow a pleasant space where senior citizens and mothers with young children could leave their flats and safely go. This was just a small matter but for the people who lived there it relieved a lot of tension. Today they have a beautiful garden with shrubs and flowers and seats on which to sit and admire the beauty. When we talk of improving the quality of life, this is one way.

A similar situation arose when property developers with their intolerable arrogance wanted to purchase Dulwich Woods from the council in order to build luxury flats and houses. Their application was received with repugnance. When I visited the woods and saw the majestic oak trees, the abundance of flowers, especially rhododendrons, in full bloom, and the birds, I believed one would have to be non *compos mentis* to allow this irreplaceable treasure to be destroyed. A group of Dulwich residents was just as adamant, the developers were seen off and one bright morning we all gathered at Dulwich Woods to renew our pledge never to allow its destruction and to rededicate it as a haven for wildlife and a place of beauty as it has always been since Celtic times. When the people came out against the construction of a road through Roxley Corner, I supported their protest and understood their passion.

On the 15th March 1984, the Lord Mayor and the mayors of London, led by HRH Princess Michael of Kent, took part in an oak tree planting ceremony at Kew Gardens at the launch of 'Beautiful Britain'. This was a memorable occasion, and I was presented with the spade I had used. This was followed by a lunch with the Princess given by the management of Kew. By the 3rd April, I was to be in the presence of royalty once again, welcoming Princess Margaret to the Research Centre for the opening of the Parkinson's disease unit at Windsor Walk, Denmark Hill.

In 1977, the year of the Queen's Silver Jubilee, the borough reserved a special enclosure in Rotherhithe for various of its workers and employees on the day the Queen would be there. My wife and I were included, and we had the opportunity of the Queen speaking to us in the manner, shown to me in a dream a few nights before, that even if the Queen passed, she would return to speak to me. I was to be in her company again on the 9th May, 1984 at the completion and opening of that great engineering marvel the Thames Barrier, built by the GLC to counter the danger of flooding in low-lying areas of London. The following day saw Princess Anne at the Royal Albert Hall presenting degrees to the successful university graduates. I was included with others in the reception which followed. It had always been my wish to meet the Duke of Edinburgh for two reasons: he was a military man and he would say what he thought but for protocol. The opportunity arose when it fell to me to welcome him when he disembarked from his launch at Cherry Garden Pier, Rotherhithe. He wanted to see the developments that were taking place in the Docklands but at the time there was a dispute between the Docklands Authority and the council. Having done that, I left for another appointment.

Southwark borders the River Thames from Southwark Bridge to Rotherhithe Tunnel, and in the good old days of shipping, up to fifteen ships could be in the Pool of London around Butler's and Canary Wharves unloading and loading their cargoes from around the world. The borough therefore had a traditional relationship with the captains and officers of these vessels, usually in the form of invitations to the ships, and of course there would be reciprocity from the council. The mayor is the one who normally invites the officers to the parlour.

HMS *Belfast*, which took part in the battle of the River Plate in December 1940, is now permanently moored on the lower side of Tower Bridge. When I was invited to the inspection and a cocktail party, I noticed that there was a long walk along wooden planks to the ship. The mayoress had some difficulty controlling her dress as there was a high wind. While we were on board, a Dutch cruiser, HNLMS *Wolf* came alongside the *Belfast* and we were asked in, so I had to jump from the *Belfast* to the *Wolf*. The *Wolf*'s captain was invited to the parlour in return and he came bringing me a plaque which now hangs in the mayor's parlour.

The HMS *Shetland* was not a small ship; it was a destroyer capable of carrying missiles on board. The captain and officers escorted us around, pointing out the modern features which I found mind-boggling. NATO warships on exercises sometimes make a courtesy call, as was the case with the *Stanvfocha* a magnificent ship on which I was also invited for a cocktail. I was pleasurably surprised at the reception we had on the French ship the *Panthère*. The drinks and hors d'oeuvre were excellent. This prevented me from telling the captain of the horrible food and unsanitary conditions on the SS *Cuba*, the French troop ship. I was getting to know my way around and through the *Belfast* with all these invitations. The next and perhaps the last two were the cocktail party on the HMS *Osiris* and the reception on board the HMS *Exeter*. In return, my mayoress and I played hosts in the parlour to the commanding and liaison officers from most of these ships. This was done without pomposity and formality but at the same time was a polished performance.

The parlour was kept busy with calls for many reasons. Quite a number of interviews, chiefly with the newspapers, were done in the parlour as I was there more than at home. Martin Buckmaster joined me for an interview by the BBC about community Christian Radio which I had fought hard and long to establish. It was the first time I met Martin Buckmaster, but I had already heard of him as one of those who was effective in stopping Nazi Germany winning the war. He would have been good at that because his bushy eyebrows could hide the movements of his eyes and the expression on his face.

Donations to the mayor's charity from the police were also usually presented in the parlour. I can recall receiving a cheque from the Knights of St Columba there. They felt at home, even asking for a drink before I could offer one. Schoolchildren from the borough as well as from abroad came to the parlour to see and learn about the history surrounding the regalia: the robe, the mace and the chain. A few meetings of individuals and a small group were scheduled for the parlour. It was in the parlour I met Roger Scott of the BBC for a meeting regarding the Gospel broadcast and the problem of obtaining a licence. Before the annual service of the unfurling of the United Nations, a meeting of all the representatives taking part takes place in the parlour.

Other meetings in the town hall over which I presided were held in Room D as the Committee of the Common Good Trust. The Trust is the charity arm of the borough's community relations policies to which the Labour group subscribe and which I as a councillor made great effort to support. There were some positive achievements and successes but as in other political affairs there were some frustrations.

In the area of education, the failure and underachievement of children, especially black pupils, had been in the forefront The underlying causes had to be found and addressed: unemployment, poor housing and racism in schools were evident and initiatives and measures were put in place to tackle these problems, including liaison with black teachers and an effort to ensure the participation of parents in all aspects of the child's education. Grants, under Section 11, were made available to schools with a high proportion of pupils with language difficulties and other problems. Facilities were provided for Saturday schools attended by a diverse group; there was a summer school for the less academic where organised games and sports, art, pottery, visits to museums, galleries and the seaside and other excursions were encouraged and supported. The youth clubs around were resourced and the Youth Training Schemes offering skills for jobs received much emphasis and focus of attention.

All managing agents should operate with equal opportunity in mind; therefore it was proposed that staffing should include ethnic minority representatives on the Manpower Board. Housing officers should report harassments and there was a joint venture with the local authority social services and the police in support of parents whose juveniles fell foul of the law. In the year 1983–84, over thirteen hundred referrals were made to the Juvenile

Bureau. Community projects involving centres for the elderly members of ethnic minority groups, Asian women's training, day nurseries and refugee communities were funded. I was committed to all these objectives and I not only attended the meetings but was instrumental in maintaining stringent monitoring. It was therefore expedient for me when I became the mayor to have community spirit as the theme for the borough: to continue to foster and promote educational opportunities without distinction of age, sex, race or religion and to provide facilities for recreation and leisure with the object of improving social welfare and conditions for all residents of the borough.

I could not be nonchalant; my ears and eyes were put in top gear which was never changed down. One Saturday evening the mayoress and I were at the Elephant and Castle Recreation Centre for the International Basketball Competition and to present the prizes. The manager of the centre was chosen from a shortlist of five, six months before, when I was on the interviewing panel. One of the candidates, I remember, boasted of his relationship with his large staff of thirty black cleaners but when he was asked if he had ever thought of promoting one to being a doorman, he was confounded. The Peckham Rye Gala organisers had made a request to have a pig roasted on the common. Much to their surprise, I refused to give permission as there were some who would object on moral and religious grounds. Later in the evening of the Gala, a police officer asked that I get the revellers to reduce the noise. I took the microphone and said, 'Now hear this, I would like the sound system turned down now.' I left. A few days later I saw the officer, who said, 'Thank you, Mr Mayor, they didn't disobey you.' There must be equal opportunity as well as the equal regard without which the concept of equality is a myth. To have a purpose and to make it known, one has, at times, to be a Daniel.

The central government under Mrs Thatcher had introduced a system of rate-capping which their manifesto stated would curb the extravagance of the high-spending councils in the interest of the ratepayers. When this was mentioned in the February council meeting, it was met with disapprobation, an indication that there was trouble ahead. There was some understanding in the ruling Labour group that at the April meeting the rate for the ensuing year, 1984–85, should be set so that the annual estimates could be approved; if not, councillors would be surcharged. Some streetwise councillors planned to defy the government and vote against setting the rate, whatever the cost, although the chief executive at each point advised what the council could legally do. One councillor was heard to say he had nothing to lose because he only owned a record player and a radiogram. I personally was going to go by the book and not risk the roof over my head for which I had toiled night and day.

As mayor, I presided over the meeting of the council scheduled for 7 p.m. on April 25th. There was a deliberate attempt to scuttle the debate by moving numerous amendments which had to be seconded and debated before putting to the vote. Although the councillors realised that at the end of the day the rate would have to be set or they would be charged for dereliction of duty, the meeting was prolonged until 2 a.m. Some councillors were half-asleep and just put up their hands to vote willy-nilly as their running mates summoned them. At last the whip motioned that the meeting be adjourned for another week when the rate would be set in a special meeting. This was carried. This would take us right up to the wire, but after seven hours in the chair I was relieved... well, not just yet. I made a dash for the gents just left of the council door but in my haste almost entered the ladies. The alertness of the mace-bearer tugged at my jacket and directed me next door. I just made it without further embarrassment.

At the next meeting, the older and wiser heads like Ann Lowe, Jesse Fairweather, Mike Stevens, Barry Brown and others like Jim Greening stood up for common sense and within an hour the rate was set, resulting in some falling-out among councillors over tactics. While the people of Southwark may have had their own idea when it came to the next local election, the councillors escaped being charged and barred from office for five years as were those in Lambeth. The council received less grant from the central government and at the same time could only increase council rents in line with inflation; therefore some services had to be trimmed in line with the budget. We got through the year with complaints from employees, council tenants, schools, cleaning departments and libraries, as there had to be a large-scale reassessment of services in the borough.

Chapter Twenty-One

I was the deputy mayor the following year and by the law of averages should not have had to preside over a similar rate-setting meeting in 1985. On the day in question, while at work I received a telephone call from the chief executive at around 3 p.m. The mayor of Southwark would not be available to preside at the last meeting on 30th May to set the rate; his car had broken down on his way from Brighton. I gave my assurance with the request that the car be sent early so as to give me time to study the agenda. He was pleased that I would be there early as a group of political activists were planning to block the entrance so that certain councillors could not enter and the mayor and the deputy mayor were on the 'stop' list. However, he said an unusual arrangement had been made for me at the council meeting, so I should be prepared. That had me guessing but it takes more than words for a war man to lose his nerve.

The mayor's car arrived with the mace-bearer. A postman asked for a lift in the official car and for a peaceful life I obliged. Years after, I saw him with his family and, pointing at me, he said to his grandson, 'That's Mr Mayor – I had a ride in his chauffeur-driven car with a guard.'

I was first taken home for a bath and a change of apparel. Then the mace-bearer produced an overall and asked me to put it over my suit. Nearing the town hall, he diverted to Southampton Way, pulled up at the back, and I walked like a building workman to the back door, which was manned.

He quickly opened the door and I was smuggled inside to the mayor's parlour where I was able to get myself in the frame of mind and body ready for the council meeting at 7 p.m.

At 6.55 p.m., I was immediately behind the mace-bearer to hear him announce as we entered the chamber, 'Be upstanding for the deputy mayor, the chief executive and the officers of the council.' When the news reached the agitators at the entrance and they realised that their guns had been spiked and the council was in session setting the yearly rate, they were livid. Their wooden banners were being used as a weapon on the doormen but the police almost outnumbered them and were in control. The press and television cameramen who were out there waiting for trouble and excitement were equally disappointed. I was called all the black names in the book and racially abused by the National Union of Public Employees shop steward – Mary Dean – for backing the decision to set a rate. It was the tenth acrimonious, bad-tempered and hostile meeting, totalling thirty-four hours, before the council agreed a legal rate by twenty-six votes to twenty-three with eleven abstentions a day before the district auditor threatened to make the councillors personally pay over two hundred and fifty thousand pounds that Southwark had lost in interest by not setting the rate. Neither the local nor national papers could, this time, say that the loony left had won the day in Southwark council. While some councillors were sent 'In Loving Memory' cards with a white feather attached, I was hailed as a conquering hero who had stepped in when the mayor was wounded in battle or may be gassed.

I was not opposed to a demonstration by the residents of Southwark, because they were under severe social and economic pressures on the rebound from the massive cutbacks which had to be imposed. It was the lack of civility and respect, the unrestrained and confrontational behaviour to which I entirely objected.

I personally felt the consequence of the economic stringency when, thank God, I did not end up with a heart attack or an ulcer but a hernia, albeit a painful one. My hospitalisation to have it treated was arranged by my specialist in June of 1984. On arrival on the appointed date and time, I was politely sent back home, whereupon I wrote to King's Hospital requesting the reason for the cancellation of my minor operation. The reply was that because of cuts in government expenditure and the unavailability of beds, I was one of one hundred and thirty-four patients turned away from surgery so far. Three weeks later, however, I was admitted, but I could have been the victim of a strangulated hernia. I wasn't, and after two restful weeks of convalescence I was back in the saddle again, raring to go.

Indeed, as the mayor, I, with the mayor of Lewisham, paid a visit to Number 10 Downing Street to demand the return of two hundred and fifty-nine million pounds which the government had withdrawn from the three boroughs of Greenwich, Lewisham and Southwark. We also called on Mrs Thatcher to rescind the Rate Capping Bill then going through Parliament.

Chapter Twenty-Two

I am no meacock. My constitutional strength goes back, I believe, to my indomitable warrior ancestors, originally from the Ashanti tribes of Ghana, the Maroons who for over two hundred years gave the English a good run for their money. Even with the importation of the 'Miskito' Indians from Central America to fight on behalf of the English, the Maroons were not defeated and to settle the score they were given the Rio Grande Valley in Portland, although their counterpart, in the Trelawny Rebellion surrendered when dogs imported from Cuba were set on them. There are tricks in trade and when it was thought that there could be further resistance, they were put aboard a ship and transported to Nova Scotia to die of cold, but some survived.

'The fault is not in our stars... / But in ourselves, that we are underlings,' Shakespeare reminds us. I am indebted to those of us who have left lasting memories of the gallant spirits which triumphed over the evils of ignorant men. These memories must be preserved. When the Empire in the First World War was losing men in France as if a reaper was cutting down the poppies in the field, the cry of the Minister of War, Lord Kitchener, was heard in the colonies. Men in Jamaica were taken out in banana longboats singing, 'Some of us will not come back – we know that fully well.' They fought bravely in Amiens and in Turkey where casualties were very high both in the trenches and in the cold.

The war cemetery of Seaford, Sussex tells the story of how a group of West Indian ex-servicemen and women took part in the war memorial parade there in 1986. In the Alfriston Road cemetery are to be found nineteen gravestones bearing the badge of British West Indian Regiment men who died in the First World War. My appreciation goes to the wonderful lady who attends these graves. When the dogs of war were silenced in 1918, those who survived physically, maimed and mentally scarred, returned to Jamaica and died there. Whenever I visit Jamaica I take a look at the memorials in the parish capitals I visit. There is a wreath-laying ceremony on Remembrance Day at the War Memorial in the renamed National Heroes Park, officially opened by the Queen as George VI Memorial Park in 1953. I was privileged to lay a wreath in 1992 on behalf of the West Indian ex-servicemen and women in the United Kingdom.

Veterans of the Second World War, with the help of the British forces and the Jamaican government, instituted the Jamaican ex-servicemen's Association but it wasn't until the 1970s that the West Indian veterans in Britain began thinking of a comparable Association. We were all members of the British Legion but belonged to different sections and as such were not seen as a group marching at the Cenotaph in Westminster on Remembrance Day in November.

The first planning meeting of seven men was held at an address in Atlantic Road, Brixton. Subsequent meetings followed, and membership was opened to anyone serving in or retired from the services. In 1982 it was established as a legally constituted charity with our own headquarters at Manor Street, Clapham and branches in Birmingham, Derby, Manchester and Nottingham. We are given our own section at the Remembrance March and we hold our own Remembrance service. A service of dedication for the

National Standard of WIESA was held at Westminster Cathedral on 17th May, 1986. The celebrant was the Officiating priest of the Roman Catholic chaplain to the RAF. As one of the Trustees I must pay tribute to Hector Watson, one of the founding fathers of this Association, and his wife who are sadly no longer with us; with a small staff they supervised the social and cultural activities including a senior citizens' lunch club.

I'm going nowhere involuntarily. I need no abeng talking drums to communicate. I may not possess the qualities of the military tactician and chieftain Nanny of the Maroons, but I have a rough idea of the terrain; I am not coming down. I'm climbing up the mountain with God at my side.

Being a councillor and the first black mayor in the London Borough of Southwark were achievements beyond my wildest dreams, but there was one other idea I wanted to see in reality and that was a gospel radio station, the object of which was not only the singing of gospel songs but the dissemination of religious information, education and counselling in accordance with the teaching of the Christian faith. There was an inaugural meeting in the mayor's parlour, and when the idea was aired there were offers of technical support and financial pledges. Subsequent meetings took place to discuss finance, staffing, premises, and more importantly, the application of a licence for the broadcast. I was convinced that there was a demand for a local station of this nature to meet the spiritual needs and provide an outlet for the talents of the exuberant young people. So serious and intent was I that I paid a visit to the Christian Production of Toronto, Canada, and the USA where such stations are well established.

In the course of time we realised that the obstacle was going to be the reluctance of 'Pharaoh' the Home Secretary to grant a licence. And it came to pass that it was so. Our hopes were dashed when the Government announced that plans for community radio would be shelved. I am delighted that the government has now relented and Premier Radio with similar objectives is now broadcasting daily to a wider audience than what we had anticipated.

The Crossroads Christian Communications Incorporation of Canada was also exploring the possibility of instituting religious cable television for which I was recruited as the agony uncle and counsellor, but that, too, did not materialise. I did, however, present *Night Thoughts* on Thames Television, a programme of religious thoughts screened before closedown. My greatest satisfaction was when the BBC's *Songs of Praise*, produced by Chris Mann, was conducted at Southwark Cathedral on a Sunday in February 1984. My cup ran over with joy as the uninhibited black choirs exploded with pulsating vitality in the presence of an overflowing cathedral and ten million viewers. I was the coordinator, the link man drawing together thirty Pentecostal churches which stood and delivered in the most spectacular manner.

The radio station was disappointing but there were other avenues of service in which I could find expression. The Church of England realised that it was in possession of many old churches which were surplus to requirements and that valuable use could be made of them. Some of the redundant ones were sold; underused ones were shared with other denominations, but what to do with the old ones in a state of disrepair occupied the thoughts of the diocese. This coincided with the mood of central government which encouraged housing associations, particularly in the inner cities. Archdeacon Douglas Bartles-Smith was appointed to the Southwark Diocese at the right time and with foresight he launched the Southwark Diocese

Housing Association in which I was invited to serve. Housing had been one of my areas of interest since 1952 when, as the second black man to buy a house in Camberwell, I had had to deal with awkward, delinquent tenants and problems of maintenance within the laws and regulations of tenancy, so I humbly agreed.

I currently sit on the management committee of the Southwark and London Diocesan Housing Association. This appoints a director who, with his staff, administrates and oversees the properties of the diocese within and without the city of London. The Committee finds it expedient to resort occasionally to a quiet conference centre to assess the performance of the Association and to plan for long-term growth and development. The Association is consensually committed to making sure that those in need of housing are prioritised despite the enormous problems associated with irresponsible tenants and the resulting rent arrears.

Simultaneously, I was an active member of the Independent Ministerial Churches of Great Britain, visiting the black-led churches, making recommendations and supporting them in their youth programmes. With local authority grants they were teaching youngsters skills at Manor Place and Clubland, Clapham. Depending on their record of attendance and evidence of acquired knowledge of motor mechanics, these youths were encouraged to make applications to Ford at Dagenham. There were summer schools for the younger ones and I can remember assisting in the running of one at the Church of the First Born in Brixton for two weeks. We had an average attendance of eighty children after dropping leaflets and touring Brixton to take them off the streets.

I was also IMCGB's representative at the meeting of the Council of Churches of Great Britain and Ireland which usually convened at large conference centres. It was at the Swanwick Conference Centre near Derby that I had the special pleasure of meeting the late Bishop Derek Warlock of Liverpool. He was an intellectual who gave his time and abilities unreservedly to the Church. When there was a petition or request to the Central Government, he was the one to draft the proposal.

As I participated in the discussions and mixed freely in the social gatherings at these conferences, I reflected on the changing scenes of life. The day slavery was abolished, I was told that my great-grandfather collected the people of Priestman's River in the morning and headed for the Church the slaves had built, St Mark's church, Boston, three miles away, to thank God. They had never before been allowed in the church with their slave owners during the service; an almond tree had been planted near the church for the slaves to stay with the horses in the shade and hear the word of God. But for all this and more, for my hopes of heaven, I am willing to forgive my debtors and to love my neighbour.

Here is another fact stranger than fiction: at the annual civic service of the borough in 1985, I, as the borough dean, was the guest speaker at Southwark Cathedral. A summary of all aspects of life in Southwark was compiled by Southwark College and I officiated in burying the capsule under the new extension of the college; it is possible that a record of these happenings are there for posterity.

I was thrilled, too, to be in the company of Bishop David Shepherd because we had in common a love of cricket. I remember telling him of how I would have given anything to see him at the crease. When he and Parkhome had opened the batting at the Oval, I had been unable to obtain a ticket so I had paid ten shillings for fifteen minutes of watching from a house near to the gasworks. Now, I was bowled over when, as the mayor, I received a concessionary ticket to the Long Room to watch the test match between Australia and England when Bob Willis was the captain of the England team. That day, I had lunch with the officials and the captain's very tall, refined and graceful mother.

There were some relaxing if not hilarious times which intervened to break up the tedium and mental strain one encountered. The last time I played cricket was when I played in a charity match for the mayor's eleven against Tim Rice's team in Belair Park in the summer of 1983. I took four wickets for thirty-six runs and opened the batting with a former Essex wicketkeeper. I made twenty-two runs and even with the tips beforehand from the umpire whose daughter and mine were at Dulwich Hamlet school together, we lost the match. Tim was so impressed that I was given two tickets to the opening of *Evita* and an invitation to the backstage at the end.

There was not so much disappointment as embarrassment when I officiated at a prize-giving function. I had just completed my speech at the Good Neighbours' Christmas party when the matron introduced me to a well-built man whom I thought was the head of Marks & Spencer in Rye Lane and whom I had met the week before. This man looked puzzled as I spoke. My quick-witted mace-bearer saw the predicament and made some horse gestures behind him. This was funny but I got the message and corrected myself. It was a case of mistaken identity; the person was the flamboyant racing presenter John McCrirrick.

Chapter Twenty-Three

Towards the end of my term in office, the Jamaican Government, in conjunction with the *Daily Gleaner* and Air Jamaica, treated me to an extra-special two-week trip to the island. There was no problem obtaining permission from the council and I was accompanied by the mayoress and my son who thought I could not cope without him in Jamaica. He was half right, but it was on the plane that I really needed him. I had boarded the aircraft in a dark worsted suit of professional respectability, forgetting that in the tropics there is neither summer nor winter, autumn nor spring but one long scorching and blistering season. I was overcome by the heat and it was Michael who detected that something was wrong and quickly undid my shirt, summoned assistance and brought the brief but frightening and unnerving situation under control.

There was advanced publicity in the media of the arrival of 'the Jamaican Sam King, Lord Mayor of London' and I was welcomed at Manley airport by officials from the Ministry of Foreign Affairs on 16th March, 1984. My first task was to dispense with the misprint or misinformation and establish that the correctly designated position was that of mayor of the London Borough of Southwark.

A luncheon in my honour was given by the Minister of Local Government, the Honourable Neville Lewis, at the Oceanic Hotel overlooking the sea and the surrounding hills of Rockfort. In the first week, I met the Governor General, the Deputy Prime Minister, the Rt Hon. Hugh

Shearer, the editor of the *Gleaner*, the mayor of Kingston and a William Konrad, a visiting mayor from Florida. It was a welcome that befitted a prince. In my discussion with the Minister of Industry and Commerce, the Hon. Karl Samuda, I was pleasantly surprised that he was the nephew of my friend Saboteur with whom I had shared a billet in the RAF during the war. Saboteur was now a professor. The RAF Association wanted to have a fly-past but I declined and settled for a dinner instead. Two weeks were too short to respond to all the invitations but they did succeed in parading me round like a prized stallion.

Nothing could stand in the way of my visiting my village and especially my old school, Fair Prospect. The sight of those bright-eyed children staring at me as I addressed the school is forever in my mind.

Jamaica has not lost its flair for hospitality and generosity. The Range Rover, complete with chauffeur, belonging to the Mayor of Port Antonio was at my disposal during my stay in Priestman's River. The only sad thing was that I saw only one of my school friends Videt Senior, a classmate, and she was the one I did not like. They were all abroad seeking a living.

Chapter Twenty-Four

I was successfully contending with the political challenges and the demanding occupation but was not having the same satisfaction on my own in a large empty house which stared me in the face day in, day out. The question of entering into a tenancy agreement was not contemplated. I had had to deal with a fire caused by careless tenants and I had not forgotten my experiences at Castlemaine Road with having to intervene in contentious issues, quarrels, fights and complaints among tenants. The only problem I never had was arrears, as the rent charged was always within their capacity to pay. On one of my rent-collecting rounds I found one tenant in a deplorable state. Apparently her husband had attempted to roast this grotesque thirteen-stone woman like a pig. Her fat and stumpy fingers and the visible part of her right leg had been scalded with hot water and her hair singed. I vowed never to have lodgers or tenants in the house I occupied.

There was, however, an ever-growing desire for companionship which was congruous with the feelings of one who definitely did not find matrimony irksome. Apart from invitations relating to council business, I had numerous invitations to dinners, luncheons, parties and functions of all sorts and it was at these times that I yearned for a lady, not the mayoress my niece, at my side.

There was one very large organisation to which I was repeatedly invited before I became suspicious. On each occasion a certain gentleman was always very attentive, volunteering to make me tea and generally monopolising my company, engaging me in what I thought to be patronising conversations: 'I love going to Brixton, oh, I have West Indian friends' was some of his commonplace talk. I wanted to relate what had happened to the last man who had tried that sweetener on me. I was about twenty years old, seated on the train going from Desborough to Nottingham when at Market Harborough a man of about forty entered the small compartment in which I was the only occupant. He was friendly and started chatting, then asked me whether I liked girls. As a young man I brightened up at the mention of girls thinking he might 'fix me up' with his daughter. I was tired, and as the dialogue became banal I slipped into a doze, only to be awakened by the heavy breathing of this pervert within inches of my puppy-fat cheeks, puss-face as my wife would say. I sprang to life and lashed out at him. The first blow sent him to the side of the carriage, reeling like a drunken man and the second was on its way when the train came to a halt at Melton Mowbray. I gently vacated that compartment and calmly walked into another without any compunction.

I was fifty-seven years old, public-spirited and eligible, which many of the opposite sex realised. There were a few subtle solicitations but these were totally ignored. The polite message was that accessibility did not go hand in hand with the good nature I portrayed. In saying this, I hope I have not given the impression of being selfish or callous, pompous or sanctimonious; I simply did not want to enter into a disastrous relationship in which many have been shipwrecked. Discretion is the better part of valour, as I had learned to appreciate.

I wasn't wrong in my judgement; a year or so later the man from the organisation was murdered by his same-sex friend. His body was never found.

I attended a church rally one evening and spotted a charming young lady, Myrtle Kirlew, seated at the piano, and as the event progressed I realised that my attention was on her and not on the entertaining programme on stage. I had known her before but this was the first time my emotions and affection were aroused. I was drawn to her in a profound way and at the social which followed, we chatted. A nineteenth century poet wrote these lines: 'There are two different kinds, I believe, of human attraction: one which simply disturbs, unsettles, and makes you uneasy, and another that poises, retains, fixes and holds you.' The latter, surely, is the one any sensible person would voice.

Myrtle had a trim figure, modest and affable. She wore little make-up, certainly no lipstick, but was full of vitality, was politically aware and conversationally stimulating. One thing I discovered was that she was a very private and independent person. In my efforts to get a foot in the door, I telephoned and offered to prune the roses but was turned down flat. 'Sorry,' she said, 'I have already done it.' Yet she was considerate with sincere emotion, making suggestions as to how I could improve on my speech-making and in knowledge of the Scriptures. She did not object to accompanying me to see *Evita* and it was there I held her hand for the first time. It was like a charge of electricity going through my body. This was confirmation enough: my mind was fully made up and I had no reservation in wanting another bite of the cherry. After a few months I made my proposition of marriage which was coolly accepted. I had no reservations.

On 27th October, 1984 we joyfully exchanged vows, to have and to hold, in sickness and in health until death. This was bliss and still is, I never knew that there could be such joy and happiness reserved for me. Life begins at fifty-eight.

It was the opportune time, just when I was bogged down with engagements which claimed all my waking hours and much of my sleeping time. I needed to take stock of my personal welfare, which was neglected, and who else could have brought this to my attention but a caring, intelligent and loving wife.

She was just as convinced as I was that marrying me was the right thing to do. In fact she received the confirmation one day while climbing the stairs of her house. As plain as day, she said, a voice behind had her said, 'You are going to marry Sam.' She had been alone in the house. She had looked behind but there had been no one there, so she had run in the room and fallen on the bed laughing. That happened before I proposed to her.

My wife is a philanthropist, a good hostess, always full of smiles and good-humoured; in fact, often indulges in peals and peals of laughter which make one want to be in her company. At times she will laugh herself to sleep, wake up and laugh again; then I will say, 'Shut your eyes and go to sleep.' We are from similar Jamaican farming backgrounds and I can identify with the stories she tells of her happy childhood in a large, close-knit family. There is a sense of nostalgia as we talk of the animals on the farm, the long grass, the rivers and streams and of course the laden fruit trees, the grinding of sugar cane, the making of sugar and just about everything pertaining to country life. It sounds like the garden of Eden. We differ on a few insignificant details like names and uses of certain products as we are originally from different parishes over a hundred miles apart.

Since I wanted hot dinners and cake, I had to move to my wife's address in Eltham. My commitment to the work of the borough had not diminished. I was halfway through serving as the deputy mayor and still held my job with the

Post Office in Borough High Street. Travelling, which could have been the obstacle, was not a problem as my wife unfailingly chauffeured me to the office every morning en route to her work in Stockwell.

Before I left Jamaica in 1944 and again in 1948, most parts of the island were only names to me and I was confined to Portland on the few visits I had made so far. It was therefore agreed that in the summer we would go to meet the families on both sides and embark on an adventurous and exciting enjoyment of sand, sea and scenery when I would catch up on the Jamaica I had missed. My wife would show me the place in four weeks of our first holiday together.

In a hired car we left base early one morning and headed for Portland, travelling easterly through winding roads and St Thomas, one of the most mountainous parishes. When we got to Yallahs, the large and swiftly flowing river was in spate but we crawled through the fording and travelled through the fertile valley until we arrived at the bridge over the Plantain Garden River, which was almost impassable. However, we bravely and cautiously negotiated our way across. All the while my concern was for my courageous wife who was too busy making suggestions and giving instructions to be nervous or fearful. At one time we got lost in the cane fields and we just paused by the roadside and had some lunch until we worked out our bearings.

We spent a week in Priestman's River, which my wife hadn't known, and I was delighted to show her around Port Antonio, Somerset Falls and the interesting Spring Garden once owned by the Hogg family of Britain and where the mongoose was first introduced into Jamaica. We went swimming in the sea, had lots of walks on the property between showers, picking and eating the fruits. We had visits every day from people who wanted to see my new wife.

From Portland, we went along the north coast in the direction of Montego Bay through green fields of sugar cane, banana plantations, coconut and citrus groves, stopping at Dunn's River, situated in a landscaped park where the sparkling water cascades over the rocks and empties into the sea. The most thrilling part was joining the crowd of locals and visitors climbing up the six hundred foot waterfalls. I was sorry that I couldn't help that American lady who lost her glasses going up the falls.

Time did not allow for stopping at the White River or the Roaring River as my wife said that one could not bypass the Green Grotto, developed as a tourist attraction. She was right. I never realised that such a place existed in Jamaica. It is a vast cave with compartments giving the impression that one is entering a huge house of many rooms. Stalagmites and stalactites to which Biblical names are given are everywhere. This cave was used by the slaves for secret meetings to plot rebellion and as a hideout from the masters. It was used as a secret church for the missionaries as well. Entry was by conducted tour, otherwise it would be difficult to find one's way out. At the bottom of the cave was a large, deep pond.

On the highway to Ocho Rios we came to the protected reserve of Fern Gully, so called because of the vegetation and profusion of ferns which make it cool and damp; with the high banks on both sides, the ferns form a canopy for the three miles of drive on the slope. This was another outpouring of natural beauty that I had never seem.

We diverted from the main road and took a five mile stretch of winding rough road leading to Union Hill, the property of my wife's brother who after early retirement had resorted to planting bananas and rearing beef cattle, displaying as much competence and efficiency as he did as a Detective Superintendent of Police. This man generates his own electricity and a gravity feeding system is in place for the cattle. We had a great time of conviviality, fresh steaks, abundance of fruits and walks in the undulating fields followed by the seven dogs which pranced and rolled over, snapping at the butterflies and chasing the frogs. We walked in the expansive pastures and viewed the hefty and healthy animals grazing in the lush green grass, whilst the sounds of wildlife could be heard in the shady woodland. This, at fifteen hundred feet above sea level, presents an almost temperate ambience in what is supposed to be the tropics.

It takes discipline to keep abreast of schedule. We had to be on the move again, so we loaded the nippy little Starlet with jelly coconuts, fruits and ripe bananas and set off on another leg of the tour. It was not such an effort now as we were running downhill; only the potholes kept one's eyes glued to the road until we joined the main road going west to Montego Bay. Along the way could be seen golf courses, tennis and badminton courts, equestrian trails, great houses including the famous Rose Hall, beautiful hotels and the deep blue sea never out of sight on the right all the way. Pressed for time, we had to forego the planned rafting on the Martha Brae River.

The picture I had of Montego Bay, going back to my youth, was not a commendable one due to the sordid stories associated with that town. But all this vanished as we approached it. Montego Bay is far removed from what it was in the time of the Spaniards when pig butter – lard – derived from the vast herds of wild hogs which used to roam the place, was shipped to Latin America and elsewhere. Nor is it exclusively for the wealthy and mighty, a coterie of like-minded people who used to arrive on the banana boats from mainly England and the USA. On the contrary, Montego Bay is breathtaking, the second city of Jamaica, with a modern airport and scores of cruise liners bringing tourists to the area for a healthy dip in the warm sea especially at Doctor's Cave. We booked into a hotel in full view of the sea, then strolled around the shops and boutiques, ice cream parlours and restaurants before retiring to bed. We were dead beat but my wife had enough energy left for an hour at the table tennis board.

The following day we had fifty-two miles of drive to Negril, at the western tip of the island where I had not been before. It was a pleasant journey by the coast and through farmland on smooth flat roads unlike what we left behind. There was another big surprise for me. Negril formally had the reputation as hippyland where hippies from far and near used to gravitate for the smoking of ganga; some also brought hard drugs which they used freely in the wooded area they 'captured' until the police moved in and ruthlessly threw them out. Now Negril is in competition with Montego Bay and is a potent rival. The hotels and guest houses are fanciful and glamorous, adjacent to miles and miles of the finest white, sandy beaches. Because Negril was at the other end of Jamaica, I conjured up a picture of it being like Port Antonio or Morant Point: drab and uninteresting except for the sea, but when I set my eyes on the place I was absolutely stunned. We checked in at the Teawater Hotel and awaited the evening meal of seafood while watching the rapturous sunset before the fire-eating and limbo dancing.

Although I was fascinated by the incredible beauty of Negril, I was keen to set foot in the place from a historical and military point of view. British ships travelling to England were assembled in convoys in Negril Harbour or Bloody Bay. It was there, too, that the British ships waited in the mangrove swamps to attack Spanish ships had they strayed into the waters around. History shows that a fleet of fifty English warships and thousands of men assembled under Sir Edward Packenham to seize Louisiana, resulting in the defeat of the British in the Battle of New Orleans. The assemblage of Admiral Benbow's squadron against the French Admiral DuCasse in 1702 was on Negril beach. There is now no trace of these exploits; commercial enterprises have demolished all evidence leaving the white sands for revellers, not sailors in action.

We walked a few yards from the hotel onto the beach and into the warm and tranquil water where we spent an hour before the 'eat as much as you like breakfast' each morning. It is advisable to have some miles on the clock before the sun's heat gets too uncomfortable, so before the sun had even risen we were on the way heading for Mandeville, ninety-two miles away. We journeyed along the south coast through the seaport town of Savanna La Mar at the edge of the sugar cane plantation, then on to the fishing port of Blue Fields, another historical bay where English ships sailing in convoy rendezvoused. I was totally absorbed with the acres of grazing lands, pimento trees, mangoes and breadfruit as one passed from village to village, each with its distinctive character, until we arrived in the sleepy seaport town of Black River which takes its name from Jamaica's longest river which meets the sea there. We made a stop in the town for a fish meal and then to view the historic structure of the parish church of St John the Evangelist, built in 1837 in the centre of the old English town. My wife has a particular interest and affection for this town, having spent some years teaching in the local all-age school and taking many a trip to the mineral spa and to the beach where there were sometimes sharks around.

It was on to Middle Quarters next, where one was almost forced to stop because the traders stepped in the road brandishing their strings of crayfish and lobster freshly caught in the mangroves and morasses. As one slowed down, others with their trays of mangoes rushed forward to begin bargaining as the wise purchaser never pays the first price asked. This took us on a scenic drive through bamboo which formed an archway for about three miles. I was really enjoying this because my wife was doing the driving so that I could acquaint myself with the scenes to which I was a stranger, although at times I had to remind her that Jamaica has speed limits! Saying this, I was once the one stopped by the police and fined four hundred dollars for speeding when I tried to pass another motorist in a no overtaking zone, at my wife's instigation, on the North Coast. She laughed all the way.

Without coaxing, we were gradually slowing down. We had began climbing the prominent Spur Tree Hill which crosses the Don Fifuerero Mountains and which rises one thousand feet for every half mile. In the old days before the motor car, mules, oxen and sturdy Jamaican ponies used to pull carriages over the hill. When we approached a truck laden with cement coming in the opposite direction, I was scared, but my wife said, 'What would you have done before the road was widened?' It occurred to me then that it would have been a great achievement if a tunnel were built instead of or as well as the road. That's food for thought.

On the brow of the hill, pause and take a backward look: there, before your eyes is the spectacular view of the St Elizabeth plains, the breadbasket of Jamaica producing a variety of vegetables, corn peanuts and cashews. The bauxite mining works are also clearly visible. From there we cruised into Mandeville, noted for its cool climate, greenery and a variety of flowers: lilies, bougainvillaea and hibiscus are everywhere. A large proportion of expatriates make Mandeville their home primarily because of the climate, its central position and the low level of crime; consequently, land and house prices are comparatively high, in some cases higher than those in Beverly Hills and Stony Hill in St Andrew.

Beauty apart, the town holds many man-made historical landmarks. The courthouse is a fine example of indigenous architecture, built of limestone blacks cut by the slaves. Then there is Mandeville Hotel built on land which was originally the garrison for English troops, and Mandeville Rectory, the oldest house in the town. One had to take a walk through to the market, not so much to buy as to look at the products and to listen to the market jokes and conversations. There are some excellent schools and colleges to add to the town's characteristics and attractions. We thoroughly enjoyed the two days in the town before the straight run down Melrose Hill on the way home. Once off the hill we were obliged to stop at the wayside booths displaying bundles of fruits. There was also roasted corn and yam available but we just bought strings of oranges, tangerines and star apples.

Spring Village, our base, was a quiet farmstead where nothing but the chickens disturbed the peace and quiet. I had a shower and went to bed. By the following day we were in Kingston visiting the Bob Marley museum, friends and relatives, taking lunch at Devon House, a complex which includes craft shops, restaurants and the best ice cream flavours. The building is surrounded by flower beds, flowering shade trees and gracious outdoor seating arrangements.

Time was now running out and my wife reminded me that one could not go to Jamaica and not visit the world famous Milk River spa on the banks of the Milk River. The water, the most radioactive mineral bath in the world, is nine times as active as Bath in England and fifty-four times that of Baden in Switzerland; consequently, bathers are limited to no more than fifteen to twenty minutes in the bath. The water does not come from the river but from a saline spring in the hills. It flows in and out of the baths at a temperature of about ninety degrees Fahrenheit.

Many more vacations to Jamaica were to follow but this was the most enjoyable and indeed revealing and educational; it was therapeutic, a belated honeymoon. We were abstemious and parsimonious in nothing and I came away humming the song of the Jamaican-born Harry Belafonte:

> This is my island in the sun
> Where my people have toiled since time begun,
> I may sail on many a sea,
> Her shores will always be home for me.
>
> Oh island in the sun,
> Willed to me by my father's hand
> All my days I will sing and praise,
> Of your forest, waters and your shining sand.

It was a long haul; I reflected on the joy of discovering so much of Jamaica and slept for most of the duration of the flight back to England.

Chapter Twenty-Five

Southwark was regarded as my political home, but, *ceteris paribus* – all things being equal – I had to adapt not only to a change of residence but also to serving in a new environment. There were a few discreet stares when I was seen one moment getting in my wife's car to go to work and the next into one with the crest of Southwark at my gate.

At the first opportunity, I went to the ward meeting at Westhorne Avenue where there were about forty people in attendance. I introduced myself as one who had recently moved to the area and, presenting my paid-up card, I expressed my wish to transfer my membership from Ruskin ward. I was warmly welcomed. I imagine some enquiries were made, because at the next meeting someone referred to my political background, leading up to asking that I join the governing body of one of the local schools, but I declined because I was fully stretched as an elected councillor in Southwark until 1986 when the Labour Party was informed that I would not stand for re-election in the forthcoming local election. I was approached to be a candidate in Greenwich but I felt that I should give way to younger blood. Looking back at sixty, one is just approaching political maturity. I did not stand but I canvassed diligently to increase the responsiveness of the electorates to the Labour candidate. Labour won control of Greenwich council.

The need for school governors was again on the agenda at the ward meeting and I accepted the political appointment as a governor at Haimo Road Primary School in Eltham. It was the time when the central government introduced decentralisation into the education system which meant that in future schools would manage their own budget. The governing body was allowed to co-opt two others with special ability or experience. Our first task, I remember, was to find someone with accountancy and management skills, which wasn't an easy exercise. As an experienced person in this respect, I took the lead in coordinating the Labour group and discussing aspects of the agenda half an hour prior to the governors' meeting. Later on I was elected the chair of governors.

It was the first time I had found myself in what could have been a serious political quagmire. In response to an advertisement for a post there was a number of applicants of which three were shortlisted. The post was given to the candidate whom the interviewing panel thought best, but a particular lady had the preconceived idea that the panel should rule in her favour and accused me of being biased. As one who follows procedures and statutory requirements to the letter, I had nothing to fear, but it wasted much valuable time in having to defend the panel and myself against the appeals that were made to Greenwich's education officers.

It was, however, a pleasure working with a school with a committed staff and an excellent head who was abreast with good strategies and practices. The curriculum was wide, purposeful and lively with emphasis on learning. Sports, recreation, health and safety were well staged. Children were made aware of the environment and ecology in a practical way, so much so that the celebrity and naturalist

David Bellamy, whom I was delighted to meet, paid a visit to the school, giving it media publicity.

In September 1988, I accepted another appointment to the governing body at the large mixed comprehensive school Eltham Green, with over one thousand pupils on roll. Following the Education Act of that same year, governors were expected to focus on administration, ensuring that at every level the school itself functioned for the development and education of each child.

To undertake this responsibility, time was allotted for governors to receive training, especially in health and safety matters and in finance. At one of these training days, when I introduced myself and said I had seen active service in the Second World War (I always love to make this little appendage) I noticed there was a raised eye brow. At the end of the session, the lady lecturer said to me, 'Mr King, according to your statement you are at least sixty-two years old.' I said, 'Yes' to which she retorted, 'How can you? You do not look more than fifty – how do you keep so young?' I said it was clean, contented living, good food and daily exercise. I did not tell her my wife dyed my hair.

I am neither dim-witted nor naive when it comes to the effective use of resources for education provision, and this has been helped by attending the courses on finances. As one who has been deprived of fundamental learning I invariably summon common sense to the aid of my logical deductions. On one occasion I could not see where the Section 11 funding was being used for its intended purpose so I asked that at the next meeting a report be tabled. The person in charge was visibly uncomfortable but the matter could not be deferred nor side-stepped. The subject was pursued and it was found that the entire allowance was being merged with the main budget. Shortly after, a teacher was employed with specific responsibility for equal opportunity among staff and pupils to warrant the consideration of continuing categories of funding. There were a few behavioural problems which merited suspension and expulsion. At the start of the next school year I was voted the deputy chair of governors.

Problems are a *sine qua non* in all schools and Eltham Green was no exception, but they did not stand in the way of the school achieving some excellent results, especially in the field of sports. In the London Schools Athletics Association Championships at the West London Stadium, Eltham Green shone in many fields, achieving national standards and best performances in shot-put and discus, and in the same year they won three gold medals, one smashing the long distance UK record for under-17s in the All England Schools Athletics Championships in Birmingham. There were other facilities at the school such as the Kart Racing Club which prepares pupils for the legitimate use of the road, and others for academic, social and vocational benefits.

Though I was no longer a council or in Southwark, I was still involved with the Diocese Housing Association, being the borough dean, and I had embarked on a course of New Testament studies at Goldsmiths College which entailed much reading and attending the lectures twice a week. It was regrettable, therefore, that something had to give. I resigned from the governorship at Eltham Green and concentrated on Haimo Road Primary. I could now visit the school more often and make the necessary recommendations. One area of concern was preventative healthcare, despite frequent health inspection by the school nurse. This received full attention, giving support to parents and the homes of the children in need of such care. Another was safety in the playground. This was brought to the attention of the school, but before the officer could inspect the play frame, a child fell off and was hurt. I was also head of the premises committee and both parents and teachers responded positively to calls for renovation work and other areas where the assistance of parents would be welcomed. I objected to the treatment of the head who had made this oversubscribed school one of the best in Greenwich. He was forced to relinquish his position; my resignation was also tendered.

Chapter Twenty-Six

To wrench oneself from a place which has been almost a second home for thirty-four years is a very painful and unpleasant thing to contemplate, but this was my experience on my last day at the South Eastern District Office one Friday in February 1987 when I retired from the only permanent post I had held since being demobilised from the RAF. It was a job for which I had had to pass a test, serve a probationary period of six months and pay five shillings for what was the Civil Service Crown Stamp to seal my record – a job for life, not just for Christmas.

I remember the day I went to the Peckham Labour Exchange and asked for a form to join the Post Office. I stood at the counter filling in the form when the clerk stopped me in the process. She said, 'The information you are giving will follow you throughout your working life in the Post Office – sit over there.' She directed me to a table and chair in the corner. 'Fill this form up in your best hand writing.' She was right and I thanked her for that advice. This was the beginning of a career which was to take me from an appointment as a postman to a sorter and to an executive position from which I was to retire, leaving me with many interesting and lasting memories of people and events. Some of these haunt me in dreams; some amuse in retrospect.

When I was at the Eastern District Office in Whitechapel, I once accompanied a fellow sorter to the Blind Beggar near London Hospital. On entering the pub he said to me in a low tone, 'Mind your own business in here – people break other people's legs in this drinking hole.' A few minutes in that place was enough. I could not stand the coarse jesting, the ribald humour coming from mouths dripping with intoxicating drinks and the gaze of stuporous red eyes barely visible through the cloud of smoke emanating from cigarettes and cigars which would tarnish my smart uniform. I ejected myself and never returned to the place where to me only the blind or the beggar would venture.

There was, too, at this office a rather eccentric pre-war sorter, Cliff Morgan, who gave us post-war ones the cold shoulder; exchanges with us were kept at a minimum. He wore the badge of his regiment on his blazer every day to work, then transferred it on to his brown working coat. The opposite to him was John Jones, the talkative and bragging sorter who had worked on a British submarine in the East China Seas. He was forever telling stories of voluptuous Chinese women and his exploits, wishing he was back there. He was the first and only sorter to have invited me home to see his grape vines.

When I arrived at the head office at South Eastern District, I told none of the sorters that I had already done four years in the Post Office, so they were all very helpful, especially Fred Barlow. On my first Sunday there I was assigned to the registered post enclosure. Fred was there, telling me how hard it was in that area and that he would do the duty for me, but I denied him the privilege. My balance that day was only twelve items. He was lying for five hours of double time rate of pay. Fred was very jovial and we became good friends. Most weekends he brought me flowers for my wife until I missed him for a week, soon to hear that he had died suddenly and been buried. As soon as I heard I went to see his family, just his wife and a daughter with one kidney. I knocked at the door and a crying girl and a sobbing wife came out. She said, 'You must be Sam.' She asked me in and in the discourse she told me that Fred had died intestate and that the Inland Revenue had sent her a letter demanding taxes. We sat down together, filled in the form and wrote an explanatory letter. A month later, I received a letter of thanks. She had been exonerated.

Another of my associates at the head office whom I could never forget was a regular night sorter of Italian descent. He was a man of about five foot six inches, not very attractive physically, but he had a charming smile and was a reliable worker. At break he would go by himself to his locker and out would come a well-seasoned, roasted pig's head with its mouth turned up, on a plate; he would return for the condiments of pepper and salt and fresh bread and sit down to eat. This would last him three days. The first time I beheld this performance I was flabbergasted and turned aside but he called me over and insisted that I have a piece. To be courteous, I selected a bit of the well-done, grizzly and crispy ear. Even that I found hard to swallow as it reminded me of the head of John the Baptist on the platter.

Without being censorious, there were some colleagues who were not particularly nice, but on the whole there was a congenial and sociable atmosphere created partly by the hobbies around which people grouped and shared ideas. These were photography, gardening, sports, crosswords, art and winemaking, to name a few. They were all amateurs but usually very good in their field of interest. No wonder there was a sinking feeling when I had to face the thought of my retirement, which would mean a severance from the activities and people I had grown to appreciate over the years. In the penultimate year of my retirement I was given a one day course designed to prepare me for coping with the trauma, how to handle my finances and, more importantly, how to utilise the extra time profitably to my advantage. It was when the union representative and I sat down to plan the retirement party in earnest that it hit me that my days at the office were numbered. I had made numerous donations to retirement parties over the years without thinking that one day it was going to be me.

My record of the area for which I was in charge was carefully checked, and the supervisor remarked that from the day I had taken responsibility, that department had had no problem.

On the day of my retirement, I was taken from home in the postmaster's car. Normally I would go through the staff door but on this occasion I had to enter by the front door and receive a visitor's name tag. My heart was at breaking point. I proceeded to empty my personal locker for the last time, just to check, then to the supervisor's lounge to the tumultuous cheer of two hundred guests. The formalities began with very moving speeches, including one from the chairman of compliments and praise for a job well done. Among my specially invited guests were Mr Ashpole, my former manager who guided my training in the post I then held, and the Lancashire man, Norman Smith, the mayor of Lewisham who, because of his devotion to the borough, was made mayor for a second time. The presentation was made of a set of Black and Decker tools and a Sharp stereo. My wife was ill that day and, regrettably, was not present to receive her large bouquet. In my reply of thanks, I had to divulge my only unhappiness of the Post Office not taking into account the eight years I served in the RAF when my pension was being calculated. A big buffet with free bar was in waiting but I left sombre and sober; I have been drunk only once and that was the effect of eating a poisonous Jamaican trunk-fish.

The last thing was to say goodbye to the proprietor of the paper shop where I had always bought my *Daily Telegraph*. I also paid my last visit to the flower shop at the corner of Borough High St and Great Dover Street. The florist was a lovely lady who told me the story of how her family came from Ireland and when her father could not get a job in the building trade he had started the flower shop which she had inherited after his death.

I left the Post Office with a good record. The assessments of my service was almost identical to those from the RAF: supervisory ability, personal qualities, leadership and cooperation ranged from very good to excellent. The only adverse comment was in reference to my voice which was a little loud. I have a strong voice, and with the noisy machines in the work area one had to speak above the normal to be heard. My conduct was judged as exemplary and my dress as very smart.

The changes that had taken place over those thirty-four years had been phenomenal. This was noticeable in the composition of the workforce. Twenty-five years before, I was the only black sorter along with about four cleaners. On the day I left there were three middle managers, one a woman and scores of black sorters. Other changes were more striking as the years went by resulting in the Post Office moving from a loss-making to a profit-making enterprise for the first time in 1985. A series of innovations was at the cutting edge of such a breakthrough. These were all labour-saving devices such as the introduction of the postcode in 1959 when mail sorting was streamlined. Before that, letters were sorted three times, firstly according to destination then, towns and villages and lastly for precise streets. This was time- and energy-consuming. A further update was the segregator for separating parcels, packets and letters, later replaced by the fantastic E40 letter-sorting machine, and with the two-tier posting introduced in 1968, mail sorting accelerated. Now machines are capable of reading typed and printed addresses and postcodes at the rate of thirty thousand per hour. The mechanisation of the 70s also boosted the morale of employees and employers alike. Equal pay for women, which came on stream in 1975, was another improvement and was long overdue.

On the downside, there were some unfortunate happenings in those years as well. The Great Train Robbery in 1963 of £2.6 million and a walkout of twenty thousand workers demanding a six per cent pay rise were setbacks. Another blow was a strike in 1971 for a fifteen per cent pay increase to match that of the miners, railwaymen and local government workers. The sea-change continued with the Post Office becoming a public corporation splitting into two large organisations: the telephones which became British Telecom in 1981 and the postal. The GPO ceased to be a civil service department in 1969. The government was now entitled to a share of the profit which in 1988 was one hundred and sixty-seven million pounds. We, the employees, were not in favour because we had to pay proportionally more into the pension scheme beside losing the status of civil servants. Before I bowed out there was another upheaval brought on by the Post Office Act of 1986 which divided the PO into Girobank, PO Counters and Royal Mail letters and parcels (Parcel Force). Rowland Hill would be astonished to see the multiplier effect of his dream.

Until recently, I often returned to farewell functions, but mechanisation continued apace, forcing the closure of the office. I, however, attend the luncheon for retired managers quarterly at the Union Jack. I must admit that it was not as easy as I thought to come to terms with not getting out of bed and going to work at the usual time.

Chapter Twenty-Seven

I was not exactly in the bloom of youth for a dog of my age. Sixty-one is not a pup, but I was in the pink of health and form when I retired. The option was to offer myself for re-employment elsewhere, but then I had to consider the problems of coping with new situations, demands and people. The conclusion was that money, for which I had been a slave all my life, was not the criterion. My service at the Post Office was *fait accompli*. I had a mind for learning; therefore whatever I chose to do had to be something which satisfied my soul. My involvement with schools and church activities continued unabated but my mind was proactive. I thought of academic studies, English literature or History, which I find stimulating and engaging, but I doubted my ability to pursue these to any length especially in a controlled situation.

The uniting body of the Pentecostal Churches, the International Ministerial Council of Great Britain, was affiliated to the British Council of Churches. Through this recognition, the need for black ministers and pastors to be theologically better equipped in order to raise their status of understanding with mainstream churches, was highlighted. The IMCGB conference thought it expedient to recommend a course in theology. This was taken on board, culminating in the launching of Theological Education jointly with Goldsmiths College, University of London in 1984. Having participated in the discussions which led to this and being convinced of its advantage to me as a layman,

I decided to become a student once again. On 23rd September I paid my registration fee of thirty-two pounds and attended the inaugural session for a three-year course in New Testament studies at Goldsmiths College.

Attending lectures twice per week was demanding enough, but added to that was the voluminous amount of reading and essay writing, the art of which I had to learn and learn quickly. But it was exciting and thought-provoking. 'Describe and discuss', 'illustrate', 'show the significance of', 'compare and contrast': these were some of the terms I had to learn to handle. So were the concepts, contradictions and interpretations, the symbolic and the realistic; all required a great amount of research for background knowledge and elucidation. It was in this area that I received a considerable amount of practical assistance from my wife. Through discussions we teased out and grappled with ideas. She helped me in organising my thoughts, correcting my spelling and grammar and generally encouraging me all the way.

The twenty-two ardent students in the class bonded and developed a close friendship. Sister Hannah was a nun who had married and had to leave the convent. She was an outstanding scholar, writing her essays in Greek. There were frequent tests and a final examination at the end of the third year. For this I prepared to the best of my ability yet was apprehensive and nervous waiting for the results. The day they arrived by first class mail, I broke out in a cold sweat, but with modest composure I opened the envelope. I had passed. My wife and I were filled with a pleasant elation. 'Nothing tried, nothing done,' she said.

It was, for me, a great achievement on the day of graduation to receive the Certificate in New Testament Studies, authenticated by Goldsmiths College, University of London. I was advised to see the principal about further studies as my grades were good but I declined. The moderator of IMCGB suggested that I be ordained as a pastor. To this I reply with a quotation from Romans: 'How can they preach unless they are sent?'

There have been times when my feet slip as I continue my climb up the mountain. Footsore and mouth ulcerated, I press on as I have developed an affinity to the rock to which I have been clinging for life and put up an extraordinary battle to survive. Now and then there has been a pause for a picnic lunch and a glance at the wonderful landscape. Inhospitable in parts the mountain may be, it lends itself to versatility and to retaining the consciousness of being human with the ability to reflect.

One of these reflective moments occurred in 1988, the fortieth year of the arrival of the MV *Empire Windrush* to Tilbury bringing five hundred immigrants from Jamaica. It was forty years and forty winters, contrary to the pronouncement of the Rt Hon. Creech Jones that we would not last but one winter. Even if we had had a repeat of the terrible winter of 1946–7, when snow was on the ground for many days, and the miners' strike which led to coal being rationed, I believe the position would have remained the same.

I was on sick leave from the RAF staying with my English 'parents' in Bulwell, Nottingham, during those times. I was one with the locals, scrounging for orange boxes and old furniture and ripping out wooden fences to get the fire started for heat and cooking. At around 11 a.m., I remember hearing an unusual stir in the street and found there were women looking knackered yelling, 'Coal at Beestan Gasworks.' I noticed that some of the women had perambulators with no babies in them, some had bags or basins and just about any kind of container available. There was only Fred's twenty-year old pram in the shed, so I took it, got a bag and an old pail and just followed the line of women to Beeston gasworks. I had to pay two shillings to get through the gate and on to the coke which normally would be used for building roads, not for burning. When Mam arrived home at 6 p.m. she found the fire burning in the hearth and the kitchen stove lit. She beamed with delight and said, 'Sam, you are a good boy.'

Forty years on, and the immigrants whom death had not removed were still in the United Kingdom, so we announced that there was going to be a celebration which began with a church service at Southwark Cathedral. The interest of the media was aroused and they entered the arena. As protagonist, I had numerous interviews by national newspapers including the *Times* and the *Daily Telegraph*. Lambeth commemorated the arrival of the *Windrush* with a party at the town hall and a week-long exhibition. There was an oral history project planned by the London Sounds and Video Archives. Lambeth Services, together with the *Voice* and South London Press, combined to produce a booklet entitled *Forty Winters* detailing the memories of Britain's post-war immigrants from the Caribbean. It was sold out in June 1988 and was reprinted in December of that same year.

The climax for me was the invitation to appear with Vince, another *Windrush* passenger, on Terry Wogan's chat show on the BBC. Vince was a boy of thirteen accompanying his parents on the ship. I remembered him well, a bright boy with such confidence looking forward to an English education which was more than the average boy of his age would receive in Jamaica. There was only one other immigrant child, as far as I can recall, a girl of about eight. The strangest thing is that she now disclaims all knowledge of ever been on the *Windrush* although Vince sees and recognises her. Perhaps she does not want to reveal her age. Before this, I had not known very much about Wogan. My television viewing is chiefly sports, news, documentaries, a good film and *The Bill*.

For the sake of comparison we revisited Tilbury. The changes were incredible. It was such a different place from the Tilbury of 1948 when it was a thriving port on the Thames. Today we saw only a Polish cruise liner in dock and a few containers with hardly any men in the port, compared to the hundred when we landed in 1948. The whole area was a ghost town with very little commercial activity. It was sad to see the demise of a port which had given such hope forty years before, when people were engaged in a variety of work.

To verify that I was indeed Sam King, I was visited at home by Wogan's researchers, and on the appointed day, accompanied by my wife, I was chauffeured to the BBC studio. We were escorted to the hospitality suite for refreshments and a preliminary meeting with the charming and entertaining presenter in whose presence all signs of nervousness vanished. Then it was into the studio with the cameras trained on Vince and myself as we were introduced; Vince as a lecturer at Brixton College, I as the former mayor of the London Borough of Southwark and both as among the first set of immigrants on the *Windrush* to arrive in England, to loud applause.

Vince recalled his first day at school, how he had a fight with a boy who called him racist names and how he went on to do well because be was clever. My experiences were somewhat dissimilar, but I expressed the view that in my estimation one third of the people of the UK believed in their superiority and that that was why a small island with fifty-five million people were able to rule a quarter of the world; another third were tolerant and kind and the rest possessed a *laissez-faire* attitude, unconcerned about the world as long as their football team won on a Saturday or England beat the West Indies or took the Ashes from the Australians in cricket. I continued to say that my quality and standard of living had improved and my perspective on life had changed since making Britain my home because as the first son I was marked out to be a farmer planting bananas and rearing cows.

Two young black comedians in the role of railway porters provided the humour and brought the show to an end when I delivered the message from my Irish sister-in-law to Terry that the leprechauns were watching over him. He replied in kind.

On 22nd June, 1998 it will be fifty years since the *Windrush*; the five hundred immigrants have grown and multiplied many times over. Taking into account nature's work and the reverse immigration now in operation, there still remain many thousands who are staying just where they are, as a fallen tree. The celebrations commemorating the fifty years will be spectacular, uniting even those who have chosen to be anonymous in the Diaspora, and will provide a dramatic opportunity to mark the continuing contribution to Britain's cultural heritage. It will be a lasting tribute to those who have successfully climbed up the rough side of the mountain.

It is very important that the history of an individual or nation should be preserved, and when I was approached by the Museum of London Oral and Audio-Visual History archive for a recording of aspects of my life, I agreed to make that contribution for posterity, to be used for educational, research and study purposes. The recordings and transcripts are available to private individuals and bona fide educational establishments for teaching purposes, publication and broadcasting.

Chapter Twenty-Eight

Where I grew up, the aspirations of boys revolved around being a cricketer, a farmer or a truck driver. When the banana truck was laden with bananas on a Monday morning, I used to stand under the coconut tree and watch it take the bend with a change of gear on its way to Port Antonia. That truck was the only vehicle in the district, taking not only bananas but pimento and other produce to Kingston. It was used as a bus and even as an ambulance in times of emergency.

The sound of the revving engine and the circular movements of the driver's hands were firmly fixed in my mind and would be imitated around the house and in the yard. Whilst I was absorbed in doing this one day, my mother asked what I wanted to be when I grew up. I thought she knew, but I said I wanted to be a truck driver. I listened for her to compliment me on being so ambitious. Instead, she surprisingly took hold of me with her strong arm as she sat at the side of the barbecue. 'Look at me,' she said. 'Unnis Webber owns that Maple Leaf truck which he employs people to drive while he sleeps in his bed. You start thinking of how you are going to be the owner of a truck, be it Maple Leaf, Bedford or whatever. Anyway your father expects you to be big a farmer.' I was about ten or eleven then, but it stuck with me.

Until I left Jamaica for the RAF, there was a total lack of mechanical or engineering knowledge on my part, and I was clumsy at the start of my training even though the theoretical did not present much difficulty to understand. I knew, for instance, a motor engine that is based on compressed air, mixed with fuel vapour and ignited to cause a combustion in a chamber, then expelled to give motion, but was at a loss if something went wrong.

My first car was a second-hand, four-door saloon Wolsey with thirty thousand miles on the clock, four new tyres and body in good condition. The salesman assured me that it was on the market because the owner had died and his wife could not drive. The test drive confirmed performance and efficiency as satisfactory. For the first time I would be taking my family in a car on holiday, so I was really looking forward to being at the wheel of my car in England. We were going to Devon. The children were just as excited, playing and fighting in the back, singing and playing games. Nearing our destination we were descending a hill and I slipped into second gear but the car accelerated, careering down the hill. I realised that I had a crisis on hand but I kept my nerves, gently applied the brake and brought the car under control. The gears were faulty. I hardly wanted to continue the journey when I thought of how the entire family could have been wiped out. That spoilt the holiday as we were confined to the immediate vicinity of the farm, although we did more walking than was planned. The car was coaxed back to London and returned to the garage, but I was not reimbursed in full. I was, however, satisfied with my next vehicle, a second-hand Land Rover which the children loved, especially on a long journey when they would be put in the back with a blanket and two pillows.

As the owner of a car, I could do the basics, but as for removing and resetting spark plugs with the feeler gauge, check the state of charge, cadence breaking, suspension and shock absorbers, valve clearance and other car maintenance skills, I had only a limited and, in most cases, no idea. It is never too late to learn, and since my wife was determined never to let go of her old Vauxhall Cavalier and perhaps would need my help with simple mechanical trouble, I turned to car maintenance.

It has always been my philosophy that a man should not be obsessed with the pursuit of his rights to the detriment of his responsibility, and part of being responsible is to be a handyman, willing to indulge oneself in what one may term the mundane: install shelves, decorate, cut the hedges and the lawn, sharpen the tools, clean the brass, check the deterioration of the car if possible. The latter was now slotted into the time now vacant with the completion of my New Testament studies. Once a week I attended the class at Crayford Manor House, set in the pleasant surroundings of a manicured lawn, herbaceous borders and flowers.

It would be difficult to find a better instructor than the one we had in the person of George McKay. He started off, he told the class on the first evening, as an apprentice on the Clyde, Glasgow, and continued his training in the armed forces with the Royal Electrical and Mechanical Engineers. Before being employed by Bexley council he worked at Ford at Dagenham. The mixed class of eighteen was very fortunate to have had him. Students were encouraged to bring their cars in for practical work. The ladies especially were surprised to see how quickly a wheel can be changed given the instructions and tools. We learned so much and built up a rapport which was nurtured by the end-of-term social occasions when home-brew and cakes were brought in. At the end of the year we all had a pub lunch together. One year a weekend trip to France was organised.

Intriguing stories of driving experiences came from lorry drivers, firemen, teachers, security guards, retired folk, dispersing the inhibitions. Even the two young men in their twenties wearing earrings were happy with us. I was specially close to one of the ladies because her birthday was the same as my wife's. We looked forward to her cake but we would also have a little something and a card for her. We continued the class in another venue, Crook Log in Bexleyheath, for the next two years; then I ceased attending, having learned enough to cope with basic mechanical or electrical problems. So far, I have not been put to the test because the car is serviced at intervals, as instructed, in addition to frequent checks I make. On the whole, car maintenance has been engrossing and challenging. Each time we take the car out, I mentally rehearse the sequence in which to proceed in case there is a mishap: check the electrical works, then the petrol feed.

A holiday is always a stimulant, so at the end of the course my wife and I went on an extensive holiday, firstly to Jamaica to recapture that memorable time of our first visit together. From there it was a short flight to Florida, where relatives and friends chaperoned us to the Everglades, the beach, the malls and Disney World. The trip was an experience not to be missed. We flew up to Washington DC, designed by the Frenchman and the African American as commissioned by the President George Washington in 1791. The view of the sunset across the Potomac River is indescribable, and so were the historic buildings: the White House, the Senate, the Jefferson Memorial and the numerous museums. The most captivating was the Air and Space Museum which is as the name implies. We took a boat ride on the Potomac to the home and estate of George Washington in Virginia. Our last trip was to the grave of President Kennedy in the

Arlington Cemetery. The malls with their food halls have much to commend them. After a month we were almost too tired to return, but were too broke not to do so.

Chapter Twenty-Nine

Retirement for me is a shift in focus from one particular activity to another. I have been trying out the principle of matching my activities to the physical and mental strengths at my disposal whilst ignoring all the weaknesses in the process. Ultimate success should have been the product of this. Looking back, I should have tried to correct at least some of my weaknesses. I have been incautious, trusting people without analysing motives on a number of occasions, resulting in my being taken for a ride around the mulberry bush and abandoned. I would take individuals at their word, imagining what it would be like to be in their position of need. I would refuse help to someone only if a positive response would lead to a diminishing, a lessening of my productivity or self-esteem. One could say I was blind to the cynicism, inconsideration and dishonesty which dwell in the heart ready to be unleashed. When this comes from friends, it is damaging beyond repair.

When one such friend requested a short-term loan for a deposit on a house until the bank had cleared his application, I did not think twice; after all, a friend in need is a friend indeed. How else could I treat one with whom I had been in the RAF? Well, it is now fifteen years and I have not been repaid. In fact my so-called friend disappeared until he was found in a wheelchair.

My second clients were two persuasive property developers who came with plausible schemes that would convince, I dare say, the professional legal mind. I fell for it.

They produced collateral security, giving a receipt and a promissory note drawn up by a solicitor. Again, taking them at face value, I did not investigate and made a substantial loan to be repaid with or without interest. It is now ten years and not a red cent. What is the point of taking them to court when they are today without house or home?

With hindsight, I should have been able to detach the sentimental from the logical. In other words, I should have freed my spirit to make a moral judgement. I am not just a biological individual. I have a moral side, and by this extension expresses my social significance in my roles and functions. This is what to me is a good citizen, carrying out the functions of a human being. It should be possible, therefore, for people to live together in ways sympathetic to the interests, consequences and needs of others, leading to mutual trust, but I overestimated the capacity of some to do this. It takes empirical trials like these to learn, but I am not going to worry or fret; I am going into my garden; who steals my purse, steals trash. My good name is far more important, more than silver or gold.

I have not experienced a lowering of energy levels and boredom thresholds with the onset of age. I surprise myself with the capacity I possess for fresh knowledge; therefore, I am making every effort to retain my mental acuity by challenging my mind, but a healthy mind exists in a healthy body, so with that I have been paying maximum attention to a healthy daily diet prepared by my keen and attentive wife. There are also chosen exercises which fit into my lifestyle. There is no line of demarcation between work and leisure. They fuse. I have personal freedom in choosing what and when I do things. With this ability to choose, I do not find work dull or tedious. There is a measure of pleasure and satisfaction in doing it, adding colour to my life and providing an escape from the dictates of 'time and motion' and from the 'organisation man'. Now I have time to practise being a farmer.

We were fortunate to have inherited a ready-made garden, although looking at it critically, there is room for improvement. After ten years it has not altered very much in design, but there are a few additional flowering shrubs. It is not big – one hundred feet long, of which a third is lawn, bordered by roses and shrubs, vines and perennials. It is no Japanese garden with waves of azaleas and oases of serenity, although I do contemplate or rather meditate when I am working in the garden and find it therapeutic and calming. It is in these moments that I am likely to be disturbed by my wife, who creeps up behind me and gives me a fright, setting her off in fits of laughter.

To be truthful, my knowledge of English gardening was very minimal, and because work had taken precedence over this type of activity, I could not improve on the little I knew. The 'Führer' – a colleague in the Post Office – used to give me some valuable tips for cultivating roses, but this was not put into practice until I retired and moved to my present residence where there is more space and time to explore new grounds. Plant surgery – cutting back to rejuvenate – was not previously considered, nor did I take time to learn that a different approach is required for growing a variety of plants.

As for the physical structure of the garden, it was left as it was, since there was nothing intrinsically wrong with the original. Now I find ways and means of giving a new look to fences, walls, sheds, paths and trellises for climbers which are effective in brightening and enlivening but not necessarily inexpensive.

Herbs in the corner of the garden remind me of the kitchen garden which used to be the pride and joy of my mother. The climatic conditions are dissimilar, but some of those herbs thrive in my garden. The thyme and mint which hug the ground and spread are aggressive and have to be kept under control. The spinach, garlic, tomatoes, squash, beans and fennel all find a place in the kitchen garden. In the autumn I reward myself by having a sip of home-made wine from the abundant apples while my wife sets to work making healthy drinks from the blackberries and blackcurrants and pastries from the apples and pears.

I share my garden time with the church I attend. I am the groundsman, cutting the very large lawn, assisted by my wife. I plant flowers, bulbs and shrubs, and recently vegetables have been included.

My garden falls short of what I desire, however. As a rustic, a peasant, I would have to make my garden in the country where the continuous activity of the creatures could be admired in the hedges, trees, tall grasses and flower beds, with the birds replacing the nocturnal animals in the day, twittering, chirping, squabbling and feasting on the berries or searching for worms and insects. My favourite animal, the rabbit, would be free to date, mate and give birth. It would be a place where I would observe the drama of the cat chasing and pouncing on its victims, and the metamorphosis of the caterpillar and the emerging butterfly. I would watch at leisure the bees feeding on the sweet nectar of the honeysuckle and foxgloves, the camouflage of the spider and the consequent entrapment of the prey, the stealth of the frog sitting in the shade flicking its tongue and catching moving insects. The fox would be banned, but the humble hedgehog would be at liberty to wander and clear the place of slugs and snails. I may never possess a garden such as this, but I am reading the relevant literature and watching the garden programmes on television to improve what I have. I have not yet hung up my harp.

Leisure or retirement, for me, is not drifting or wandering like the clouds or waves of the sea, for then life would be sterile. My voluntary contributions to the management committee of the Southwark and London Diocesan Housing Association and the West Indian Ex-Servicemen and Women's Association continue and I will persevere with these as long as I am privileged to do so. I also have a good working relationship with the present mayor of Southwark whom I represent when he is unable to fulfil his appointments.

I am a life member of the London Labour Mayors' Association, founded in 1920 and in the past boasting the distinguished memberships of Clement Atlee and the famous Lamorbey who was sent to prison for defying the central government. I remember him whenever I pass the park and buildings named after him in Sidcup.

One of the advantages of belonging to this association is that it keeps us active and in touch with each other. The information desk is kept very busy despatching news of functions to which we are invited, and as a solid gold chain gang we merrily troop along while our secretary sniffs out interesting places for visits we otherwise would not have made. I refer to such places as the Police Academy in Hendon, Alexandra Palace, Mansion House, Royal Ascot, some embassies and High Commissions in London.

It was on one of these light-hearted occasions that a lady mayor told me of the wonderful holiday she had had in Jamaica. One morning, she said, while having breakfast outside the hotel under a large mango tree, a beautiful, rosy mango had landed in her lap. She had cut short the delicious breakfast of mackerel and boiled green bananas and had had the mango instead.

There is great comradeship among us and a feeling of loss when one passes through the veil. Norman Smith and the ninety-five year old who died as result of fighting off an intruder were sadly missed. There were always jokes and reminiscences of episodes when we were mayors.

Speaking of recollections, I remember two Nigerians, with flattering speech of how great I was, once wanted me to open a large new factory in my name in Lagos which they thought would help their bicycle-making business. They nearly convinced me, having offered to pay my fare and show me a possible ancestral home. They overlooked the fact that I must have had some common sense for the people of Southwark to have made me the first citizen of the borough. Even my medical and police records had been checked to verify that I was of sound mind and free of impropriety.

The best time we ever had together was the five-day trip to Europe organised by Richard Balffe, Member of the European Parliament. This was informative, educational and pleasurable as we visited the EEC Parliament in Brussels and Strasbourg. As I had undergone surgery two months before, my movements on the sightseeing tours were somewhat restricted, but I did go to the house of Karl Marx. I was more disappointed than my wife when I could not take her out to dinner one evening in Frankfurt as planned because of the panic attack I had at seeing blood in my urine. She of course thought it was normal because of the nature of the operation. She just laughed and I was calmed. My Myrtle was right. A German man did give her a bunch of flowers.

Going through Belgium, there was a tinge of sadness when passing Bastogne where the last major battle of the Second World War was fought in 1944: the Battle of the Bulge. A few German Panzer tanks and air raid bunkers and shelters could still be seen as a reminder of the terrible price that was paid for freedom from tyranny and injustice.

After fifty years, I am at a stage where I can reflect on those who have faithfully urged, willed, cheered, and even dared me to go forward. The effect has been that my emotional consciousness has been kept alive and this has provided the consistency to satisfy the objective and the subjective even when I have been out of sight.

The organisation in a community is influenced by forces generated from within, but away from this group one has to contend with influential forces from outside. The intelligent and normal human being will therefore gravitate towards a situation which offers him spontaneity of expression and fulfilment. As a gregarious person, I found this in a group of friends who by their willingness to share and reciprocate were a preserving influence. Prior to this, there must have been a driving force which gave motivation in the first place and then to continue without being desultory in the face of many obstacles. My postulation is that this stimulation was rooted in the past. As the first son, I had an obligation toward my family, an impulse to recompense my parents and to be a big brother to my siblings. Associated with this was the pain and deprivation that was the experience of my fellow men, something which I wanted to avoid at all cost.

It could be that this character trait was inculcated at a much earlier stage in life through various gratifications which reinforced a particular behaviour and attitude. I refer to the immense satisfaction I had as a teenager in managing people and property and in the praise and admiration of my parents. This had the desired effect of boosting my confidence and security enough to participate in the learning process to which I was exposed in a new environment half a century ago. What I perceived my self-image to be was of prime importance in maintaining and enhancing my behaviour patterns. It was an integrating factor in my personality. I can trust myself in a conflict situation as I accept myself for what I am. I have found myself in such situations because my limited education did not furnish me with the cognitive strength and power to remove the mountain, but I did not run away or look for a scapegoat; I climbed the mountain knowing that nothing that man does or plans is set in stone. In time even iron rusts. To sit back and attribute blame in many cases is a sign of fear and perhaps ignorance and laziness. The past, with its pain and needs, are negatives which limit us if we allow then to dominate our anticipation of the future. We fool no one if we resort to castigating others for all our failures. Abraham Lincoln's well-known dictum is that, 'You may fool all the people some of the time; you can even fool some of the people all of the time; but you can't fool all of the people all the time.'

Someone once postulated that 'the successful research scientist is nearly always a man and he is more likely to be a first son.' To this, Freud adds that 'a man who has been the indisputable favourite of his mother keeps for life the feeling of a conqueror, that confidence of success that often induces real success.' This may be true in my case, and although I am no scientist or psychologist, I would say one should find a positive for every negative and view a setback as a challenge. To do this, one's mind must be geared to learning, otherwise one becomes a boor, with an empty mind and heart and will give way to the drag and the inertia from which it is difficult to extricate oneself. It boils down to being in control of one's will, and its exertion in a positive direction is often rewarded, in time, by a rise above circumstances. Life is paradoxical, succeeding in what it seems to fail.

Chapter Thirty

History abounds with a myriad of examples of those who have risen above the odds leaving the mountain trail littered with messages of hope. Pamela Burrel was left to bring up six children after a divorce and after suffering the loss of the family's wooden house in a fire. The operative word of encouragement to her children was 'stay': 'I am going to stay on you'; 'stay in school'; 'stay out of trouble'. Stanley, the older boy, listened to his mother, but he had never forgotten his father's observation and advice when he took his sons to the races. 'There are winners and losers in every game. I expect you to be winners but you have to size up the situation and play the angle,' were his father's words.

Stanley grew up to be a streetwise kid from the black ghetto and took to dancing to the captive audience on the tarmac outside the local sports stadium in California. The owner of the Oakland Athletics baseball team was drawn to this young lad who was only twelve years old and offered him a job as an errand boy taking team announcements around the club. For this he got five dollars per game, supplemented by washing players' cars and lacing up their shoes, not omitting the one-man dance show in the locker rooms. One day one of the players told him that he looked like the king of the basketball players, a man nicknamed Hammering Hank. Stanley stuck with his job, now paying $7½, and at seventeen was promoted to the office announcing results of the games on the phone. His dream was shattered when, given the chance of joining the team, and trying very hard, he did not succeed in becoming a player.

Stanley was recruited in the US Navy at the adolescent age of nineteen and was trained as an aviation storekeeper. The commander overheard Stanley making critical remarks about the drill leader and called him to the office. Stanley admitted his misdeed but justified his action by saying that a weak leader makes the team look weak. 'And you think you can do better?' the commander asked. Back came the reply, to the commander's amazement, 'I do, sir.' With this he was made a drill leader, a job he executed with great skill, and he was a model of organisation and efficiency using the technique of intimidation.

After leaving the Navy, he visited his mother one day and found his brother and a friend reading aloud from the Bible. This to him was anathema but he accepted an invitation to the Pentecostal church the following Sunday and was deeply impressed by the fervour of the music and worship. It occurred to him that there was something more important than winning. He joined the chair and began writing gospel songs, popularising then in the inner city by rapping to conventional tunes, and this prospered. Stanley adopted the stage name of M.C. Hammer, selling literally millions of albums, each one including a religious number to say thanks to the one above. He has not forgotten his humble beginnings: charities are generously financed; several family members and friends from his old neighbourhood are employed by him. Hammer sized up the situation, played the angle – whatever that means – and has become a man of substance, showing others how to scale the mountain and win.

In a transforming world, hopelessness and helplessness should be confronted and not be allowed to take root in one's repertoire of development. How we as individuals construe and anticipate events leads to failure or success consequently one should take responsibility for managing his journey through life given that there is access to opportunities for learning and social welfare provisions facilitating the steps along the way.

When St John the Evangelist had his vision on the Isle of Patmos, the angel told him to write down what he was seeing and hearing. Had he not done so, we would not have learned of the destiny of the individual and history – what is biblically termed eschatology, although no one claims to understand it. In writing this story I want to say that I have not lost my way up the mountain or I deliberately wandered off into verdant valleys or cosy eaves. As a feeble mortal, I am entitled to sleep but just for enough to revitalise and renew my mental and physical powers. Only God doesn't sleep; He rests. I have not attempted to record all what has happened to me since I left my mother's womb, for that would be quite impossible. I have selected what is authentic, relevant and pertinent to encourage others in the persistence of the good and to deter irrational impulses and dissipate tensions.

The mistake the native Americans made was not to leave their history in writing. The battles we see played out on television were lost to the cowboys who have not admitted to being trounced as the invading enemy at Little Bighorn. They just told pejorative stories and made themselves heroes. We have seen the actions but not the thoughts of the American Indians and my slave ancestors; therefore we lost the design of the pattern that action and thought interwoven would have produced. For this to be possible it is necessary to retreat from external standards of value, from the expectations even of friends, withdraw from the pressures of social conformity and develop an independence of mind to search for what is right and essential and discard the rest.

My writing this did not come just from a moment's thought; it did not spring by chance out of my mind. It involves my consciousness, my experiences, my environment and my inheritance and contains years of adventures, surprises, stresses and strains of passion and will in collision with circumstances, and, I must say, the rich rewards which make my life worthwhile. There have been times in my life when I have had misgivings, when I have halted and hesitated, when I have almost succumbed to temptations of various kinds. Once, I had to conduct an enquiry into a lost parcel in the Post Office and this took me to an address in Herne Hill. As I left, a man from across the road came towards me, shook my hand and said, 'You are the mayor of Southwark – you must be a lodge brother to get that position. Come into my house and let's talk.' I pointed to the Post Office crest on my briefcase and told him I could not accept his hospitality; besides, I was not one of his lodge brothers although I was a brother to anyone who is in Christ. With me, there were no secret deals.

These distractions are but mountain mists, but before me there is a steady light which injects new vigour and irrepressible optimism to press towards higher moral and spiritual endeavours which lead to a life of full unity between my head and my heart, that is, between reason and faith. I knew my life had its plan, which became more obvious as the years unfolded. It was for me to adhere to the fundamental principles that gave my thoughts a definite order for movement and direction. Without this order, my life would be left to chance and would be filled with impracticable dreams and evanescent desires. I would be 'loafing' with no plan and hence no end to be attained, or should I say no ideal to aim at, because man at his best only moves towards an ideal which is never fully reached. There is always more to be known and better to be achieved, a recognition of the limit of one's knowledge.

My writing stems from a heart inspired and a life actuated by love – the meeting point of God and man. I believe that love solves all the enigmas of life and thought and it is this conviction which gives me the courage to face evils and challenges. My belief is that love begins as a constituent element of man's nature and expands through life, taking different forms in the socialisation process as we think and act. The heart which can love is therefore an essential precondition of all worthy attainment.

By logical deduction, experience and common sense, I conclude that love is as a primal power in us as reason is, giving meaning to life and making us members of a physical and spiritual kingdom. It kindles the passion for one's country, arouses pity towards the suffering and steers one away from selfishness and ignorance towards truth and goodness, knowledge and benevolence. No one can claim to be truly emancipated unless one moves towards this realisation where there is a permanent outflow of helpful deeds for the sake of fellow human beings. Every person, good or bad, is obliged to have some practical attitude towards his fellow men, and if one is guided by the spirit of love and reason, selfishness diminishes and society becomes a place where one articulates one's view of what is good. This is the ideal which, along with loving people, we should strive for, when the self expands until joys and sorrows, defeats and victories are felt as our own. I reckon that is what St Paul meant when be wrote 'Bear ye one another's burdens' or Jesus in his command to 'Love one another as yourself.' This love transcends all limitations of sex, age, race and creed. It transcends, too, the limits of finite existence and becomes a spiritual principle of aspiration and surrender to God, loving Him first, thus making it possible to love others to the extent outlined above, for as it will be God radiating through us. God is love.

This love has impelled me to serve the Mother Country in the war and to honour the pledge to make provision for all my three brothers and four sisters to join me in Britain in the pursuit of a better life, and to offer myself with all my energies as a servant in various capacities. Financial and intellectual gain would be folly and futile and would be worthless for me and the family without the essence and worth of things: love. I would not be able to forgive my enemies and debtors without this. We move from ignorance to knowledge, evil to good and bondage to freedom not by the process of evolution but through love and hard work in a world where these exist, and since evil cannot be eliminated altogether, work becomes a permanent activity upon which the preservation of life and liberty depends. My enthusiasm for work is intrinsic, and whether I was in South Africa or the Deep South of America, I would be engaged in the social and economic struggles of the disadvantaged.

Techniques and strategies are no good without emotional attachment to produce gratification, so one gets involved in occasions which bring people together: births, deaths, major events, literature and music. When my wife and I had a holiday in Turkey some years ago, I started a conversation with a Turk while my wife was riding the camel. He asked me where we were from and I said England. With surprise on his face he replied, 'You are not English.' I said we were originally from Jamaica. 'Jamaica? Where is that?' I didn't offer any geographical explanation; I just said, 'Heard of Bob Marley?' 'Oh yes, I know,' he replied. The curiosity and one-sidedness seemed to melt away and instead of two worlds there was one.

Before that diversion I was praising work, but I must now debase idleness which is ruinous to man because it sustains misery and is incompatible with moral life. It stultifies hope, paralyses effort and plays a perilous trick on the intellect, checking its growth. To place rest above effort puts stagnation above progress; therefore one should revolt against idlers who condemn themselves to a life of bondage, pessimism and powerlessness. The idle mind centres on unproductive thoughts which ripen into all manner of wickedness and remorseless actions, exonerated as the weakness of man and therefore a losing battle to resist. Moral life is seen as a mere figment if one accepts this view.

I am particularly concerned with the purposeless waste of life and resources and as a mentor would appeal to the youth to be discontented with idleness, laziness, call it what you will, for to be so is the first stage of breaking out of a state that is inadequate, imperfect and wrong. A life deprived of moral potency and purpose is worthless. My philosophy of life is that every individual has a hereditary predisposition from the remote past which rises to the surface, and as part of the whole has his place and function in his environment. Everyone also has a trust laid upon him which he may, out of choice, violate or keep. My advice to anyone who may be wavering is that it is your duty to keep this trust. When youth is in one's favour, one has the wherewithal, the power, the energy and the concentrated might to fight one's way inch by inch. It is my experience that one gains nothing except through conflict. I have never been an idle spectator of this conflict but rather one who pulls out the power and the energy, enters the field of battle and find that victory hangs on the valour and vigorous decisiveness of each combatant.

I will further stress that one cannot afford to be lukewarm about this: whatever one is playing for, stake it boldly and take a resolute stand against vice. Never be an instrument of evil, else you may find yourself measuring your power against what is morally good and at work in society and the world instead of recognising this good and making it valid. By saying this, I am leaving no room for indifference, neutrality or a surrender to idle optimism. Listen and you will hear the trumpet calls through the noise of battle, for the sound reverberates and wafts back on the wind. If God is with us in the conflict, victory is in every blow, but we are not to condemn the world. Nothing is what it ought to be, for, indeed, everyone can find a flaw in his highest achievement. That's where humility begins.

There is no room for arrogance in the struggle of life. When Jesse Jackson suggested to Arthur Ashe, God rest his soul, that he was not arrogant enough, Ashe's cool and calculated reply was, 'I don't think my lack of arrogance lessens my effectiveness one bit.' We cannot wisely condemn things simply because they do not happen to answer to any conception which we may have chosen to elevate into a criterion that may just be an empty notion without an objective validity. An individual's actions are not understood and can have no validity and moral meaning whatsoever except in the light of the purpose which has given them being. We know the man only when we know his creed – what he believes in. This is his ideal, and his purpose is an endless progress towards his ideal or goal. I say endless because it is never achieved in most cases but effort is a step in the direction of self-realisation.

These are facts to arouse sensitivity to the hidden truth, although it may be now, as it was then, that after the prophets have left us we believe what they have said, but as long as they are with us, they are voices crying in the wilderness.

I have made mention of the fact that my motivation and drive may have been the result of the interplay of nature and nurture, but that explanation would be inadequate as it would account for only one side of the equation, the push. There is also the pull, the centripetal force coming from another source, the leader who is not weak. In life, good leadership promotes a mutual influence between the leader and the led and is a part of the dynamic system of this mutuality. My leader evaluates my needs and capabilities, showing himself to be supportive, directive, achievement-oriented and participatory in every task and assignment. The empathy is there as He arbitrates and conciliates. The impact of this motivates me to the point of altering my behaviour or giving up my personal freedom if need be. The more I subordinate myself to this leader, the wiser, stronger and more obedient I become, for obedience is inherent in the subordinate and full obedience is the service of a necessity which is within and requires more than intellectual demonstration. Knowledge of this ripens into wisdom and becomes a disposition of the heart.

The leader I follow cannot be described as democratic, autocratic or *laissez-faire*. He cannot be categorised, but His legitimate power which makes for righteousness penetrates through the divine endowment of will and reason which rule my life. The battle against evil can therefore be won by the application of the power of the will which manifests itself in thought, desire and deed. Here lies my optimism not in my healthy body and disposition but in the goodness of God which satisfies the finite hunger of the soul. My belief in this fact makes me able to transcend the discords, scepticism, selfishness, antagonism, hypocrisy and many more undesirables with the despair they bring. My leader,

God, is no Lost Leader who 'broke from the van and the freemen and sunk to the rear and the slaves.' He did not lead me into rocky solitude to wrestle with the dragons of objections, threats and hopelessness; instead, He gave me a sturdiness of heart and a predisposition to see the sunny side of life, and through this optimism I can be reconciled with my world, believing that my wants, needs, and claims will always be met, and in this I not only find happiness but blessedness.

Faith in God gives me a profound conviction of the evanescence of evil, teaches me to reject compromises, releases my belief in the universal brotherhood and enables me to rise above the demands made on optimism and belief. If these are not part of my way of life, I am a mere dreamer. Faith as hope and desire is something I cherish and nurture, otherwise it would lapse into doubt and crumble into dust beneath the blows of discouragements and vice. It has sustained and strengthened me in confronting the contradictions of life, otherwise I would be questioning the path along which He has taken me but as it is I cannot justify the ways of God to man. All actions imply belief, and the ardour and vigour of moral action can only come from a belief which is wholehearted. Faith cannot give an account of itself, but it is most secure and is illuminated in the manifold experiences of my life in which influences of our complex environment are continually absorbed. I grow by means of them. Though faith possesses all my faculties, I cannot express it through the channel of speech.

Chapter Thirty-One

It was thought that the early immigrants, given their backgrounds, 'didn't have a chance' in this civilised, industrialised society, but our attitudes and belief, for me Christian belief, were the techniques of survival from the day we stepped off the *Windrush*. We had no stake, no investment, but we had hope, that hope that the poet describes as springing 'eternal in the human breast'. Poverty may be a cause of crime, but it is not a sufficient explanation in this land which may not be as egalitarian as some would like but is still a land of enough opportunities to keep one's head above the water.

Having a stable work record, a fixed address with a family, being committed to the values of thrift and making myself available for community service were long-term goals which I knew I could achieve through hard work, deferred gratification and rational planning. Immediate gratification would be the antithesis of these values, which were not reckoned to be the aspirations of only the middle classes and were given high priority. Not everyone will be successful, but we all can try in an honest way. My integrity has been threatened on many occasions but ulterior means to achieve material goals would only impair my vision as I climb up the mountain.

The law works through the exercise of common restraints to produce a degree of uniformity in behaviour, but there are ways around these corrective measures. I am not one who assumes that all deviance is the product of things outside my control, be it biological or sociological, because that would be denying my moral status. It is partly a social artefact but this 'cannot-help-it' idea in defence of the nonconformist should be taken with a pinch of salt. I regard myself as an autonomous moral being, responsible for my actions, and in preserving myself as such I impose stringent discipline on myself which induces a rational aversion to idleness and vice. There must be sanctions and control for man to survive with dignity in his social environment.

In November 1945, while waiting for the gliders to return, the ground crew responsible for repairs was informed that the gliders were not coming back. So as not to waste time, we were put in a coal fatigue party taking coal on a lorry from Witham railway station to Rivenhall, Essex. A week into this assignment, I detected that of the twenty full bags of coal, only eighteen were unloaded. We had been stopping at the Wild Boar on the return journey for a drink and I had begun to suspect something fishy. My dedication to the task diminished and I started to work noticeably slowly. The leader of the working party thought I was indolent and reported me as deliberately malingering. This was serious. If I had been at the front line I could have been shot. The officer in charge questioned me as to the reason for my reluctance when my behaviour and discipline had been exemplary and my work record excellent. I told him I didn't like working on the coal fatigue party. I thought he treated me fairly and sympathetically; I was rescheduled to another job. Two weeks before Christmas, the Wild Boar was broken into and the fatigue party was interviewed by the police because it was found that drinks were being sold in the billet. The leader of the party had been stealing the coal and doing deals with the pub landlord but had felt short-changed, which was why he burgled. I always knew someone was being dishonest and that was the reason for my malingering. Despite the pleadings of his vicar brother, the thief was given two months imprisonment and a dishonourable discharge from the RAF. When thief thieves from thief, God laughs.

Responsible behaviour, punctuality and regularity were inculcated very early in life and were rigorously reinforced in the service of the RAF and the Post Office. At no time did I ever frown or question the discipline enforced. I can always go back to childhood and find some experience to match. One day, everyone had gone to the farm and I was left with my four year old brother. My father had given me clear instructions to keep my eyes on a nine month old pig in reserve for Christmas which was tied to a coffee tree. No sooner had he left when my friend Reggie came for me to play cricket about five hundred yards away. We played for hours and then a man passed by and said that Joe Williams had just killed a pig that was in his potato field. I was frantic and ran to where the pig had been tied, but it wasn't there. The village knew of the slaughter so my father was also aware before he got home and he arrived in a bad mood. 'Sam,' he said, 'come here. Where is the pig?' I was dumb. He reached for the broom by the kitchen door and started to whack me on my legs. My mother intervened: 'That boy is wrong and foolish but you should never punish a child when you are angry,' she said to him. With that he stopped and that was the last time my father punished me. I was twelve then, and I never again gave him the opportunity to scold me; I took my responsibilities seriously.

As a worker in adult life, I realise that I am expected to defend the values as well as to execute the functions entrusted to me. A disciplined person is most likely to make the most of his potential and is less likely to be bugged by insecurity, depending on the image he has of himself. My uniforms in the RAF and the Post Office were not merely clothes; they were badges of membership and rank which were not susceptible to the flexibility of etiquette outside of these associations. There was an intensity of feeling associated with them which gave expression to the standards incorporated in the behaviour I wished to maintain.

I remember as a young serviceman, after an evening out in the town, an equally young and pretty girl suggested that we spend the night together in the air raid shelter. I started walking with her when she noticed I was not going in her intended direction. I took her home and handed her to her mother who was very impressed that a serviceman could be so considerate. To have gone to the shelter with a weak girl would be evil without palliation, cruel, brutish and mean. I was invited in and given a cup of tea. I returned the compliment a few days after by taking a box of sewing gadgets for her – chocolates were not available then, and in any case I don't think I could have afforded them. The fact is, I equated her with my sister and would not like anyone to take advantage of her; besides, I felt that it would be morally wrong.

Standards of discipline extend to showing deference and respect to those in authority without any qualms, otherwise the system would not survive. This is the word of one who is a passive person; far be it from this war man. I approve of assertiveness and active mastery of a situation rather than a passive acceptance of it, and allow tolerance of frustration, personal identity and individual relations where the weight is on the side of equality rather than hierarchy, except in certain areas like the military where the latter is not a mark of subservience but an indication of courtesy and discipline. These to me characterise a well-adjusted person with faith in himself and of course in God. The value and strength of faith corresponds to the doubts it has overcome. Those who never went to battle cannot come home heroes.

I would say I am a realist who has developed a sense of responsibility, especially in moral judgement, though I am not by any means a perfectionist. My work shows that I seek results not perfection. I have made many mistakes which cannot be recounted, and even if I could, the purpose it served would be difficult to state succinctly. As a strong young man ready to demonstrate prowess, I was keen on group relationships, and as we know, group situations generate differential effects of significant consequence. I was at a critical period when adjustments to new situations had to be made, and I bowed to the pressure of the group which emphasised similarity. I was afraid of disrupting and hindering the flow of good relations and of being labelled a cissy or an eccentric. Nothing hurts a young man's pride more than being marginalised and being accused of divided loyalty, and I desperately wanted to be consistent with the ties of belongingness and conformity, so the appropriate reaction was to gratify my ego by conforming to the norm which on one occasion was to be tattooed.

I was on leave from RAF Swannington, and members of the group escorted me to London Road, Manchester, where I chose the pattern of a cobra wrapped round a woman. I watched with my influencing friends as the tattoo artist put a carbon paper an my left arm, traced the design on and then cut it in with an electric needle. It bled a little, but I was tough and would have taken more than that had I been captured by the enemy, I told myself. It was a foolish thing, and years later I realised that it was not only foolish but wrong when I found a reference to it in the Bible: 'Do not cut your bodies for the dead or put tattoo marks on yourselves: I am the Lord,' (Leviticus 19:28).

I fell for the novelty of the situation to avoid ostracism and the unfavourable attitude of the group. It was meaningless behaviour which left me with a guilt feeling, but on the other hand, on reflection, it was a small price to pay for the solidarity of friendship we enjoyed. The relationship was a strong bond and is of lasting significance.

A group of us in RAF uniform were returning from the Queens cinema with our girlfriends one very cold winter's night and came face to face with some American soldiers of the Ranger unit, equivalent to the British Commandos. Everyone knew that this spelt trouble, and one of them deliberately collided with one of ours. He took hold of the blonde girl and said, 'I'll take you home, baby, you should have nothing to do with niggers.' An argument ensued, and we were all going to take on the American when one of the Jamaicans, alias Pig, five foot eight, muscular, fearsome-looking, weighing about two hundred pounds and a Kingston waterfront man said, 'Boys, stay out of it, this is my fight.' He had spent many hours on the beach with his Chinese friends, practising karate kicks. The American threw a punch but the Jamaican blocked it and landed a telling upper cut with his right hand which felled him. As he was recovering, Pig got him by the right hand and tossed him away. It was spectacular. American number two entered the fray to close with him, but this Hercules let him come and then side-stepped and walloped him over the back of his head, despatching him to the ground before he could wink.

The police were quickly on the scene and arrested the Jamaican for fighting and being a troublemaker because he had beaten up three GIs at a dance hall in Long Eaton a month before. Why didn't they ask why? By this we had telephoned Syston and an officer arrived to take Pig away. Pig was put in a cell.

The sergeant did not want to hear from us, but a local civilian couple came forward and confirmed that it was the Americans who were the culprits. Pig was let out with a warning. He did marry his blonde and was deprived of her only by death.

It is now our turn to honour and stand by Pig at the West Indian Ex-Servicemen and Women's Association, where distance is not maintained. Each member considers it his or duty to support, emotionally and otherwise, those undergoing the anguish of irreparable loss, fear and loneliness which come thick and fast now that most of our members are living on borrowed time, that is, over three score years and ten. The social convention which discourages adults from returning to the childlike state, a tearful parting after half a century of togetherness, is widely ignored. Because I enjoy pre-eminence within the association, my views carry weight when interceding with outside agencies and in bureaucratic situations.

We in the association are not looking for change or alternatives. We participate because we feel the need to maintain strong social and cultural ties. Only then can our presence be seen as a distinct entity and our commitment be both effective and affective in preserving our identity from being submerged in the avalanche of change for the benefit of our children and fellow men. Our identification with the symbols of a common struggle for survival is the key to the cohesion and consensus of the collective. The relationship to which each submits voluntarily, therefore, aims at influencing and persuading, not coercing. But we do not see our fellows any less as individuals as opposed to the wider society which generalises, seeing us more as members of an aggregate, plainly and simply as immigrants.

After fifty years, whenever I go to Nottingham I still feel at home just as I would going to Priestman's River, Jamaica.

You could say that I grew up on the banks of the river Trent, where most people were accommodating and hospitable. They gave emotional support during some of the worst times of my life. There, as in other places, I recognised that I was accepted and wanted. I did not need to be continually on guard; I could be myself. This helped me to develop an image of myself, and the continual relationship sustained this identity and softened the impact of external forces.

Admittedly, there were other friendships that were weak and did not have the moral fibre to sustain them which were therefore transitory. Coming from a large family, it is easy for me to make friends as I regard the family as the prototype of the groups into which one is later incorporated or affiliated. I am broadly tolerant and at ease with all kinds of people, and just as there is a sense of pride in any accomplishment in the family, conversely there is discomfort and disappointment when a friend commits a folly which spoils the relationship. That is the behaviour of a 'let-down artist'.

Chapter Thirty-Two

We all have our prejudices and fears which, if not confronted and dealt with honestly, are channelled into neurotic reactions: hatred, bitterness, vengeance, the forces which shut us up within the boundaries of ethnic groups, religion, class and dogmas causing direct and violent trouble and noises of conflict that drown the still small voice of reason and the silences of the tolerant mind Friendships and relationships can be preserved if we stop being afraid. Fear breeds misunderstanding, resulting in suspicion, injustice and even murder. We need to talk, to communicate. Consistent communication educes a tendency toward conformity within a normative pattern, thus breaking down barriers.

Personal experiences precluded, one can always find exterior mechanisms or events to trigger a successful conversation which helps bring people together. As one with a wide-ranging mind, I love to talk and express my feelings about matters which are personal and which may not be for the best. In other words, I do enjoy taking refuge from things in people. By so doing, I contain my feelings. This my be a product of habit or perhaps a defence mechanism, trying to avoid extreme inhibition which creates tension.

The problems caused by immigrants are always highlighted, and whilst I am not denying or condoning the recalcitrant and deviant, fifty years domiciled in Britain have made me see two sides to the coin. I was never one for

Marxism, believing in or anticipating the decline of nationalist feelings on the grounds that they could not coexist with the sharing of benefits and redistribution of wealth. Nationalism is not doomed as long as each person has a nationality, an internalised, emotionally-felt membership of a country, a belonging to a culture which endows him with an identity which he carries with him in his conduct and expression and which makes him prefer to be with those of the same nationality. These factors are second nature to individuals, and with the multiplicity of linguistic, religious and cultural groups here in Britain, for coalescence to be a reality it will take a very effective government and sound education given that literacy among ethnic groups is not a minority accomplishment.

The original new entrants were markedly distinguishable by virtue of our skin colour and were seen as inferior, barbaric and outlandish, consequently being treated with suspicion and hostility. This provided the means for exclusion from jobs, clubs and housing. If this was allowed to continue, there would be a strong incentive for different groups to conceive of themselves as separate without endangering their material benefits. Whilst it is difficult to change one's culture, it is impossible to change one's pigmentation; besides, there is nothing in the nature of things which decrees that any society must only contain members of the same pigmentation, hair or eye colour. We are aware of the disaster in places where this has been law, and I am delighted that the Commission for Racial Equality has replaced the Race Relations Board and the Community Relations Commission as a stronger unified body in terms of power to deal with complaints effectively and to advise the government on policies.

I am convinced that prejudices, superstitions and fears will decline with the progress of learning, wealth and industry. Some of our children suffer from the divergence between the languages of home and school, having a vernacular lacking in usefully applicable idiom. The result here is that these children, not in possession of the language of modern organisations, industry, government and educational machines, lack identification and therefore cannot be loyal and effective citizens.

Given how it was, I could never believe that I would live to see the indigenous people opening up to the richness and knowledge of other cultures. Ideas and skills are beginning to be shared and valued and people are accepting the fact that Britain is a multi-cultural, heterogeneous society. Some ethnic practices are appreciated and adopted by the dominant culture: carrying babies the African way, certain dances and music are but a few. Mass communication and travel have aided this process, which shows no sign of abating.

This acculturation is a two-way process as the immigrants acquire new practices. The new generation born and bred in Britain no longer sees the culture as strange and threatening nor themselves vulnerable; it is absorbed, accent and all – they are British West Indians. They play football, cricket and rugby and involve themselves in athletics with the same confidence, dedication and expectation as anyone. One should be open and straight and be approachable without prevarication. Life is basically difficult and I do not wish to spend my brief days being pessimistic and negative, otherwise I'd never be able to cope, let alone solve any problems. 'As for man his days are as grass; as the flower of the field, so he flourishes. For the wind passes over it and it is gone and the place thereof shall know it no more.'

Chapter Thirty-Three

My concentration now is not an adjustment, adaptation and acculturation, of which I have done enough already, but on my best friend, my wife, with whom there is total intimacy, with no secrets and the greatest pleasure in activities with each other. Although intimate, this does not encroach upon our individuality. There is no dominance of one over the other; we allow common sense and compromise to prevail and because we are so close we acquire a stable way of dealing with each other. My wife is by nature yielding rather than dominant, except in the kitchen where she never gives way, except as a participant, to my doing the cooking, although the only meals I can prepare from start to finish are soup and porridge. She is companionable and self-confident, with a sense of duty. I am flexible, but not when she wants to cut my moustache. That is one distinguishing feature that will remain until death – the other is the parting in my hair on the left side. Happiness and satisfaction correlate closely which, for both of us, is a product of a very happy childhood in a large family, so we understand each other.

We both make friends very easily, are considerate of others and are not lone wolves; we engage in most activities together and confide in each other about everything, providing I promise not to repeat what we discuss. Our income level is not as important to us as the personal characteristics of prudence, thrift, stability and financial management on which my wife can give me a lesson any day. She shops with discretion and I don't, so I joyfully relinquish that aspect which she does with delight and consideration, purchasing everything she thinks I may need. Usually they fit or match perfectly, be it shoes, shirts, socks or ties. If it were up to her I would do nothing, as she is quite happy for me to sit back, watch her work and listen to the funny stories she tells. Even if one is repeated, it sounds new.

If one should ask, I could not identify one area of difficulty. Oh, yes, my wife always checks on the water level in the bath. I tend to be economical from experience and lessons on conservation of everything, including water during the war years, but I don't mind – I love the feel of her soft and gentle little hands on my body. I could get around this by using the shower but I don't like showers except only in the tropics. And there is another thing: the number of times I have beaten her at chess would be counted on one hand and I never come near to winning at Scrabble. She is even catching up on dominoes, trouncing me 6–0 once. To take matters further, she frequently baits me for a rough and tumble, but how does one engage in horseplay with an egg? The obsession with conflict, desire for social recognition, economic advantage and hedonistic aspiration do not exist in our home. We are too busy thinking of others and being thankful.

We have an automatic give and take policy which benefits and balances both sides equally, for she is no captive wife. Complacency on my part would cover me with opprobrium like an outcast or a hanger-on. Just as it is incumbent on the honourable citizen to carry out his duty through an elaborate and detailed working of the system, so too am I constrained, not through instinct, intuitive impulse or sentiment, to submit to my obligation to reciprocate. The equivalent repayment and advantage is not of an economic nature but stability and love which will not be sacrificed for anything. I do love her relaxed and cheerful company. Whenever she is out, I am like the cat she once had – alert, listening for her footsteps, waiting at the door at the appointed time of arrival. One night, my wife was very late home. I was so anxious that I was about to call the police when she opened the door, laughing.

You may be wondering why I haven't been mentioning my wife by name all the time. This is because I keep seeing reflections of so many qualities in her: sometimes she is Myrtle, that evergreen shrub shedding the fragrance of the knowledge of the love of God; then there is Clarabella, given at birth; Miriam, the brave lady who led the people in singing after crossing the Red Sea, and Little Mother, so attentive and responsive. She was reserved for me, I know without the shadow of a doubt.

I am not bored with life; if this happened it would be a sign that my faculties were dying and endurance was at an end. My wife and I expect to continue enjoying some pleasures: the daily and weekly newspapers, a cup of tea whenever and wherever, including in bed, good books, a holiday near or far and a good restaurant now and then. These fantasies for us are rewarding and rich, as we have been brought up to settle for a minimum which is not purely economic but emotional, intellectual and spiritual, doing as much good as we can considering the irreversibility of time. We have no illusions about life; everything is significant. As much value is placed by us on gifts of sensual or aesthetic value such as flowers as on goods of individual and non-essential consumption value.

It has been refreshing and heartening reflecting on the past, and although as a result of wholesale linguistic deprivation which has made it difficult to translate what I have known into thoughts and words some areas may even be clumsy, I have set out to clarify my experiences. I hope that what has been written here illustrates how much I believe that meaningful thought and behaviour depend upon the ability to reflect; otherwise, one is merely responding to stimuli or just manifesting a blind habit.

The valley may have narrowed; there may be more steeps and impassable rocks to climb, but I am not exhausted or demoralised and my knees haven't given way. My eyes are on the leader, the anchorage of my faith, which can be summed up in these inspiring words:

All the way my Saviour leads me,
Cheers each winding path I tread,
Gives me grace for every trial,
Feeds me with the living bread.
Though my weary steps may falter,
And my soul athirst may be,
Gushing from the rock before me,
Lo, a spring of joy I see.
This my song through endless ages:
Jesus led me all the way.

PEACE AND LOVE.

Names and Ages of the 492 People from Jamaica who Landed at Tilbury on 22nd June, 1948 from MV Empire Windrush

Hubert Adolphus	24	Martin Barrett	50
Wallace Aitcheson	25	Olga Barrett	22
Rupert Allen	21	Linda Barrow	38
Kenneth Amos	21	Cecil Baugh	39
Dudley Anderson	23	Joyce Baxter	21
Ebank Anderson	34	Stephen Beaumont	37
Gerald Anderson	29	Frank Beecher	22
Herman Anderson	22	Florence Bell	25
Alva Angus	32	Hylton Bell	23
Herbert Angus	20	Eric Benain	38
Walter Aquart	32	Thomas Benjamin	40
Gladstone Archer	27	Vincent Benjamin	31
Henry Archer	26	Ductor Bennett	28
Joseph Armstrong	24	Robert Bennett	32
Edison Austin	25	Vincent Bennett	23
Allan Auxilly	25	Delisser Bernard	20
Alan Baker	18	Hugh Bernard	28
Charles Baker	23	Frederick Black	26
Frank Baldwin	28	Wentworth Blair	26
Edward Barnes	20	Frederick Blake	47
Tino Barovier	19	Linton Blake	42

Mixford Bloomfield	44	Arnon Burrell	36
Amelius Bonthorne	28	Edwin Burrowes	17
Septimus Boothe	33	Lenval Callendar	29
Leslie Brady	20	Robert Callum	29
Arthur Braham	24	Norman Cameron	37
Moira Bramwell	31	Alpheus Campbell	21
Lloyd Branch	22	Gerald Campbell	17
Terence Brennand	23	Gofflett Campbell	20
Fulton Briggs	22	Margaret Campbell	63
Leslie Broadley	50	Wilmot Campbell	36
Cleveland Broderick	38	Aubrey Carthy	21
Alfred Brooks	19	David Carton	28
Clarence Brooks	23	Jessie Carton	22
Maurice Brooks	22	Catherine Case	22
Allan Brown	44	Lloyd Case	28
Aston Brown	31	Easton Chambers	37
Aubrey Brown	26	Leslie Chambers	25
Eric Brown	20	Oscar Chang	22
Joscelyn Brown	21	Ellis Chen	21
Joseph Brown	24	Leslie Chin	24
Joseph Brown	33	Calton Chinnon	36
Nellic Brown	26	William Chong	19
Vincent Brown	35	Lawford Christie	21
Wilmot Brown	36	Ivan Chung	22
James Browne	42	Vincent Clare	29
Lisco Bruce	26	Clarence Clark	23
Robert Bruce	28	Eric Clarke	23
Chudleigh Bryan	25	Gilbert Clarke	19
Stanley Buckley	27	Winston Clarke	23
Charlotte Bunting	26	Hubert Cleghorn	24
Newton Burgess	27	Carold Cobbett	49
Donald Burgher	25	Wesley Coke	23

Lester Cole	25	Thomas Douce	22
Mary Collacott	28	Glen Doughlas	28
Claud Collins	23	Rupert Doughlas	32
Melvin Collins	25	Leslie Downer	20
Rudolph Collins	17	Eric Drysdale	22
Beatrice Colthirst	38	Eliza Dunkley	29
Cebert Cooper	21	Hubert Dunkley	39
Hezran Cooper	27	Olive Durk	35
Timothy Cooper	23	Mabel Eames	43
Augusta Cornes	35	Leonard Earle	24
Herbert Cornwall	40	Alfonso Eason	28
George Coward	23	Noel Edward	22
Frederick Cragie	38	Clinton Edwards	21
Kenneth Crossgill	21	Granville Edwards	27
Alvin Crossman	25	Cecil Evans	23
Delvus Cunningham	21	Edwin Evans	21
Ali Curling	20	Leopold Evans	45
Alexander Da Costa	22	Patrick Evans	24
Glenville Daley	22	Ansel Everal	23
Calvin Darby	24	Albert Ewar	20
James Davis	40	Roslyn Ewen	33
Barbara Day	34	Henry Falconer	29
Ernest De Pass	21	Arthur Falkes	49
Yorke De Souza	35	Alvin Farrer	25
Vernon Dehaney	34	Richard Ferguson	36
Quintin Delmar	24	John Fisher	18
Edith Demetrius	47	Cecil Fong	21
Adorish Dennis	47	Frank Forbes	24
Vivian Dennis	25	Willimina Forbes	30
Oswald Denniston	35	Aston Francis	28
I Doeman-Howel	33	Kenneth Francis	28
Ainsley Dolphy	34	Maxwell Francis	29

Clifford Fullterton	38	Rex Haye	25
Nellie Gabourel	22	Leeroy Haynes	19
Alford Gardner	22	John Hazel	21
Gladstone Gardner	23	Canute Hemmings	26
Cecil Garrick	40	Alice Henriques	26
Oswald Garrick	24	Aubrey Henry	26
Charles Gatehouse	51	Floyd Henry	23
George Gaynor	24	Richard Henry	34
Ferdinand Gooden	21	Ronald Henry	30
Sikarum Gopthal	28	Egerton Hermitt	32
Harold Gordon	37	John Hibbert	23
Reginald Gordon	32	Keno Hibman	29
Hall Grace	15	Margaret Hinds	35
Cryil Graham	38	Alpheaus Hines	25
Joscelyn Grant	24	Helond Holdsworth	22
Joseph Grant	29	Evelyn Holgate	29
Rupert Grant	36	Alphonsus Holness	28
Victor Gray	23	Dorothy Hopwood	38
Clifford Green	20	Howard Hopwood	53
James Gregory	22	Martin Hudson	29
Fredick Grey	34	William Hue	21
Herbert Grey	21	Edward Hughison	16
Alvin Guy	28	Mavis Hunter	25
Stafford Hague	36	William Hunter	38
Elsie Hall	48	Iva Hylton	23
Norman Hamilton	24	Lloyd Hylton	23
Lionel Hanchard	27	Alton Jackson	26
Lucilda Harris	31	Leonard Jackson	25
Harold Harrison	29	Lloyd Jackson	22
Astley Harvey	28	Roy Jackson	23
Neville Harvey	24	Sidney Jackson	34
Carlton Hauchtol	34	Arthur Jarrett	25

Henry Johnson	33	Harold Lue	24
Willis Johnson	28	Edward Lym	21
Clinton Johnston	23	Archibald Lyn	24
David Jones	22	Kenneth Lynch	21
Obadiah Jones	52	Louis Maillard	20
Robert Jones	38	Ivy Mair	42
Percival Josephs	38	Anna Malcolm	38
Samuel King	22	Joseph Malcolm	25
Bertic Kong	20	Granald Male	29
Joseph Laing	28	Roy Maragh	28
Lubert Laing	21	Standford Markland	27
James Lambert	28	George Marshall	41
Henry Lawrance	27	Heather Martin	22
Daniel Lawrence	26	Mortimer Martin	31
Edward Lawson	21	Owen Martin	21
Sidney Lawton	23	Reginald Mason	21
Clinton Lecky	25	Verley May	26
Edward Lecky	22	Hepburn Mayne	34
John Lee	23	Albert McBean	25
Martin Lee	37	Seadford McCalla	30
Arthur Leigh	26	Wilbur McCrea	33
Stanley Leon	38	Harold McDonald	23
Eugene Leslie	46	Joslin McDonald	24
Dudley Levy	26	Vincent McFayden	26
Kenneth Levy	26	Alvin McKenzie	19
Winston Levy	27	Oswald McKenzie	24
Eric Linton	36	Aston McLachlan	8
Glenford Linton	25	Edward McLachlan	19
Charles Llewellyn	20	Godfry McLachlan	18
Roy Lloyd	25	Marjory McLachlan	14
Stanford Locke	38	Mary McLachlan	46
Leslie Lowe	16	Ansel McLaren	32

Gordon McLarty	22	Doris Nelson	26
Winston McLean	20	Kenneth Nelson	20
Renfrew McMurrin	25	Leonard Nelson	28
George McPherson	16	Wimston Nelson	23
Lyndon Meikle	28	Lester Newell	19
Mezzil Meikle	21	Richard Nosworthy	29
Uriah Meikle	33	Rudolph Nunes	34
Roland Menzies	38	Astley O'Meally	34
Lawrence Miller	42	Festin O'Meally	22
Christopher Minto	20	Ageande Ogilvie	40
Arthur Mitchell	25	George Palma	27
Terry Mitchell	16	Bertram Palmer	25
Veron Mitchell	28	Calvin Palmer	20
Claudius Montague	21	Arthur Paterson	22
Wilmot Montague	33	John Paterson	34
Egbert Moore	38	Julian Paterson	25
Ivan Morgan	42	Clement Patterson	22
Arthur Morris	28	Everard Peart	30
Clarence Morris	41	Caleb Peterkin	37
John Morris	28	May Phillips	32
Marguerite Morris	23	Clement Philp	27
Ivan Moses	29	Allan Plummer	21
Sydney Mowatt	27	John Porter	30
Sterling Mullings	43	Muriel Poultney	23
Constance Munroe	31	Curtis Powell	23
Rosell Munroe	49	Gerald Powell	23
Cecilia Murphy	25	Eric Prendergast	25
Kenneth Murray	19	Norman Preston	24
Bevis Nair	25	Rena Quinn	21
Vincent Nam	21	Doughlas Rae	16
Beresford Nasralla	23	Henry Raffingston	40
Aubrey Nelson	20	Evelyn Ramm	25

Alphonso Raphael	21	Leslie Shim	20
Stephen Raynor	21	Dennis Simms	22
Alphonso Reece	18	Karl Simms	26
Calvin Reid	24	Henry Sinclair	42
Edna Reid	42	Sylvester Smart	28
Eustace Reid	40	Keith Smellie	20
Hemsley Reid	24	Rynold Smikle	40
Vincent Reid	13	Arthur Smith	29
K Rewachandan	24	Charles Smith	21
John Richards	22	Henry Smith	23
Vernon Richardson	19	Jeffray Smith	26
Halbert Ricketts	24	Reuben Smith	41
Manley Ricketts	37	Wilford Smith	39
Rudolph Ricketts	21	Austin Snow	30
Wellesley Ricketts	28	Vernon Sollas	18
Roy Riley	23	Joscelyn Sommers	30
Reuben Ritchie	26	Beryl Spence	29
Llewellyn Roach	23	Eustace Spence	36
Aldwin Roberts	26	Renford Spence	22
Arthur Robinson	26	Bertran Springer	19
Aston Robinson	25	Delroy Stephens	28
Louis Robotham	29	Franklin Stephens	26
Ernest Rochester	28	Leslie Stephens	23
Lorraine Rochester	18	Owen Stephens	21
Joseph Rose	27	Vincent Stewart	23
Simoin Rowe	24	Charles Stimpson	26
Franklin Russell	35	Clarence Sullivan	22
Hopeton Samuel	28	Ena Sullivan	35
Edwin Samuels	26	Mavis Swaby	27
Sydney Sang	34	Staunton Swaby	21
Mortel Scott	27	Wilton Swire	21
William Sekrie	21	Clifton Synmoie	22
Aston Senior	22	Alfred Sharpe	47

Maurice Tait	19	Rudyard White	24
Abraham Tanquee	24	Sydney White	22
Webster Tapper	23	George Whyte	29
Lambert Taylor	24	Aston Williams	23
Lester Temple	21	Barrington Williams	23
Felix Thomas	36	Edgerton Williams	21
Guy Thomas	26	Edward Williams	20
Harold Thomas	38	Edward Williams	25
Vincent Thomas	27	Loyal Williams	19
Egbert Thompson	29	Mais Williams	36
Ishmael Thompson	33	Marilyn Williams	34
John Thompson	22	Ronald Williams	24
Melton Thompson	26	Rudolph Williams	24
N Thompson	37	F Willoughby	23
Ronald Thompson	22	Harold Wilmot	40
Egbert Tingling	22	Rudolph Wilmot	21
Lloyd Tomlinson	28	Gerald Wilson	18
Raphael Tomlinson	22	Grayville Wilson	21
Egbert Townsend	22	Jeanne Wilson	28
Cleveland Valentine	27	Lascelles Wilson	24
Allan Vanzie	23	Clive Winston	19
Lilian Vautier	51	Irwin Wong	30
Gloria Vaz	20	Holland Wood	29
Samuel Walker	25	Charles Wright	25
Vivian Walker	35	Leslie Wright	31
Adolphine Wallen	21	Louis Wright	23
Adrian Walters	44	Reuben Wright	32
Aubrey Walters	26	Dudley Yapp	19
Ishmael Warren	47	Clarence Yin	23
Ferdinand Watson	34	David Zayne	24
James Wentworth	33	Doreen Zayne	22
David White	26	Herbert Zayne	20